D0609358

COMPUTER-ASSISTED INSTRUCTION IN ECONOMIC EDUCATION

COMPUTER-ASSISTED INSTRUCTION IN ECONOMIC EDUCATION

A Case Study

William I. Davisson
and Frank J. Bonello

university of notre dame press
notre dame & london

Library of Congress Cataloging in Publication Data

Davisson, William I
Computer-assisted instruction in economic education.

1. Economics–Study and teaching–Case studies.
2. Computer-assisted instruction–Case studies.
I. Bonello, Frank J., joint author. II. Title.
H62.D256 330'.028'54 76-642
ISBN 0-268-00715-2

Manufactured in the United States of America

CONTENTS

ACKNOWLEDGMENTS

Many persons have assisted us in our activities over the last few years. Consequently the final product of these activities, this monograph, must begin by recognizing their contributions. Our largest debt is to the Alfred P. Sloan Foundation. The foundation's financial support allowed us to complete the computer assisted instruction system, to enlist the cooperation of other educators both here at the University of Notre Dame and at other institutions, to purchase and develop evaluation instruments, to collect and process data, and, finally, to publish this monograph. In particular, Mr. James D. Koerner, program officer for the foundation, was extremely helpful, offering suggestions and accepting changes in procedures as the project developed.

We are indebted to many persons here at the University. Professors Thomas R. Swartz and Roger B. Skurski offered support above and beyond the call of duty by developing a substantial portion of the computer materials and by allowing us to implement the experiment in their classrooms. Professor Dennis J. Dugan also allowed us to invade his classroom and assisted in the initial attempts at applying the evaluation methodology. Professor Kenneth Jameson was helpful in a number of different ways. He was a coauthor of a paper in which the learning model used here was developed, he is a coauthor of one of the chapters included in this book, and he served continuously as interested and insightful colleague. The cooperation of John Goldrick, director of admissions, and Richard Sullivan, registrar, were essential in the construction of a large portion of the data base.

Our thanks to the Alfred P. Sloan Foundation for making possible the study of CAI in economics as well as the publication of this book.

1

AN OVERVIEW

A. Introduction

It is not surprising that certain sectors of society, recognizing the impact of technology on the ability of manufacturing industries to produce goods, should turn to technology for advances in their own domains. The case in point is education. The last several years have witnessed an extensive effort to incorporate the computer into the educational process in the hope of improving teaching effectiveness. Instructional computing is now found in almost all academic areas.[1] We have been and continue to be a part of this effort centering our activities in the area of economic education.

The development of a professional literature paralleled the expansion of interest in and use of computer-assisted instruction (CAI). Initially this literature was limited to illustrating various approaches, applications, and techniques that could be or had been developed. More recently the emphasis in the literature has shifted to evaluations of CAI. This type of progression was, of course, to be expected. However, it is our opinion that at the present time the hard evidence on the effects of CAI is largely fragmentary.[2] This fragmentation appears in two ways. First, evaluations of CAI tend to focus exclusively on cognitive achievement, ignoring the impact of CAI on student attitudes and educational costs. This too is to be expected, for cognitive achievement is the presumed essence of education and, indeed, isolation of this element alone is difficult. In addition, the attitudinal area is relatively new ground for educators lacking both instruments and methodology necessary for assessment. Nonetheless, a complete evaluation of CAI demands that the effects of CAI in all three areas–cognitive achievement, student attitudes, and educational costs–be determined.

This is not to say that the evaluations of the impact of CAI on cognitive achievement are not without problems, for it is here that the second type of fragmentation arises. In this context the standard procedure has been to conduct controlled experiments, that is, to divide students into two groups, one of which uses CAI. Performance of the two groups on various types of examinations is then compared. Increasingly these comparisons are accomplished through regression analysis so that other differences between students can be controlled. We find no fault with this larger research design. We are concerned with the variables included within the regression model. Because these models do not proceed from a well-articulated conceptualization of the learning process, important variables can and have been frequently omitted.[3] Finally it would appear that the beginning work in the attitudinal area may be afflicted by the same problem.

This monograph is an evaluation of the CAI system employed in a two-course sequence of Principles of Economics at the University of Notre Dame. In the evaluation we have attempted to avoid the two types of fragmentation mentioned above. To this end we have devoted separate chapters to a discussion of the instruments and methodology of evaluation in the cognitive and attitudinal areas. These chapters should be of general interest, for they apply to the evaluation of other types of educational innovation besides CAI. We have utilized these elements in the evaluation of CAI and included a separate chapter on costs. These chapters will be of particular interest to persons concerned with CAI. We by no means wish to imply that we have settled all the questions regarding either the methodology of evaluation or the impact of CAI. With respect to methodology, we have provided, let us hope, a base that others may build upon or, at the very least, have stimulated sufficient interest that an appropriate base can be established. The CAI results herein presented may be subject to some generalization but are limited in that they refer to a particular CAI system used in particular introductory economics sequence.

Before proceeding to these discussions we must delineate the characteristics of the system and the courses into which it was introduced. These topics along with a general description of the research design and the students in the courses constitute the remainder of this chapter.

B. Description of the Courses

Although the Economics Department of the University of Notre Dame offers several different introductory courses, the largest is the sequence numbered Economics 223-224 and entitled Principles of Economics I and II. Two sections of 223 are offered during the fall semester and two sections of 224 are offered during the spring semester of each academic year. Each course is a three-credit course and consists of three fifty-minute class meetings each week. Two of these meetings are lectures presented by the course instructor, while the third meeting is a discussion session conducted by graduate teaching assistants. The lectures represent a common core for the approximately 300 students in each section (two sections of 223, each with 300 students). The discussion classes are small-group activities consisting of approximately twenty students. For a given section of 223 or 224 there are normally sixteen discussion classes. Four teaching assistants are attached to each section, and each of these teaching assistants handles four discussion classes. In terms of format this sequence can best be described as conventional, much like the format of large introductory sequences found at other universities.

The first half of the sequence, 223, focuses on macroeconomics, while 224 concentrates on microeconomics. The courses in the sequence are independent; neither course is a prerequisite for the other. Within this overlay the basic objectives of the sequence are: (1) to help students understand the nature of certain economic problems and institutions, (2) to help students master certain tools of economic analysis, and (3) to help students develop an ability to apply these tools. Again within this context the sequence is conventional with respect to other introductory economics courses.

The specific content of each course has been subject to some standardization over time, particularly in the theory areas. However, there are normally some differences between the two sections of each course offered during a given semester. With this in mind the topic outline for a particular section of each course offered during the academic year 1973–74 is shown in the Tables 1.1 and 1.2. The number in parenthesis indicates the number of lectures devoted to that topic.

The lectures in any given section define a common core for all students in that section. The lectures are complemented by a single "conventional" text, *Economics*, 9th ed., by Paul A. Samuelson. Because there are differences in lecture content and emphasis between sections of both 223 and 224, there are also some differences in text assignments. Over time and in any given semester, the major changes and differences are found in the discussion classes. One change occurred in both sections of Economics 223 and 224 during the 1970–71 academic year so that the student's grade is determined solely on the basis of his examination scores. Thus no credit was given for attending the lectures or discussion classes or for completing any outside assignments. This was done to make grade determination consistent for each and every student in the two sections of Economics 223 and 224. Grades are based on two one-hour midsemester examinations and a two-hour final examination. The examinations normally consist entirely of multiple-choice questions developed by the instructor.

Another change concerns the use of supplementary materials employed in the discussion classes. These have ranged from workbooks, to various "conventional" introductory readings books, to films. During the experimental year the discussion classes were focused in an entirely new direction in order to implement the CAI experiment. These alterations will be discussed

TABLE 1.1

Economics 223, Section 62
Course Outline Fall 1973-74

I. General Concepts in Economics
- A. Meaning and Methodology of Economics (1)
- B. Basic Economic Problems and U. S. Macroeconomic Goals (1)
- C. Two Basic Economic Laws (Diminishing Returns and Increasing Relative Costs) (2)
- D. Supply and Demand: The Concept of a Market (2)

II. The American Economy
- A. An Overview (1)
- B. The Role of Government (1)

III. Macroeconomic Theory
- A. Measuring Macroeconomic Activity (1)
- B. Aggregate Demand
  - 1. Consumption (1)
  - 2. Investment (1)
  - 3. Government (1)
  - 4. Role of the Demand for and the Supply of Money (1)
- C. Aggregate Supply (1)
- D. Determination of Income, Employment, and Prices (2)

IV. Macroeconomic Policy
- A. U. S. Economic Performance since 1960 (1)
- B. Traditional Instruments and Agencies
  - 1. Fiscal Policy (1)
  - 2. Monetary Policy (2)
- C. Economic Policy since August 15, 1971 (2)

V. Two Views of Poverty
- A. Poverty in the U.S. (2)
- B. Poverty in the Rest of the World (2)

TABLE 1.2

Economics 224, Section 63
Course Outline Spring 1973-74

I. The Product Markets	
A. Supply and Demand	(1)
B. The Concept of Elasticity	(2)
C. Marginal Utility Theory and the Demand for Products	(2)
D. Theory of Production and the Supply of Products	(3)
E. Alternative Product Market Structures	(1)
II. The Factor Markets	
A. Theory of Production	(2)
B. The Demand for Factors	(3)
C. The Supply of Factors	(2)
D. Public Policy and Microeconomics	(2)
III. International Trade	
A. Balance of Payments	(1)
B. Theory of Comparative Advantage	(2)
C. Protection versus Free Trade	(1)
D. Current International Problems	(2)
IV. Comparative Economic Systems	
A. The Economic "Isms"	(1)
B. The Functioning and Performance of Alternative Economic Systems	(1)

below. In spite of these changes, the functions of the discussion classes have remained constant: to give students an opportunity to ask questions concerning lecture and text material, to promote discussion of topics which students find difficult, and to stimulate interest in economics by using techniques and devices not suitable to the large lecture sessions.

The courses as they stand represent what we feel are "conventional" introductory economic courses. They employ a lecture-discussion format typical of large classes, seek objectives common to introductory courses, cover content that has become fairly standardized, utilize a widely sold textbook, and employ an examination technique that is typical both in large classes and in introductory economics. Such a sequence can be found at many other institutions. One might go so far as to say that the sequence such as Economics 223-224 is not only "conventional" but has become "traditional."[4]

C. The System of Computer-Assisted Instruction

The major component of the Notre Dame computer configuration consists of an IBM 370/158 with both batch and time-sharing capabilities. The time-sharing facilities at the time of the experiment consisted of forty terminals located in three different campus buildings. It was the existence of these facilities which created the potential for large-scale use of CAI. The time-sharing mode establishes virtually instantaneous communication between the computer and the computer user, and appropriately designed programs can be utilized by the student without computer-programming knowledge or the preparation of cards. The existence of time-sharing facilities and the materials that we have developed require only that the student master a procedure, which establishes communication between the terminal and the computer, and then to access and execute the various individualized programs. These procedures are extremely simple and require perhaps ten to fifteen minutes of instruction for most students.

The CAI system consists of three different types of programs, all executed in the interactive mode. The first type of program is called a *review routine* and consists of a series of multiple-choice questions normally grouped together in terms of a particular chapter in the Samuelson text. This method for grouping the questions was selected because it allows each lecturer in a given semester to identify which routines were to be run and when they were to be run. We also felt that this method would facilitate the use of our system in other courses both here at Notre Dame and at other institutions. Finally this grouping method gives the student a textual reference base to turn to if he encountered difficulties in answering the questions in the routine.

Each review routine operates in an identical manner. The computer begins by printing out the number of questions in the routine and the chapter in the text from which the concepts are drawn. The computer then prints out the first multiple-choice question and asks the student to select the correct answer by entering the number or letter preceding his chosen distractor. The student enters his selection. If he has chosen the correct answer, he is told his response was correct and is given a reason why that response is correct. The computer then proceeds to the next question. If the student has selected an incorrect distractor, he is told his selection is incorrect and given an explanation of why it is incorrect. Then he is asked to choose another response. The process is repeated until a correct response is obtained. When the correct response is obtained the computer prints out the reinforcement, then moves on to the next question. The procedure is repeated for each question until the student completes the routine or otherwise discontinues operation. When the student completes the routine he is given an evaluation of his performance based on the percent of correct answers given as initial responses. In addition the student is informed of his relative performance; that is, if the student answers 80 percent or more of the questions correctly he is told his performance is good; if the student answers between 60 percent and 80 percent of the questions correctly, he is told to review both his text and the questions within the routine; and if the student answers less than 60 percent of the questions correctly, he is told that results indicate that he has not read or mastered the material and it would be advisable for him to see his discussion-class instructor for assistance. The routine ends by giving the student an option of reviewing any (or all) of the questions.

In addition to the logic of the chapter references at the beginning of each routine and the general format of the routines, it is important to note the logic of several other features of these routines. First consider the rational for the prompts, the explanations of why distractors are either correct or incorrect. The prompts for the correct answers are necessary because students should know if the reason he selected the correct distractor corresponds to the "appropriate" reason. In effect the prompt operates as a positive reinforcement. The prompts for the correct answers are also advantageous if the student has selected the proper response for the wrong reason or if he was just lucky. The need for prompts to incorrect responses is more self-evident, providing "corrective instruction" at the moment an error is made.

The function of the evaluation feature is also fairly self-evident. Students like to know how well they did and whether this type of performance is adequate and, if not adequate, what might be done about it.

The option of reexamining questions was included because we visualized the situation where a student was undecided between two distractors. He might by good fortune select the correct response. He finds that his reason for including this distractor as a possible correct answer is consistent with the prompt, but the prompt may not tell him why the other distractor was incorrect. At the end of the routine, then, he can return to this question and select the other choice to obtain an explanation of why it is incorrect.

As their name implies, the review programs were predicated on the belief that the student would utilize them after listening to the appropriate lecture and reading the corresponding text material. The routines would give the student an evaluation of his knowledge, allowing him to test himself and remedy deficiencies by means of the prompts and further study. At this point one might ask if this procedure is more properly administered via a computer or through a device such as a discussion class or a workbook. With respect to a discussion class we feel the computer approach has certain advantages. First the student can use the computer routines when he is ready for them rather than when his discussion class is assigned. This then allows for self-pacing. Second, the computer routine may act in a more personal manner in the sense that the student is not forced to listen to discussion of questions to which he already knows the answer. He simply reads the prompt to that question to check his reasoning. It is also more personal in the sense that the student might be reluctant to ask why each of the incorrect responses was incorrect for fear of wasting class time or revealing his lack of knowledge to his fellow students. Such inhibition would not prevent a student from going through a computer-review routine and obtaining prompts for all incorrect distractors. In large measure, these arguments in favor of review routines do not apply to workbooks or programmed texts. The major advantage of the review routines over these alternatives is its instantaneous positive reinforcement or instantaneous correction. In addition, the computer has an advantage over these devices in the sense that it represents a new medium and, as such, may be less boring.

Finally it is important to note that the routine is printed out and the student may take his printout with him to use as a study guide. This allows the student, at his own convenience, to refer to questions before examinations without revisiting the computer. This review should highlight areas that are troublesome and encourage the student to reexamine lecture notes and text materials in these areas. As deployed, the system contained nineteen review routines for the macroeconomic course (223), with a total of 141 multiple-choice questions, and 23 review routines for the microeconomics course (224), with a total of 191 multiple-choice questions.

The CAI system also includes a group of programs called *demonstration routines.* Actually this group of programs can be divided into two subgroups –one aptly defined by the term *demonstration* and the other, perhaps, more appropriately described as *calculation routines.* The first subgroup takes a particular quantitative concept, provides a detailed discussion of the concept, and then using a given set of data the program presents a numerical or graphic example. Students are given an option at the end of the program to change the basic data set and obtain new numerical or graphic results based on their own data. With the second subgroup, students are given economic models or basic formulas and then must supply data to obtain output. These programs are designed to relieve the student of the burden of making numerical computations. At the same time, however, these programs can be used for demonstration purposes. This is either accomplished by having students knowingly switch between models with appropriattely assigned data sets or to make changes in a systematic manner in a basic data set. Because the calculation routines can be used for these purposes we have included them within the category of demonstration routines.

From a functional standpoint the demonstration routines, in the narrow sense, allow for a more detailed and systematic analysis of a quantitative concept. In addition these materials provide the student with approaches to concepts that differ and thus supplement those found in the lectures or in the text. Take, for example, the concept of diminishing returns. Most lecturers and most texts will not begin with a specific, appropriately constrained production function. This is done because the use of an appropriate production function involves calculation difficulties. A computer demonstration performs such calculations very quickly and thus allows an explanation of this concept from its logical starting point. Even without this possibility the demonstration routine provides another explanation and application of the material which is beneficial for many students; at least many students continuously request additional material of this nature. The student is largely passive as the routine proceeds through its initial phases–discussion and the original numerical example. The opportunity to change the basic data set gives the student the chance to become actively involved. But in addition to this feature, it allows the student to experiment with assumptions; for example, in the diminishing-returns routine the student may change the constraints on the production function to obtain constant or increasing returns and to change the quantity of the fixed factor employed. Each time an assumption is changed a new numerical example is printed out and the student, by comparing the various numerical outputs, can isolate or verify the impact of such changes and thereby reinforce the logic developed in the lecture or the text.

The calculation routines perform one basic function: they allow for ease of calculation in assigned problems. For instance, in macroeconomics, certain models imply that a dollar's increase in government expenditures has a more expansive impact on national income than a dollar decrease in taxes. Once an instructor presents these models, indicating their particular properties and establishing the conceptual bases for drawing conclusions from these models, he might seek to reinforce this lesson with a series of numerical examples. Indeed these examples might compare the results of these models with the results established in other models. To do so during the lecture or as a homework assignment generally involves too high a cost in terms of student time. However, if the student has access to a computer terminal and is able to call a routine that will make the necessary calculations, the series of examples can be processed in less time than would be required to complete a single example manually.

The CAI system contains five demonstration routines for the 223 course and five demonstration routines for the 224 course. Again all routines were operated from the time-sharing mode and students could save their results as they were printed. The number of routines may create the impression of limited coverage, but the calculation routines normally included a series of increasingly more sophisticated formulas and models. Thus a given demonstration routine of the calculation subgroup could be used repeatedly as the level of sophistication increased.

The third type of routine is called a *game simulation.* The basic function of these routines is to provide the student an opportunity to apply his knowledge in solving problems as presented in a simulated "real world" of data provided by the computer. The operational elements of each simulation are identical. First, the computer provides a description of the type of simulation to be developed specifying objectives as well as the variables which students will control. Second, the computer prints out the "initial state of the world," basic data describing the state of the goal variables, tool variables, and other selected variables. Third, the student acting as a decision maker must manipulate the tool variables in an attempt to achieve desired values of the goal variables. This manipulation is based on the student's theoretical knowledge as reinforced or supplemented by his examination of the initial state of the world. Fourth, a new data set emerges that embodies the results of the student's decision. At this stage the student can ascertain the results of his decision and his success as a policymaker by viewing the "new state of the world." The simulation routines either terminate at this point or provide for further decisions with additional output.

Although the operating procedures in the simulations are basically the same, there are important differences between them. One difference concerns the type of changes which take place within the simulation. In simpler simulations the only source of change is a policy decision made by the student. Typically this policy decision is accomplished by changing a tool variable. In more complex simulations there is systematic variation in nonpolicy exogenous variables as well. Indeed the student is required to recognize such changes if he is to make correct policy decisions. The most advanced simulations include random change. These changes are added for the sake of realism; that is, the future is not perfectly predictable and consequently even the most carefully designed policy can be frustrated by unanticipated changes in behavioral patterns. The simulations also differ in other respects including the number of goals to be achieved, the compatibility of the goals, and the number of tool variables over which the student has control.

The advantages of game simulations lie primarily in the experience which the student obtains in attempting to solve problems on the basis of his knowledge and ability. In the process of playing the game, the student not only gains such experience but also demonstrates for himself the necessity and usefulness of theoretical knowledge in isolating behavioral patterns and in determining the appropriate changes in tool variables. These games, of course, may be played without a computer but then their scope must be significantly reduced in order for the student to determine the results of his decisions. Specifically, computer game simulations allow for much more complex, hence more realistic, games than those which can be used in discussion classes or in workbooks.

The system contained four simulations for the Economics 223 course and one simulation for Economics 224. Again all routines are run from the timesharing mode, and students have a complete printout of their activities. As such, these routines do not allow for interaction between groups of student decisionmakers. Games with this capability usually require batch processing and thus were considered as inconsistent with the CAI system we envisioned —completely time-sharing and single-student operation.

This then represents the CAI system. It employs the computer in a variety of ways—reviews, demonstrations, and simulations—and does not represent merely the playing of the same game simulation over and over again. The end product of our CAI system emphasizes the review function. Several factors explain this emphasis. One factor is the relative newness of the review concept and lack of testing regarding its effects. In addition, we felt that the students would identify the review routines as the most beneficial to them. These programs can immediately isolate the extent of the students' understanding and provide immediate instruction directed toward their weaknesses. The educational output of the simulations, however, is much less evident to the student and, by the same token, are extremely difficult to construct. The demonstrations, of course, fall somewhere between these two extremes. In addition, elements such as time constraints both in the construction of materials and the amount of time necessary for their execution by the students, favored the review routines. Nonetheless, the system as it was introduced employed the computer in a range of pedagogical techniques and, as such, would provide a better test of the effectiveness of CAI.[5] By the same token the results of the experiment itself would provide suggestions for the improvement of the system.

D. Research Design

To determine the impact of CAI on cognitive achievement, student attitudes, and educational costs, it was decided that a controlled experiment would be undertaken. Thus the students using the CAI system were classified as experimentals, while the remaining students were classified as controls. The means of determining which students would be controls and which would be experimentals was a random selection of discussion classes. Simply, the list of sixteen discussion classes for each section of each course was arbitrarily designated as an experimental or a control class. The experimentals were then given an introduction to CAI including a description of the various routines which were available and the proper procedures for logging on and executing routines. Each of these students was given a user number. By means of an accounting system employed by the computing center, we were able to determine the number of times each number was used and the time spent with each logon. The controls, on the other hand, were to meet in their regularly scheduled discussion classes. It was decided that if the results of the experiment were not to be biased, then the controls must have access to the multiple-choice questions contained in the review routines. If these materials had not been made available to the controls, one could have argued that the experimentals should have performed better than the controls in the cognitive area since they were exposed to a mass of multiple-choice questions specifically prepared for them. Thus at each meeting of a discussion class copies of the multiple-choice questions without the prompts were distributed to the students. The discussion classes were free to review these questions, with the teaching assistant rather than the computer supplying information regarding the appropriate answers and the reasons why the distractors were either correct or incorrect. The teaching assistants were required to use their own words in explaining the "logic" of the questions rather than simply repeating the prompts.

In more specific terms the instructions to the teaching assistants with respect to their discussion classes were as follows: (1) ask students whether they had any questions regarding lectures and answer any as they arise, (2) ask students whether they had any questions regarding assigned text material and answer any as they arise, (3) distribute the multiple-choice questions and discuss them, if desired; and (4) proceed to discuss any questions that are considered relevant.

With respect to the experimentals, the first semester involved two different approaches. One approach, called *forced experimental*, was structured so that groups of students would meet at assigned times in a room equipped with time-sharing facilities. Each week the teaching assistant would meet the class and assign the appropriate routines that were to be executed that week. The students could then use this time to run the assigned materials. The other approach was called *free experimental.* These students were required to meet as a group only once at an assigned time. At this meeting they were introduced to CAI and given a time-sequenced list of CAI routines much like the course schedule and text assignments distributed in lectures. The students were then "free" to utilize the CAI materials whenever they wanted to; they were not to meet as a group again. During the second semester the two different approaches to the experimentals was abandoned, the students, were divided into controls and (free) experimentals. This is the design used in the 1973-74 academic year. These results are presented in the next six chapters.

The breakdown of the number of students according to this classification based on initial enrollment figures is shown on Table 1.3.

The function of a controlled experiment is, of course, to take a group of otherwise identical subjects or groups of subjects and to change the treatment to which they are exposed in one dimension. The research design was constructed according to this specification. The students in a given section of either 223 or 224 would listen to the same set of lectures and have a common textbook. The treatments would be varied in terms of discussion classes; certain students, controls, would be exposed to the human element by having

TABLE 1.3

Student Enrollment

Economics 223 (First Semester–Macroeconomics)		Economics 224 (Second Semester–Microeconomics)	
Total Students	634	Total Students	573
Section 61	328	Section 63	286
Controls	109	Controls	142
Forced Experimentals	111	Free Experimentals	144
Free Experimentals	108		
Section 62	306	Section 64	287
Controls	134	Controls	138
Forced Experimentals	56	Free Experimentals	149
Free Experimentals	116		

teaching assistants, while other students would be exposed to the computer element, the CAI system. The controls would see the same multiple-choice questions as the experimentals, but these questions would be processed in entirely different ways. In addition the experimentals had access to the demonstrations and game simulations while the controls did not. This "advantage" was offset by the give and take possibility within the discussion class. All students were given hours when the teaching assistants and the lecturers were available for assistance. This was done to insure "equality of opportunity" for help outside the formal mechanisms. All students were told that the only elements considered in grade determination were the three examinations given in each section of each course. Attendance was at the discretion of the student and would not be considered in grading.

The controlled-experiment design implies control over test conditions. In our case complete control was not possible. It was impossible to insure that the controls would never have access to the routines available on the computer. A control student could exercise such a possibility by asking an experimental student for his user number or by asking for printouts of the various reviews, demonstrations, and simulations. Also there was no way we could force an experimental student to use all the available CAI material. In recognition of these problems we did engage in certain procedures that would allow us to determine the extent of such activities. As we shall indicate later, the breakdown was substantial, particularly during the 224 course.

The requirement that the various groups of students be identical or otherwise be controlled for differences necessitated the gathering of considerable data. These data include indicators of scholastic ability as measured by entrance exams, college grade-point averages, previous economics and mathe-

TABLE 1.4

Selected Characteristics for Various Aggregations of Students
Economics 223
(Standard Deviation in Parentheses)

	MSAT[a] $\bar{X}$	VSAT[b] $\bar{X}$	Projected[c] GPA $\bar{X}$	Cumulative GPA $\bar{X}$	% B.A. Majors	Total $\bar{X}$
All Controls	615.07 (78.948)	545.69 (90.278)	2.74 (0.459)	2.93 (0.459)	69.3	13.525 (3.825)
All Experimentals	607.29 (76.611)	546.430 (78.303)	2.74 (0.583)	2.94 (0.438)	68.5	13.621 (4.291)
Free	503.28 (75.570)	552.72 (71.868)	2.75 (0.438)	2.93 (0.600)	71.77	13.670 (4.195)
Forced	612.97 (77.971)	537.48 (86.099)	2.74 (0.439)	2.95 (0.439)	64.37	13.556 (4.430)
Section 61	606.41 (78.664)	535.35 (81.371)	2.72 (0.439)	2.92 (0.560)	76.0	13.312 (4.097)
Controls	604.45 (79.668)	528.37 (88.366)	2.71 (0.436)	2.91 (0.539)	79.8	12.863 (3.723)
Experi-mentals	607.37 (78.347)	538.75 (77.730)	2.72 (0.441)	2.92 (0.571)	74.0	13.545 (4.260)
Free	601.55 (80.383)	547.43 (71.550)	2.72 (0.446)	2.90 (0.625)	75.0	13.717 (4.023)
Forced	613.13 (76.231)	530.16 (82.854)	2.72 (0.417)	2.95 (0.514)	73.0	13.371 (4.498)
Section 62	615.72 (75.872)	558.85 (82.745)	2.77 (0.448)	2.95 (0.578)	61.1	13.870 (4.132)
Controls	623.59 (77.879)	559.89 (90.070)	2.77 (0.477)	2.96 (0.548)	60.4	14.053 (3.844)
Experi-mentals	609.21 (73.788)	557.97 (76.405)	2.77 (0.424)	2.95 (.603)	61.6	13.723 (4.355)
Free	605.89 (71.274)	558.39 (72.287)	2.77 (0.403)	2.96 (0.403)	68.1	13.628 (4.402)
Forced	617.93 (80.308)	556.88 (87.284)	2.79 (0.479)	2.92 (0.669)	48.2	13.925 (4.287)

[a]Mean score on the mathematics portion of the Scholastic Aptitude Test
[b]Mean score on the verbal portion of the Scholastic Aptitude Test
[c]This is a projection prepared by the Admissions Office and is based on MSAT, VSAT, and rank in high school class
[d]For Economics 223, Part I, Form A was used for the precourse test

TABLE 1.4
(continued)

TUCE Precourse Test[d]					
Recognition and Understanding $\bar{X}$	Simple Application $\bar{X}$	Compact Application $\bar{X}$	% with some prior College Economics	% having classes using Computers	% having some College Mathematics
5.343 (1.737)	4.458 (1.666)	3.725 (1.851)	32.8	38.1	71.3
5.548 (1.930)	4.428 (1.765)	3.647 (1.839)	33.8	41.6	74.6
5.674 (1.893)	4.353 (1.687)	3.643 (1.881)	34.1	41.2	76.5
5.377 (1.972)	4.531 (1.866)	3.648 (1.785)	33.3	42.1	71.9
5.497 (1.848)	4.280 (1.719)	3.535 (1.800)	35.9	41.9	75.1
5.294 (1.596)	4.265 (1.768)	3.304 (1.652)	36.7	38.5	76.1
5.602 (1.955)	4.294 (1.701)	3.649 (1.865)	35.2	43.8	74.9
5.868 (1.942)	4.208 (1.478)	3.642 (1.953)	35.2	42.6	75.9
5.333 (1.940)	4.381 (1.903)	3.657 (1.780)	35.1	45.0	73.9
5.448 (1.873)	4.585 (1.727)	3.836 (1.874)	31.7	37.9	71.9
5.391 (1.846)	4.602 (1.581)	4.060 (1.934)	29.9	38.1	67.9
5.494 (1.900)	4.572 (1.840)	3.657 (1.811)	33.1	37.8	75.0
5.496 (1.843)	4.496 (1.867)	3.637 (1.837)	33.6	39.7	76.7
5.491 (2.035)	4.736 (1.788)	3.698 (1.771)	32.1	33.9	71.4

TABLE 1.5

Selected Characteristics for Various Aggregations of Students
Economics 224
(Standard Deviation in Parentheses)

	MSAT	VSAT	Projected GPA in University	Cum GPA	% BA Major	Total
All Controls (280)	616.32 (76.520)	548.46 (85.474)	2.74 (0.464)	2.89 (0.562)	73.2	15.939 (3.896)
All Experimentals (293)	604.59 (78.360)	538.93 (83.945)	2.74 (0.445)	2.92 (0.570)	77.2	15.468 (3.633)
Sec. 63 All Students (286)	603.47 (74.918)	537.62 (78.622)	2.71 (0.443)	2.93 (0.566)	80.3	15.423 (3.672)
Controls (142)	601.99 (73.853)	538.67 (72.918)	2.70 (0.460)	2.91 (0.570)	79.7	15.289 (3.604)
Experimentals (144)	604.93 (76.106)	536.59 (84.086)	2.74 (0.427)	2.95 (0.565)	80.8	15.556 (3.745)
Sec. 64 All Students (287)	617.34 (79.998)	545.73 (90.599)	2.76 (0.465)	2.89 (0.566)	70.2	15.972 (3.849)
Controls (138)	633.37 (76.346)	560.11 (97.410)	2.78 (0.467)	2.87 (0.555)	66.4	16.609 (4.082)
Experimentals (149)	604.24 (80.799)	541.25 (80.050)	2.74 (0.464)	2.90 (0.576)	73.7	15.383 (3.533)

[a]For 224, Part II, Form A was used for the precourse test

mathematics exposure, and so on. In addition an assessment of CAI on cognitive achievement, attitudes, and costs also required the compilation of data. In terms of cognitive achievement the Test of Understanding College Economics (TUCE) was administered as a precourse and postcourse test in each semester and an item analysis of all examinations was obtained. In the attitudinal area precourse and postcourse surveys were administered which included student opinions regarding economics, various elements within the instructional process, as well as their opinions on certain economic institutions, problems, and policies. Obviously some of these data, particularly in precourse tests and precourse surveys, represent information regarding differences between groups of students. But the postcourse test and postcourse survey data as well as changes between precourse and postcourse are elements that were to be compared between the controls and the experimentals. A more thorough discussion of the instruments used to generate the data will be undertaken in the chapters which follow.

TABLE 1.5
(continued)

TUCE Precourse Test[a] Recognition and Understanding	Simple Application	Complex Application	% who had	% who were Econ 223	% who were Econ 22	Econ 223 GPA
5.114 (1.750)	6.246 (1.828)	4.579 (1.611)	87.1	45.1	54.9	2.740
5.034 (1.170)	6.014 (1.811)	4.420 (1.693)	92.8	28.7	71.3	2.638
5.056 (1.766)	6.091 (1.798)	4.276 (1.643)	93.8	28.7	71.3	2.785
4.937 (1.694)	6.085 (1.808)	4.268 (1.497)	92.3	34.4	65.6	2.809
5.174 (1.833)	6.097 (1.795)	4.285 (1.780)	95.1	23.4	76.6	2.761
5.091 (1.693)	6.164 (1.847)	4.718 (1.639)	86.4	44.8	55.2	2.581
5.297 (1.794)	6.413 (1.839)	4.899 (1.667)	81.9	57.5	42.5	2.659
4.899 (1.576)	5.933 (1.829)	4.550 (1.600)	90.6	34.1	65.9	2.515

E. Profile of Students

Tables 1.4 and 1.5 present detailed descriptions of various aggregations of students in Economics 223 and 224 respectively. Drawing from Table 1.4 as well as additional data we can construct a profile of the typical student in Economics 223. He is a college sophomore (80 percent), majoring in the College of Business Administration (70 percent). Indeed, the sequence is required of all business majors (the Economics Department at Notre Dame is in the College of Arts and Letters). The student is white (90 percent), male (93 percent), and Catholic (94 percent). His Scholastic Aptitude Test average 546 for verbal and 610 for mathematical. In addition he was a product of a private high school (62 percent) and has experienced success during his freshman year with a university grade-point average of 2.9 (on a 4.0 scale).

Although the student was generally taking the sequence as a required course, the student believed that economics would be useful and relevant but felt that large lectures were not a good teaching device. Students were more favorably disposed to discussion classes. Interestingly enough, odds were approximately even that the student had previous exposure to classes using computers (49 percent). This exposure left the student favorably disposed, believing that CAI was a good teaching method that was stimulating and not dehumanizing. In terms of economic opinions, students were basically in the middle of the road (on the average between 2.0 and 4.0 on a scale which measured from 1.0 to 5.0).

This then represents an overview of the CAI system, the courses in which it was introduced, the students that were enrolled, and the research design initially established to determine its impact. With these elements in mind we can begin to evaluate the impact of CAI.

2

MEASURES & DETERMINANTS OF A COGNITIVE ACHIEVEMENT

A. Introduction

This chapter begins with a description of the various instruments employed to measure cognitive achievement. Within this description we address several issues related to the particular instruments and testing in general. In the second section of this chapter, a model of the learning process is developed. Within the context of the model, the potential impact of CAI on cognitive achievement is isolated. Finally some preliminary discussion of the problems that may be encountered in operationalizing the model is presented.

B. Measures of Cognitive Achievement

The experiment relied solely on tests or examinations to determine cognitive achievement. There were, however, two types of tests. The first is the Test of Understanding College Economics (TUCE).[1] For the 223 macroeconomics course Part I, Form A (macroeconomics), was given both as a precourse test and as a postcourse test–initially administered during the first week of the semester and subsequently as part of the final examination. In the latter instance a common final examination was given to both sections of 223 with the thirty-three multiple-choice TUCE questions combined with seventeen additional multiple-choice questions prepared jointly by the two instructors. For the 224 microeconomics course Part II, Form A (microeconomics), was given both as a precourse test and as a postcourse test. Again the precourse test occurred during the first week of the semester while the postcourse test was part of the final examination. In the case of 224 the additional or non-TUCE multiple-choice questions on the final examination were not common between the two sections; each lecturer made up his own set of questions which were then combined with the thirty-three multiple-choice TUCE questions.

The other type of tests were those generated locally. For each section of each course, these consisted of a series of multiple-choice questions grouped into three elements–two one hour midsemester examinations and the non-

TUCE portion of the final examination. With the exception of the non-TUCE portion of the 223 final examination, these questions were prepared separately by each lecturer for his own section. Thus for each section of either course, the cognitive achievement of the control students and the experimental students can be compared in four different ways: performance on the first midsemester examination, performance on the second midsemester examination, performance on the TUCE portion of the final examination, and performance on the non-TUCE portion of the final examination.

The use of the independently prepared and nationally normed TUCE was deemed appropriate for several reasons. First, by using this instrument, we reduce the possibility that the examinations used to measure cognitive achievement were biased in favor of either the controls or the experimentals. Although the distribution to the controls of the multiple-choice questions contained in the review routines was undertaken specifically to avoid such a bias, it would still be possible to construct examination questions that drew heavily from the demonstration and game-simulation routines–items which were available only to the experimentals. The use of the TUCE, however, does not eliminate all potential bias, for it would be possible to construct the demonstration and game-simulation routines in such a manner that they emphasized the material covered in the TUCE. With regard to both of these possibilities, all we can say is that we did not attempt to emphasize TUCE-like material in the demonstration or game-simulation routines, nor did we attempt to emphasize demonstration or game-simulation routine materials with the locally generated examinations.[2] We believe that a careful analysis of these materials would support this claim.

A second advantage obtained by using the TUCE is an ability to determine whether CAI operates differentially in terms of facilitating learning between different "objective categories."[3] Here each form of the TUCE is divided into three groups of questions stressing different learning objectives. These groups are: "recognition and understanding," "simple application," and "complex application." The thirty-three questions of Part I, Form A, of the TUCE are equally divided between each category, while the thirty-three questions of Part II, Form A, of the TUCE have twelve, eleven, and ten questions respectively, in each category. Given this categorization the controls and experimentals can be compared in terms of their performance on the total TUCE and also on each of these "objective categories."[4]

There is perhaps a negative aspect to the use of the TUCE, and this pertains to the content coverage and skill emphasis of this test relative to the courses. Specifically, each form and part of the TUCE is also grouped into content categories, and between these content categories the number of questions as well as the relative weight of objective emphasis varies. For example six questions of Part I, Form A (18 percent of the test) are devoted to "policies for stabilization and growth." In addition all six of these questions are in the "complex application" category. The 223 course does not deal in such detail with this topic, and so far as growth is concerned whatever is learned follows from extensions of the income-employment model. Although this is an argument against using the TUCE, it is a problem which operates evenly on both controls and experimentals. This imperfect matching of content and objective emphasis operates to bias TUCE results for both groups of students downward, retaining the validity of comparison between the groups. In the more general sense, however, there is a correspondence, indeed a fairly close correspondence, between both the objective and content emphasis of the TUCE and the courses.

Another point of potential concern is the use of the same form of TUCE in a given section as both a precourse test and as a postcourse test. We offer the following points to justify our procedure. The national norming data indicates, at least with respect to Part I of the TUCE, that there is no significant difference in postcourse test results regardless of the form of the precourse test.[5] Only postcourse test data were collected on Part II of the TUCE, and thus no such judgment can be made on this part. In addition, for both courses the TUCE postcourse test was part of the final examination with the order of the TUCE questions changed and with the intermingling of the locally generated questions. This we would believe represents a sufficient disguise for the postcourse test. Finally any advantage for using the same form for both a precourse test and a postcourse test would apply equally to both groups of students, potentially yielding an upward bias to the scores for both the control and the experimental students.

As to the locally generated questions, we encountered no problems with content coverage or objective emphasis. Presumably each instructor prepared questions that reflected the appropriate coverage and emphasis of his particular section. We have already raised the issue of the potential bias of these questions. At this point we can restate the two points made above: the controls received copies of the multiple-choice questions contained in the review routines, and no attempt was made to emphasize the demonstration and game-simulation routines with the locally generated questions.

Aside from this problem there is also the question of the quality of the locally generated examinations. There was no opportunity to test and revise the locally generated questions before giving them to the students. But here too we can argue that the quality of each individual question bears evenly on both the controls and the experimentals; both "good" controls and "good" experimentals will answer a "bad" question incorrectly.

It is to be hoped that the above discussion is an adequate description of the instruments employed to measure cognitive achievement. At this point two additional issues may be raised. The first is whether only examinations should be used to measure what students learned. The second issue is a corollary of the first: are examinations which consist solely of multiple-choice questions appropriate measures of cognitive achievement? Persons who raise the first issue argue that examinations should be supplemented with papers, classroom discussion, problem sets, and so forth. Clearly, in classes of the size of Economics 223 and 224, discussion is virtually impossible, at least in the lectures. Oral activity in the discussion class is possible but would eliminate a basis for grade determination for the experimentals because the CAI system was a substitute for these sessions. For problem sets and papers, there is no assurance that the work submitted by the student was his and his alone. In addition, consistency in grading of student participation, discussions, papers, and, to a lesser extent, problem sets would be a major obstacle.

Elimination of the second issue cannot be accomplished by these same practical considerations. This is not to say that practical considerations are unimportant in relying completely on multiple-choice examinations. Simply, we know of no way in which 300 essay questions (assuming one essay question on a single examination in a particular section of either 223 or 224) can be graded in a consistent manner unless an "objective" criterion is used. If this were not the case, grades and therefore the evaluation of cognitive achievement would be influenced by such presumably extraneous factors as how tired the instructor might be when he read a particular examination or the student's writing style. Beyond this, essay questions tend to be a more discontinuous measure of cognitive achievement. A multiple-choice examination yields a continuous measure of cognitive achievement in unit intervals where one unit represents a single question. Thus, for example, on the thirty-three-question TUCE examination, a student may score anywhere from 0 to 33 questions correct. In contrast it would be difficult to construct and grade an essay examination in so fine a detail. If one is unwilling to accept these arguments, then we can only state that our results are limited to cognitive achievement as measured by multiple-choice questions, but, as indicated by the "objective categories" of the TUCE, we believe these questions involve measurement of different types of learning.

C. Determinants of Cognitive Achievement

Given instruments for measuring cognitive achievement, the question now is what determines how much a student learns in a particular course. It appears to us that there are three types of factors operative in producing cognitive achievement.[6] All three center on or are processed through the student. The first of these may be grouped under the heading, *human capital* and measures the abilities of the student. The greater these abilities, all other things being equal, the greater should be the student's learning. These abilities at any point in time are a product of the student's prior experience in the educational process as well as such things as home environment, peer-group influences, and innate characteristics.

But just because a student brings a certain amount of human capital to a course does not mean that he or she will use it. This obvious statement raises the need for our second category of factors, which we will label utilization rates. Specifically we would expect that a student with a given amount of human capital will learn more the more frequently he or she attends class, the greater the time spent studying, and so on.

Utilization rates, unfortunately, capture only the quantity dimension of the student's application of his human capital. The need to capture or isolate the quality dimension of time spent on a course introduces the third type of factor. For lack of a better name we will call these elements *efficiency variables.* The argument here is straightforward: a student with a given amount of human capital will get more out of a given hour of lecture or reading a text if he thinks the lecture or text is "good." In this context "good" is interpreted as clarity or effectiveness in exposition.

This view of the learning process can be expressed functionally as:

$$CA = F\,(HC, UR, EE), \tag{2.1}$$

where

CA = cognitive achievement of the student,
HC = human capital of the student,
UR = measure of the time spent by the student with various elements in the instructional process, and
EE = student's evaluation of the efficiency of the various instructional elements in conveying explanations.

In this specification each of the independent variables—HC, UR, and EE—is assumed to operate positively on cognitive achievement, which, of course, is the dependent variable.

This view of the learning process represents an input-output perspective; that is, we view the attainment of knowledge as a production activity with the student processing all the inputs. Focusing more specifically on this perspective, we can analyze this process in terms of the conventional production-function diagram presented in Figure 2.1. Various levels of cognitive achievement or output are designated along the vertical axis, while units of time as the variable input devoted to the learning process are designated along the horizontal axis. How time is converted into cognitive achievement is represented by the curved line PF. We have drawn PF to reflect the three stages of the production process of increasing, diminishing, and negative returns.[7]

Figure 2.1 is a diagrammatic statement of equation (2.1). In terms of this equation the vertical axis represents CA, the dependent variable, while the horizontal axis represents UR, one of the independent variables. The particular position of the PF curve for any individual student is determined by the other two independent variables in equation (2.1). We would expect that the PF curve for a student with a given amount of human capital would be to the left of the

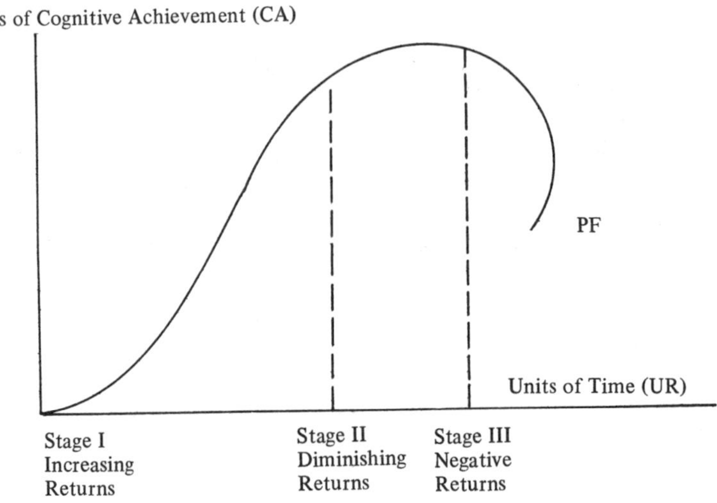

Figure 2.1. Production Function for Cognitive Achievement

PF curve for a student with a smaller amount of human capital. In similar fashion the PF curve for a student who believes that the instructional elements employed in a course were "good" would be to the left of the PF curve for a student who did not think as highly of the same instructional elements. To complete the production function analogy, HC and EE in equation (2.1) may be considered fixed factors, or inputs, and increases in either or both of these independent variables implies that a given utilization rate will yield greater cognitive achievement. Given his human capital, the array of instructional elements selected for student use by the teacher, and the instruments used to measure learning, the student determines his own level of cognitive achievement by setting his own utilization rate. This is not to say that the teacher is unimportant, for he selects the measures of cognitive achievement as well as the instructional elements that facilitate the accomplishment of learning objectives. In addition the teacher may also be able to exert some influence on the student's utilization rate.[8]

It should be noted that a student may not choose to maximize cognitive achievement. This can be demonstrated by assuming that the student knows his production function and that he or she recognizes that time is a scarce resource. A student must budget his time between academic and nonacademic activities and within the academic allocation between various courses. If the student knows his production function, he knows the amount of time that he must devote to the particular course in order to maximize cognitive achievement. He might be unwilling to devote this much time to the course, for it might imply too large a sacrifice of time available either to other courses or nonacademic activities. Restated, the decision not to maximize cognitive achievement in a particular course may be rational, for it may be consistent with alternative objectives such as maximization of an overall grade point average or, even more generally, with maximization of the student's utility function.[9]

The assumption that a student knows his production function may be described as heroic. If the student does not know his production function even if he desires to maximize cognitive achievement, he may be unable to do so because he selects the wrong utilization rate. In terms of Figure 2.1 the student operates as though his production function corresponds to PF when in fact it is below or to the right of PF. There is seemingly no solution to this dilemma unless the student is specifically aware of the contents of the instrument to be used in measuring cognitive achievement. This by definition precludes the use of examinations.[10] Partial resolution is possible by detailing the nature and coverage of the examination and by using devices which will give signals to the student prior to examination of the extent of his knowledge.[11]

Figure 2.1, as stated, is drawn to reflect the three stages of production. It can be argued, however, that the exact shape of the PF curve is sensitive to how the variables on the two axes are measured. If cognitive achievement is measured as either the number of correctly answered questions or as the percentage of examination questions answered correctly, then there are finite limits to the vertical axis. If there is a direct linear relationship between units of time spent on a course and the number of correctly answered questions (up to the point of negative returns), and if the vertical axis is dimensioned in terms of the number of correctly answered questions, then PF will appear as an upward sloping straight line. Given this same relationship, but now dimensioning the vertical axis as the percent of examination questions answered correctly, then PF will still be linear. If the vertical axis is dimensioned as percent improvement, defined as the ratio of the difference between postcourse test and precourse test scores to the precourse test score, then there may be no finite upper limit to this axis. This last dimensioning technique also generates a PF curve similar to Figure 2.1 and also the possibility of negative values for cognitive achievement.

The dimensioning problem also applies to the horizontal axis. In conventional economic terms, it is the question of selecting the appropriate production period. The horizontal axis may be constructed as hours per day, per week, and so on. It would appear that the longer the production period, the less likely one is to encounter the latter stages of production. That is, the student is more likely to encounter diminishing, if not negative, returns if he clustered twenty hours of study time in one day rather than spreading them out over the period of a week.

There is an additional problem with utilization rates in that the student may allocate time to various elements in the instructional process. For example, the student may spend time attending lectures and discussion classes, reading the text, reviewing lecture notes, and so on. Moreover, there is a limit to the number of class periods a student can devote to a given course, and these activities may be imperfect substitutes for one another. The PF curve presented in Figure 2.1 does not address itself to these complexities.

Ignoring all of these problems for the time being, the basic concepts employed in Figure 2.1 can be used to isolate the impact of an educational innovation such as CAI. As represented in Figure 2.2 the introduction of an educational innovation generates a leftward shift in the cognitive achievement–utilization rate relationship, a movement of the PF curve from PF_1 to PF_2. This shift implies that, up to the point of negative returns, the student will learn more for every given hour devoted to a course. The problem for researchers in education is to determine whether or not an educational innovation has generated such a shift and, if so, the extent of the shift. This is a difficult task, for a student who experiences a leftward shift in his production function may react a number of ways. These reactions and the difficulties they imply can be illustrated with the aid of Figure 2.2.

We can begin by assuming that the student was in position A on PF_1. By spending UR_1 units of time on a course, the student attains CA_1 units of cognitive achievement. The education innovation is introduced and the production function shifts. If the student maintains his utilization rate at UR_1 he will now be at position B and his cognitive achievement rises to CA_2. Recall that the student is free to select his own utilization rate. Thus, when the educational innovation is introduced, the student may decrease his utilization rate and maintain his level of cognitive achievement. The student in this instance moves from position A to position C with cognitive achievement maintained at CA_1, while the utilization rate falls from UR_1 to UR_2. If the educational researcher has failed to control for utilization rates, he may conclude that the innovation has not had its desired impact of raising cognitive achievement; there has been no leftward shift in the production function. But the researcher may also overestimate the impact of an innovation if he fails to control for utilization rates. Again assume that the student is initially at point A. Now the innovation not only shifts the production function but stimulates the student to spend more time on the course. The student consequently is at point D with a utilization rate of UR_3 and cognitive achievement of CA_3. Recognizing the increase in cognitive achievement and ignoring the increased utilization rate, the researcher has overestimated the "pure" shift in the production function.

Although the above argument is phrased completely in terms of the need to control for utilization rates in determining the impact of an educational innovation, the argument applies with equal force to human-capital and efficiency elements. In comparing the cognitive achievement of experimentals and controls, any difference in cognitive achievement that may be observed between the two groups may be attributable to differences in these independent variables and not to differences in treatment. Simply, we need to control for all three types of variables.

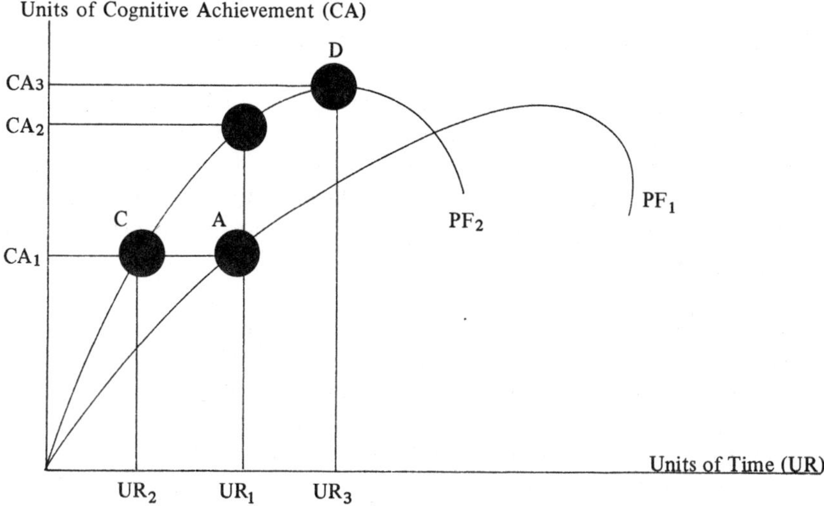

Figure 2.2. Impact of Educational Innovation on the Cognitive Achievement Production Function

Aside from difficulties in differences between groups we should also mention another problem which may be encountered when educational innovations are evaluated. Here we mean that an educational innovation may not operate evenly on all experimentals, perhaps shifting the production function out for only particular types of students. In such a situation those experimentals who are helped by the innovation are lumped together with the remaining experimentals who are not helped. There may be no perceived differences between the aggregate experimental group and the controls. It would appear therefore that care could be taken to disaggregate the experimental group to see if the educational innovation operates only for particular types of students.

D. Operational Problems

Equation (2.1) is a summary statement of our model or view of the learning process. But it is one thing to construct a skeleton and another to put flesh on that skeleton. In less macabre terms, equation (2.1) must be converted into an empirical statement. This conversion, sometimes called operationalizing the model, is the process of specifying the data items that will represent each of the three types of factors included in the equation. The importance of this process is underscored by the fact that unsatisfactory empirical results may be due either to an inappropriate conceptual view or to improper specification of the data items. With this in mind, this section presents a preliminary discussion of the data items to be included in our empirical restatement of the learning model.[12]

Any review of previous empirical work in economic education will reveal that all investigators have tried to control for human capital (although usually not explicitly).[13] Among the variables so used, the most common are student scores on college entrance examinations. In our view such scores do reflect a student's human capital and consequently we will include the student's performance on the mathematical and verbal sections of the Scholastic Aptitude Test (MSAT and VSAT respectively) in our regression equation. Even though the logic underlying such an inclusion is fairly obvious, a word or two about each of these variables is in order.[14]

The MSAT consists of questions which are designed to measure "fundamental quantitative abilities closely related to college work."[15] Within this context there are two kinds of questions. One group measures the ability of the student to apply quantitative techniques, while the other measures the student's ability to reason insightfully. These separate abilities are, of course, valuable in a sequence such as 223-224. In terms of techniques, students are confronted with graphs, diagrams, functional notations, equations, systems of equations, and so on and are required to apply them. Examples of the usefulness of insightful reasoning are harder to come by, but there is little doubt that this ability would be useful in almost any course. All other things being equal the abilities of the student as measured by the MSAT should be important in explaining his cognitive achievement. This is not to say that the MSAT will necessarily be important or of equal importance in explaining a student's performance in all economic courses or even in all portions of a given course. The reason underlying this assertion is straightforward; different areas of economics, different instructors, different textbooks, and different examinations will place varying emphasis on quantitative skills. In the larger sense, however, cognitive achievement in economics should be directly related to the MSAT.

The VSAT consists of questions that appear to be divisible into three areas: reading comprehension, vocabulary, and abstraction or "understanding of the relationships between ideas."[16] It should be noted that economics may place different emphasis on each of these skills. Specifically economics tends to use terms in a very particular way—to have its own unique vocabulary. It is not clear that a student with a strong general vocabulary and low abstraction ability would do as well as a student with a weak general vocabulary but high abstraction ability. As with the MSAT we should again recognize that the relationship between these verbal skills and cognitive achievement may not operate in exactly the same way as we move between courses or between portions of the same course. Having made these comments we will still deal with the VSAT in its aggregate form and expect it to exert a positive influence on cognitive achievement.

But in our interpretation the specification of human capital in previous studies has not been limited to student scores on entrance examinations. Such a limitation, we believe, would be unwise for two reasons; it may create a time-lag problem, and it may disregard a student's specific economic knowledge. Both of these problems arise in the current evaluation.[17]

With respect to the time-lag problem, most students take the Scholastic Aptitude Test early in their senior year of high school, while most of the students in the 223-224 sequence are college sophomores. As a consequence the MSAT and VSAT are measures of quantitative and verbal skills as they existed some two years prior to the educational experiment being evaluated. Many events, particularly those within the formal educational process, may have transpired during this two-year interim to improve these skills differentially among students. More directly the time-lag problem is the suspicion that the MSAT and VSAT are not appropriate measurements of quantitative and verbal skills as of the beginning of the 223 and 224 courses.

The second problem is much more obvious. Knowledge of economics may not affect the MSAT and VSAT, and even if it did, such knowledge is probably accumulated subsequent to the taking of the Scholastic Aptitude Test. The latter point stems from the fact that, historically, exposure to economics as a separate discipline has been restricted to higher education.

The literature provides what appear to be numerous and diverse efforts to solve these problems. To update the inventory of quantitative and verbal skills, researchers have included such data items as the number of college mathematics courses taken (but never the number of English courses taken), the student's college and/or major, the age of the student, his current year of college, his cumulative grade-point average, total number of college credit-hours accumulated, and so on.[18] To measure the student's economic knowledge at the beginning of the course, the list of options is less long: precourse test scores and previous exposure to economics at the high school and/or college level. To restate the dilemma more forcefully, the literature does not offer any unequivocal answer to the question: what data items represent a proper measurement of a student's human capital as it relates to his ability to achieve cognitively in economics as of the beginning of a course? Needless to say, we cannot offer an a priori answer to this question either. As a starting point we will use the MSAT, VSAT, the student's cumulative grade-point average and his performance on the TUCE pretest. It is to be hoped for that the third variable will solve the time-lag problem, while the TUCE precourse test should measure the student's economic knowledge as of the beginning of the course.

With respect to utilization rates—the second category of factors included in equation (2.1)—it is fairly clear what data items should be obtained.

Ideally these data would be collected on some periodic basis and in sufficient detail so as to distinguish between various kinds of course-related activity. Thus we attempted to obtain weekly estimates of lecture attendance, discussion class attendance (for the controls), time spent with the CAI system (for the experimentals), and time spent studying. With reference to the ideal data set, one might argue that study time should be disaggregated further, say, into time spent initially reading the text, time spent reviewing the text, time spent reviewing lecture notes, and time spent with other individuals. Practical considerations precluded the collection of data in this fine detail.

Turning finally to the efficiency variables, the questionnaires deployed during each semester raised numerous questions concerning the several instructional elements. All students responded to the questions concerning the instructor and the textbook, while the controls answered the questions concerning the discussion class, and the experimentals responded to those on the CAI system. In this context our problem here is somewhat similar to the problem with the human-capital specification: to select appropriate data items from among several alternatives. In other words, which of the several alternatives about an instructional element best measures its efficiency in helping the student achieve cognitively?

We can conclude this discussion of operational problems by making several comments. First, we have an ample data-base for the human-capital and efficiency categories. The problem here is to select the appropriate data items, which unfortunately cannot be unequivocally determined on an a priori basis. Second, the data base for the utilization rates is not all that it should be. The difficulty here is not in being unable to specify a priori what data items are needed, but in collecting them. Third, the regression analysis is really intended to accomplish two objectives: (1) to evaluate the explanatory capability of our learning model and (2) to allow for a more precise analysis of the impact of the CAI system on the cognitive domain.

3

THE IMPACT OF CAI ON COGNITIVE ACHIEVEMENT

A. Introduction

The purpose of this chapter is to evaluate the impact of the CAI system on the cognitive achievement of students in the Economics 223–224 sequence. This evaluation is undertaken in two ways. We begin with a relatively simple approach, comparing the average performance on the several measures of cognitive achievement of those students who used CAI, the experimentals, with the average performance of those students who did not use CAI, the controls. Next an evaluation is made on the basis of regression techniques, where the regression equation approximates as closely as possible the learning model presented in the previous chapter. With both approaches, each section of each course is examined separetely in order to abstract from the effects of different instructors or section specific influences.

B. Cognitive Achievement: A Comparison of Averages

Table 3.1 indicates the mean number of correct answers on the four measures of cognitive achievement (the two midsemester examinations and the two parts of the final examination) as well as mean TUCE improvement (TUCE postcourse test minus TUCE precourse test) for the various classifications of students in each section of the two courses. We will discuss these results on a section by section basis.

Section 61 experimentals outperformed their control counterparts on three of the five measures of cognitive achievement: the first midsemester and the two parts of the final examination. However the superior performance of the experimentals on the TUCE portion of the final examination appears to be the result of greater prior knowledge; that is, this higher score was achieved with a smaller TUCE improvement. In each of these three cases, as well as the two cases where the experimentals returned lower scores than the controls, the differences in means were not statistically significant at the 5-percent level.

TABLE 3.1

Examination Results for Economics 223 and 224
Mean Number of Correct Answers and TUCE Improvement
(Standard Deviations in Parentheses)

Course, Section, and Classification of Student	Number of Students	First Mid-semester	Second Midsemester	Non-TUCE Final	TUCE Final	TUCE Improve-ment
Economics 223						
Section 61						
Controls	103	24.1651	24.5660	11.5047	22.8131	10.0485
		(3.054)	(4.147)	(2.686)	(4.926)	(4.799)
Experimentals	211	24.1789	24.1163	11.7454	23.0185	9.4882
		(3.234)	(4.015)	(2.348)	(4.185)	(4.464)
Free	106	24.1018	24.2476	11.6944	23.4537	9.6792
		(3.174)	(3.902)	(2.350)	(4.127)	(4.155)
Forced	105	24.2545	23.9909	11.7963	22.5833	9.2952
		(3.305)	(4.134)	(2.355)	(4.216)	(4.768)
Section 62						
Controls	133	24.0606	22.7612	12.7910	23.5075	9.4586
		(3.243)	(3.205)	(2.369)	(3.767)	(3.634)
Experimentals	166	23.8605	23.2663	13.1257	23.4551	9.7349
		(3.187)	(3.335)	(2.408)	(4.089)	(4.361)
Free	113	23.7758	23.2389	13.2301	23.5044	9.8761
		(3.165)	(3.400)	(2.295)	(3.782)	(4.422)
Forced	53	24.0357	23.3214	12.9074	23.3518	9.4340
		(3.253)	(3.231)	(2.637)	(4.703)	(4.254)
Economics 224						
Section 63						
Controls	146	20.7556	19.3529	13.0074	24.2963	7.6370
		(2.672)	(4.182)	(3.080)	(3.736)	(3.940)
Experimentals	135	19.4467	19.3673	12.6443	23.5705	8.0411
		(3.347)	(3.685)	(2.980)	(3.382)	(4.127)
Section 64						
Controls	140	20.1206	18.2797	16.2517	22.6434	7.3929
		(3.239)	(3.436)	(3.013)	(3.247)	(3.665)
Experimentals	144	20.6138	18.4315	16.7603	23.6027	8.0833
		(2.398)	(3.056)	(2.846)	(3.726)	(3.769)

In this section we may also compare the controls with each type of experimental. Such a comparison may reveal that the manner in which CAI is implemented is important. The free experimentals performed better than the controls on two of the five measures of cognitive achievement, while the forced experimentals outperformed the controls on two of the five measures. None of these pairwise comparisons, controls with free experimentals and controls with forced experimentals, on any of the measures of cognitive achievement is statistically significant. In short the comparison of average performance in this section does not indicate any systematic advantage or disadvantage for students using the CAI system.

The Section 62 results support this same conclusion. Here the experimentals outperform the controls on three of the five measures: the second midsemester, the non-TUCE portion of the final examination, and TUCE improvement. In these three cases, as well as the other two, the differences between the mean scores were not statistically significant. Comparison of the controls with each type of experimental reveals no consistent or statistically significant results, both free and forced experimentals outperforming the controls only occasionally. Generalizing over both sections, the 223 results, based on these comparisons of mean test scores, leads to the conclusion that CAI is neither a superior nor an inferior alternative to the discussion classes in generating cognitive achievement. To stress the positive, CAI represents an effective substitute for the discussion classes.

As we turn to the 224 course, recall that the forced experimental structure was eliminated. Hence, for both sections of this course, the experimentals consist entirely of free experimentals. Comparison of the Section 63 controls and experimentals shows that the latter group of students outperformed the former on two of the five measures of cognitive achievement: the second midsemester examination and TUCE improvement. In both of these cases the differences in means were not statistically significant. On the other three measures where the comparison does favor the controls, we do obtain a statistically significant difference only on the first midsemester examination. These results are difficult to summarize. Certainly there is no systematic CAI effect, but we have isolated an instance where CAI appears to have generated a significant impact. Perhaps we can conclude that these results are mixed, but yield a negative view of CAI on one dimension of cognitive achievement.

Consider now the Section 64 results. Here we do obtain consistent results, the experimentals outscoring the controls on all five measures of cognitive achievement with the difference on the TUCE postcourse test being statistically significant. It would appear that the data for the two sections of 224, the microeconomics course, lead to opposite conclusions–Section 63 suggesting mixed results with the hint that CAI is inferior to discussion classes, while Section 64 indicating that CAI is consistently superior to discussion classes but that this superiority is strong in only one instance. This apparent contradiction in results raises the possibility that for the two sections of 224, unlike the two sections of 223, we may not have a random distribution of students between controls and experimentals. There are other possibilities as well, but they also suggest that the evaluation of CAI requires a more sophisticated method of statistical analysis.

Before turning to such an analysis, we can utilize the current evaluation procedure to determine if CAI operates differentially on alternative types of learning as defined by the three objective categories of the TUCE. Here we have chosen to focus on improvement, and the results for the various aggregations of students in each section of the two courses are shown in Table 3.2.

Comparison of Section 61 controls and experimentals reveals that the experimentals improved less in each category but none of these differences are statistically significant. These results do not depend on the way in which CAI is implemented. The free experimentals improved more than the controls on simple applications. The forced experimentals improved more than the controls on recognition and understanding. None of the pairwise comparisons between controls and each of the two types of experimentals was, however, statistically significant. For this section then CAI generally tends to generate less improvement in the three objective categories.

This result is in part negated by the Section 62 results with the experimentals improving less in two, rather than all three, objective categories, the experimentals improved more on complex applications. Again none of the differences in mean improvement were statistically significant. Comparison of the controls with each of the two types of experimentals yields no consistent or statistically significant results. Generalizing over both sections it would appear that there is some evidence, although not particularly strong, that CAI is a less effective alternative in generating TUCE improvement than the discussion classes, and that this is true across objective categories.

With Section 63 of 224 we begin to find evidence in the opposite direction, with the experimentals improving more than the controls on two of the three categories, while in Section 64 the experimentals improve more on all three objective categories. These results would suggest that the microeconomics portion of the CAI system is better suited to generating TUCE improvement, and this effect operates across objective categories. In short we find no evidence that CAI operates differentially among the different types of learning as defined by the objective categories of the TUCE. Rather we have found that the CAI system either increases or lowers overall TUCE improvement (the 224 results relative to the 223 results) with either effect operating more or less consistently across objective categories, although none of the differences are statistically significant. This suggests that perhaps the

TABLE 3.2

TUCE Improvement by Objective Category
(Standard Deviation in Parentheses)

Course, Section, and Classification of Student	Recognition and Understanding	Simple Application	Complex Application
Economics 223			
Section 61			
Controls	2.9029	3.6214	3.5243
	(1.993)	(2.267)	(2.283)
Experimentals	2.7536	3.4929	3.2417
	(1.951)	(2.230)	(2.433)
Free	2.5000	3.7642	3.4151
	(1.953)	(2.141)	(2.472)
Forced	3.0095	3.2190	3.0067
	(1.924)	(2.295)	(2.391)
Section 62			
Controls	2.9098	3.6466	2.9023
	(1.940)	(1.989)	(2.222)
Experimentals	2.7410	3.5843	3.4096
	(1.868)	(2.138)	(2.302)
Free	2.7257	3.7345	3.4159
	(1.843)	(2.192)	(2.178)
Forced	2.7736	3.2642	3.3962
	(1.938)	(2.001)	(2.567)
Economics 224			
Section 63			
Controls	3.9704	1.9259	1.7407
	(2.109)	(2.115)	(1.962)
Experimentals	4.0479	2.3699	1.6233
	(1.931)	(2.140)	(2.101)
Section 64			
Controls	3.1857	2.0071	2.2000
	(2.002)	(1.969)	(2.061)
Experimentals	3.4931	2.0625	2.5278
	(2.059)	(2.129)	(1.989)

224 portion of the CAI system is more oriented toward TUCE-like material than the 223 portion.

Summarizing the information from both of the preceding tables, we suspect that conditional statements are the best that can be made. Thus we will state at this point that CAI appears to generate mixed results. Assuming all other things equal, CAI represents an adequate alternative to discussion classes. But note that the manner in which the discussion classes were conducted, with a distribution of the review-routine questions to all controls, really involves a comparison of oral processing through a graduate teaching assistant with the machine processing through the CAI system. In this regard it may be surprising that CAI does at least as well, apparently, as the discussion class in generating cognitive achievement. To reword this last conclusion, under the most severe possible test of CAI, the system yields an adequate level of cognitive achievement.

C. Cognitive Achievement Regression Results

We have already presented our model of the learning process. As stated in Chapter II, that model can be summarized as:

$$CA = F\ (HC, UR, EE) \tag{3.1}$$

The argument underlying equation (3.1) is straightforward: the cognitive achievement of a student (CA) should be greater the greater his human capital (HC), the greater the time spent by the student on various course related activities (UR), and the greater the efficiency of the instructional elements in conveying explanations (EE). We have also discussed some of the problems involved in converting this conceptual view into an empirical statement, namely, to restate equation (3.1) in the form of a multiple-regression equation. This preliminary examination indicated that four data items would be used to represent a student's human capital. These variables were the student's score on the mathematical and verbal sections of the Scholastic Aptitude Test (MSAT and VSAT, respectively), the student's cumulative grade point average as of the beginning of a course (BGPA), and the student's performance on the Test of Understanding College Economics when it was administered as a precourse test at the beginning of a course (TUCEPRE). We did not, however, indicate precisely the data items that would be used to represent utilization rates (UR) and efficiency elements (EE), a task to which we now turn.

With respect to utilization rates, a student can allocate his time to several different activities. A control could attend lectures, attend discussion classes, and study. An experimental, on the other hand, while he could not attend a discussion class, could use the CAI system. Ideally then data should be obtained from each student on these various activities. The problem, however, is not in knowing what data are desired but in obtaining them. We initiated several procedures that we believed would yield the ideal data set. In fact the procedures, especially with regard to the free experimentals, yielded far less than the ideal. More specifically, the only data items that appear to be fairly reliable are those concerning discussion class attendance by the controls and time spent on the computer (connect time) by the experimentals.

Given the problems with the utilization rate data we will use an alternative measure of time devoted to the course in the regression analysis. This measure is taken from the University Course Evaluation Form. The item and its numerical values are: "Compared with other courses you have taken or are taking at Notre Dame, the work load for this course was: 4 = heavier, 3 = heavy, 2 = somewhat lighter, 1 = much lighter." Presumably this question captures the overall time effort of the student. Unfortunately it does not indicate how time was allocated among various activities. Perhaps even more unfortunate is the fact that the question is worded in a relative sense. As a consequence a student who has a higher numerical value on this question than another student may not be actually devoting more hours to the course than the second student. Let us hope that this difficulty does not occur frequently, and the question provides an appropriate ordinal scaling of time spent on the course between students. In terms of the regression equation, only one utilization rate is employed as determined by student responses to this question. The variable is identified as OUR for overall utilization rate.

The third and final category of factors in equation (3.1) are the efficiency elements (EE). We will employ three data items under this category. The first of these measures the student's reaction to the lectures. Examining several alternatives we selected one of the items from the University Course Evaluation Form: "Effectiveness of class teaching or direction." Here the student can select among four responses. The options and their numerical equivalents are: "A" = 4, "B" = 3, "C" = 2, "D" = 1 (faculty, unlike students, are not exposed to the possibility of an "F" grade). In the regression equation, this variable is identified as LE for lecturer effectiveness.

All the students not only come in contact with the lecturer but also with the text. Again the University Course Evaluation Form raises a question that can be used as a broad measure of the effectiveness of this instructional element. The item simply states "quality of readings," with response options and numerical equivalents identical to those employed for the item regarding the lecturer. For purposes of the regression model this variable is identified as TE for text effectiveness.

The remaining variable is the sex of the student. We have included this variable because several previous studies in economic education have indicated that females are at a disadvantage in learning economics.[1] The usual explanation of this result is that although males and females begin a course in economics with exactly the same academic credentials, males are dealing with subject matter that is more familiar to them and with which they feel more comfortable. This in turn is a function of the roles the students play before coming to the course and, perhaps, the roles they expect to play after the course. In the regression equation this variable is identified appropriately enough as SEX. It is of course a dichotomous or dummy variable coded as 0 for females and 1 for males. Note that the coding is not a social statement but rather a simple expedient; that is, if the above argument is correct, then the regression coefficient should be positive and significant.

To recapitulate, we have four data items to capture a student's human capital, one variable to isolate the time he spends on the course, and three variables that in a loose sense represent the effectiveness of the instructional elements. To this list we must add another variable that indicates whether the student was a control or an experimental and which in turn can be used to evaluate the impact of the CAI system on cognitive achievement. This variable is identified as EXPCODE, and like the SEX variable, it is a dummy variable. Here we have coded the controls as 0 and the experimentals as 1. Consequently if the CAI system is a better alternative then the discussion class in the production of cognitive achievement, then the coefficient for this variable should be positive and significant.

Having defined all the variables, we can now restate equation (3.1) in its multiple-regression form:

$$\begin{aligned} CA = a + b_1\ MSAT + b_2\ VSAT + b_3\ BGPA + b_4\ TUCEPRE \qquad (3.2) \\ + b_5\ OUR + b_6\ LE + b_7\ TE + b_8\ SEX + b_9\ EXPCODE + u \end{aligned}$$

where: a = constant term and
u = stochastic error term

According to the arguments presented above, and assuming that CAI is superior to the discussion class, all the coefficients (b_1, b_2, ---, b_9) are expected to be positive. For a complete summary of all the variables included in equation (3.2), see Table 3.3. With respect to the dependent variable CA, we will employ the student's score on the first midsemester examination, score on the second midsemester examination, score on the non-TUCE portion of the final examination, and score on the TUCE portion of the final examination.

Table 3.4 presents the regression results for both sections of the 223 course, while Table 3.5 presents the results for 224. We can begin our discussion of these results by pointing out that the regression data were avail-

TABLE 3.3

Summary of Variables in the Regression Equation for Cognitive Achievement

Variable	Definition	Type of Variable	Theoretical Numerical Range	Expected Effect on Cognitive Achievement
MSAT	Score on the mathematics section of the Scholastic Aptitude Test	Human Capital	200–800	Positive
VSAT	Score on the verbal section of the Scholastic Aptitude Test	Human Capital	200–800	Positive
BGPA	Cumulative university grade-point average at the beginning of the course	Human Capital	0–4	Positive
TUCEPRE	Score on the Test of Understanding College Economics administered as a precourse test at the beginning of the course	Human Capital	0–33	Positive
OUR	Overall utilization rate: "Compared with other courses you have taken or are taking at Notre Dame, the work load for this course was 4 = heavier, 3 = heavy, 2 = somewhat lighter, 1 = much lighter."	Utilization	1–4	Positive
LE	Lecturer effectiveness, "Effectiveness of Class Teaching or Direction": A = 4, B = 3, C = 2, D = 1	Efficiency Variable	1–4	Positive
TE	Text effectiveness, "Quality of Readings": A = 4, B = 3, C = 2, D = 1	Efficiency Variable	1–4	Positive
SEX	Sex of student: females = 0, males = 1	Efficiency Variable	0 or 1	Positive
EXPCODE	Status of students : 0 = controls or non-CAI users; 1 = experimentals or CAI users	-------	0 or 1	Positive if CAI is superior to discussion class

TABLE 3.4

Regression Results for Economics 223
(t ratios in parentheses)

Section 61

Variables	First Midsemester Examination	Second Midsemester Examination	Non-TUCE Final Examination	TUCE Final Examination
Constant	14.18682	6.66188	2.41058	5.09449
MSAT	0.00540 (1.905)	0.01005* (2.888)	-0.00042 (0.0167)	0.00433 (1.077)
VSAT	0.00138 (0.492)	0.00139 (0.402)	0.00574* (2.339)	0.01114* (2.800)
BGPA	1.55864* (3.806)	2.82829* (5.591)	0.92758* (2.585)	0.97018 (1.669)
TUCEPRE	0.07285 (1.439)	0.08536 (1.362)	0.10129* (2.283)	0.31992* (4.452)
OUR	-0.08677 (0.352)	-0.32444 (1.072)	0.45494* (2.108)	0.20385 (0.583)
LE	0.38866 (1.445)	0.30369 (0.914)	0.23075 (0.979)	0.30508 (0.799)
TE	0.49528* (2.306)	0.75293* (2.849)	0.19062 (1.013)	0.44530 (1.461)
SEX	-1.99160 (1.928)	-0.52852 (0.417)	-0.14311 (0.158)	-0.64502 (0.440)
EXPCODE	0.32021 (0.788)	-0.65612 (1.304)	0.14934 (0.420)	0.16842 (0.292)
R^2	0.22700	0.33049	0.16433	0.26411
R^2	0.19513	0.30245	0.12987	0.23376
F ratio	6.29756	10.42114	4.21702	7.69623
N	203	200	204	204

*Statistically significant at the 5-percent level

TABLE 3.4
(continued)

Section 62

First Midsemester Examination	Second Midsemester Examination	Non-TUCE Final Examination	TUCE Final Examination
9.30847	6.58806	4.54103	2.62422
0.00913* (3.168)	0.01237* (3.992)	0.00056 (0.265)	0.01014* (2.981)
0.00586* (2.110)	-0.00167 (0.558)	0.00136 (0.667)	0.00645 (1.960)
1.04948* (2.784)	1.62871* (3.976)	1.29036* (4.624)	1.57840* (3.511)
0.19180* (3.925)	0.10446 (1.957)	0.13905* (3.823)	0.28519* (4.867)
-0.57913* (2.236)	-0.60201* (2.126)	0.04249 (0.221)	0.01075 (0.032)
0.58535 (1.754)	1.04071* (2.862)	0.53853* (2.174)	-0.21627 (0.542)
-0.02102 (0.089)	0.09100 (0.355)	-0.42738* (2.444)	-0.02840 (0.100)
-0.23048 (0.283)	1.12656 (1.264)	1.05063 (1.730)	3.82526* (3.910)
0.09773 (0.265)	1.00222* (2.500)	0.45267 (1.657)	0.41255 (0.938)
0.39943 0.37373 13.74483 196	0.35008 0.32257 11.25185 198	0.31573 0.28676 9.63829 198	0.42770 0.40348 15.61127 198

TABLE 3.5

Regression Results for Economics 224
(t ratio in parentheses)

Section 63

Variables	First Midsemester Examination	Second Midsemester Examination	Non-TUCE Final Examination	TUCE Final Examination
Constant	11.81672	7.77264	-2.39065	0.52959
MSAT	0.00068	0.00935	0.00425	0.01204*
	(0.195)	(1.611)	(1.095)	(3.241)
VSAT	0.00505	0.00049	0.00557	0.00961*
	(1.706)	(0.100)	(1.705)	(3.074)
BGPA	2.23692*	0.92907	1.79871*	1.20322*
	(4.842)	(1.219)	(3.532)	(2.468)
TUCEPRE	0.03621	0.16753	0.11006	0.22918*
	(0.536)	(1.504)	(1.476)	(3.210)
OUR	-0.28930	-0.64751	0.10114	0.61748
	(0.839)	(1.114)	(0.206)	(1.696)
LE	0.26796	-0.56342	-0.17695	0.21658
	(0.821)	(1.048)	(0.492)	(0.620)
TE	0.07718	0.18426	0.53178	0.19695
	(0.237)	(0.345)	(1.484)	(0.574)
SEX	-1.27905	3.53324	1.76644	0.74211
	(1.158)	(1.950)	(1.451)	(0.637)
EXPCODE	-1.72486*	-1.21817	-0.84844	-0.15472
	(3.703)	(1.577)	(1.653)	(0.315)
R^2	0.40462	0.17813	0.32435	0.48294
R^2	0.36356	0.12046	0.27775	0.33728
F ratio	8.68370	2.72132	6.13394	11.93477
N	125	123	125	125

*Statistically significant at the 5-percent level.

TABLE 3.5
(continued)

Section 64

First Midsemester Examination	Second Midsemester Examination	Non-TUCE Final Examination	TUCE Final Examination
5.85666	4.86348	1.22113	5.81770
0.01020* (3.725)	0.00156 (0.516)	0.00534* (2.039)	0.00314 (1.022)
0.00041 (0.158)	0.00267 (0.924)	0.00478 (1.902)	0.01019* (3.452)
1.24950* (3.316)	1.52139* (3.700)	1.67339* (4.690)	1.19815* (3.452)
0.10172 (1.922)	0.08753 (1.500)	0.07354 (1.453)	0.24925* (4.190)
-0.05340 (0.176)	0.28868 (0.861)	0.09480 (0.326)	-0.15938 (0.466)
0.45907 (1.658)	0.99496* (3.260)	0.37542 (1.417)	0.35929 (1.155)
0.37602 (1.585)	0.49361 (1.880)	0.06979* (3.055)	0.23900 (0.893)
0.30895 (0.332)	-0.01441 (0.000)	-0.28672 (0.319)	1.01152 (0.961)
0.42622 (1.240)	-0.18817 (0.495)	0.27174 (0.823)	0.60590 (1.562)
0.30591 0.27573 8.96157 192	0.25532 0.22329 7.04779 195	0.35200 0.32413 11.16606 195	0.35947 0.33192 11.53602 195

able for about two-thirds of the students in each section of the courses. This raises the question of whether the regression sample for each section is an accurate representation of the section as a whole. We did make a comparison on a number of characteristics and the statistical tests indicated that there were no significant differences between the two groups (sample in regression and total enrollment) for each section.

To a large extent the regression analysis supports the conclusion drawn in the previous section; that is, with respect to the four measures of cognitive achievement, the CAI system is an effective substitute for the discussion classes. This is evidenced by the sign and statistical significance of the regression coefficient for EXPCODE. For the 223 course the sign of this coefficient is positive in seven of the eight regressions but is statistically significant at the 5-percent level in only one of these cases—the second midsemester examination given in Section 62. In the one case where the sign of the coefficient is negative, it is not statistically significant. In less technical terms in 223 the experimentals rather consistently outperformed the controls, but this difference is so small it can be ignored.

The 224 regression results, presented in Table 3.5, indicate an advantage for the controls. But again the advantage is so small, it too can be ignored. More specifically, in the eight regressions for the 224 course, the sign of the regession coefficient for EXPCODE is negative in five. Of these five a statistically significant result obtains only on the first midsemester examination in Section 63. For the remaining three instances when EXPCODE is positive, all three are statistically insignificant. Rather interestingly we do not obtain consistency of sign in 224 as we move between sections. For this course EXPCODE is negative in all four of the Seciton 63 regressions and is negative in only one of the Section 64 regressions.

Summarizing over both courses, one can conclude that CAI yields cognitive results equivalent to those of the discussion classes. This result obtains when utilization rates are accounted for in a general and relative sense. Because of the problems with OUR, it was decided that a more specific analysis of discussion class attendance by the controls and time with the CAI system by the experimentals was in order. What we have done is to calculate time in discussion class (expressed in hours) for the controls who were included in the regression of Tables 3.4 and 3.5 and CAI time for experimentals over various time intervals. These results are presented in Table 3.6. Here we find that there were no significant differences in any pairwise comparison in either of the two sections of 223. For example, the regression for the second midsemester examination in Section 62 on Table 3.5 indicates that the experimentals were significantly better than the controls. This difference may have been due to the experimentals spending much more time with the CAI system then the controls spent with the discussion classes.[2]

However, the comparison of discussion-class attendance and CAI time during the appropriate interval—first midsemester examination to second midsemester examination (shown on Table 3.6)—does not reveal a significant difference in time between the two student groups. Thus the conclusion here is that the significant difference in cognitive achievement was not due to a significant difference in time effort, a favorable outcome for CAI.

Although there were no significant differences in time effort in each section of 223, there were several in Economics 224. For Section 63 there was a significant difference for the second midsemester examination (experimentals spending significantly less time with CAI than controls with discussion classes) and the final examination (experimentals spending significantly more time with CAI than controls with discussion classes). In both of these cases, however, there were no significant differences in cognitive achievement and thus no firm conclusions can be drawn. For Section 64 there were also two significant differences in time effort—for the first midsemester examination and the final examination. In both of these cases the experimentals were spending significantly more time with the CAI system than the controls did with the discussion classes. But these did not translate into significantly better performances on the corresponding examinations. The evidence for this section really suggests that CAI is inferior to the discussion classes—for example, same levels of cognitive achievement with greater expenditures of time. However, we again underscore that this result obtains in only one section of one course and here in only two of the three portions of the semester. In addition, and this qualification applies with equal force to all the other time comparisons, we do not know how each student group behaved with respect to other course-related activities. It is entirely possible that overall utilization rates are the same, but the experimentals concentrated more of this total time on the CAI system. It is this very problem which makes necessary the collection of very specific time data. Again we tried, but our inability to obtain accurate and complete data on lecture attendance and study time makes the analysis less than complete.

We were able to run several regressions for the 223 course in which discussion class attendance and CAI time were specifically included. These results indicate that attendance of the discussion class and time with the CAI system were positively related to cognitive achievement. These regressions also suggest that CAI is not significantly more effective in raising levels of cognitive achievement. Thus from an overall perspective—the regressions of Tables 3.4 and 3.5, the regressions in conjunction with the time data from Table 3.6 as well as these just mentioned regressions—we conclude that although CAI is not a superior alternative to the discussion classes, it is an effective substitute.

The results presented in Tables 3.4, 3.5, and 3.6 also raise several other

TABLE 3.6

Discussion Class Attendance and CAI Time for Selected Intervals
(Standard Deviation in Parentheses)

Time Interval	Economics 223				Economics 224			
	Section 61		Section 62		Section 63		Section 64	
	Controls Average Discussion Class Attendance	Experimentals Average CAI Time	Controls Average Discussion Class Attendance	Experimentals Average CAI Time	Controls Average Discussion Class Attendance	Experimentals Average CAI Time	Controls Average Discussion Class Attendance	Experimentals Average CAI Time
Beginning of semester to first midsemester examination	2.891 (1.146)	2.516 (3.219)	2.499 (0.783)	2.655 (3.096)	2.668 (1.432)	3.418 (4.136)	2.171 (1.317)	4.214 (5.178)
First midsemester examination to second midsemester examination	1.984 (1.221)	2.198 (4.095)	2.518 (1.509)	2.995 (3.925)	2.1866 (1.145)	1.877 (2.405)	1.639 (1.363)	2.184 (3.716)
Second midsemester examination to final examination	1.323 (1.079)	1.470 (3.002)	1.263 (0.991)	1.720 (2.696)	1.041 (1.039)	1.356 (1.707)	0.700 (0.909)	1.163 (1.725)
Entire semester	6.198 (3.024)	6.185 (7.789)	6.281 (2.768)	7.370 (7.325)	5.896 (3.139)	6.651 (7.085)	4.511 (3.238)	7.561 (8.573)

interesting points. The first concerns the general explanatory power of the learning model. Here we find that, as measured by the coefficient of determination (R^2), the model, or better yet its empirical version, is subject to wide fluctuations as we move between examinations and between lecturers or sections. In three of the four sections the model performs best on the TUCE portion of the final examination and even in the remaing case it performs second best on the TUCE portion of the final examination. This might be due to several different factors, including the fact that as an examination, a true test, the TUCE is better than the locally generated examinations and the fact that the TUCE as a postcourse test should always be highly correlated with the TUCE when taken as a precourse test.

We also find that the model tends to work with greater consistency in Sections 62 and 64 and with less consistency in Sections 61 and 63. Here too these differences may be due to differences in the kinds of examinations given within a section—greater similarity in Section 62 and Section 64 and lesser similarity in Sections 61 and 63.

In the more general context we are somewhat disappointed in the explanatory power of the model. This disappointment is somewhat tempered by two considerations: (1) the data employed are not all we would like them to be and (2) we are dealing with more of a cross-sectional-type problem than a time-series phenomenon. With respect to the first point we have already expressed our dissatisfaction with the data items used to capture utilization rates and are not surprised by its inconsistency in both sign and significance. In addition, the item for the effectiveness of the text is also fairly broad. We suspect that the efficiency of the model could then be improved with better data (we must admit that we join everyone else in this excuse when an R^2 less than .9999 is obtained). We also suspect that we need to explore in greater detail the interaction between variables. Although the simple correlation coefficients do not indicate the existence of much multicolliniarity (admittedly a simple test), we believe that conceptually there is substantial interaction. With respect to the second point it is obvious that it is much more difficult to explain variation between students on a single examination than, say, over the course of the semester. Indeed when the model is applied to grades of a section, the R^2's obtained are greater than those obtained on any of the four examinations within that section. The one exception to this result is Section 63, which of course has the widest variation in R^2's on the separate examinations.

It is also interesting to note that the regression results do not support the argument that males perform better than females in introductory economics courses. Indeed, of the sixteen regressions of Tables 3.4 and 3.5, we find only one case that supports that argument, that is, where the regression coefficient for SEX is both positive and significant. Thus at least for the females involved in these regressions, they do not, in general, perform at lower levels than their male counterparts.

4

MEASURES & DETERMINANTS OF STUDENT ATTITUDES

A. Introduction

The first section of this chapter describes the various instruments employed to measure student attitudes and explains why such measurements are important. The second section presents what might be called a conceptual view of the determinants of student attitudes regarding certain economic institutions, problems, and policies.

B. Measures of Student Attitudes

We attempted to measure student attitudes in three broad areas. The first area may be generally described as student views regarding the elements in the instructional process. Here we are concerned about such things as student reaction to the instructor, the textbook, the discussion class, the CAI system, large lecture classes, objective tests, and so on. To measure these views or attitudes, we employed several different questionnaires. One, mentioned in a previous chapter, was the University Course Evaluation Form. This instrument was distributed to the students once during a semester approximately one week from the end of each course. Part I of Appendix A is a reproduction of this form. It provides information regarding the students' reaction to the instructor or lecturer, the text, and the course itself. A second instrument, reproduced as Part II of Appendix A was distributed twice during each semester to obtain information on student initial and ending attitudes regarding large lecture classes, the text, and objective tests. A third instrument, Parts III, IV, and V of Appendix A, was used only at the end of the 224 course.[1]

There are several reasons why we collected these data. Clearly the model for cognitive achievement includes student reaction to the instructional elements as explanatory variables and these questionnaires yielded the values of such variables. Also important is the fact that student responses to these questionnaires are a means of isolating both the strengths and weaknesses of the several instructional elements. Student responses can then be used to change and improve instructional procedures. Within this perspective we were primarily interested in the student remarks on the new element, the CAI system. Even if the CAI system was not found to be effective in raising levels of cognitive achievement, the student reactions might give some clues as to how the system might be modified in terms of structure or implementation in order to achieve the desired outcome. Finally, the student responses are also important for they provide still another basis for the evaluation of the CAI system. For example, assume that the CAI system did not result in any significant overall gain in the cognitive achievement of those students that used it. If on the basis of the questionnaires the experimentals reacted more favorably to the course in an overall sense as measured by the University Course Evaluation Form or if the CAI system was viewed more favorably than the discussion classes, then these would be arguments in favor of using the CAI system.

The second attitudinal area deals with student perceptions of economics—attitudes toward economics as a discipline as well as student interest in various topics within the discipline. These reactions were also measured by means of a questionnaire, which is reproduced as Appendix B. In this instance the questionnaire was distributed both at the beginning and the end of each semester.

Data generated in this attitudinal area also can be used in several different ways. First, the data are of interest in and of themselves: what are student attitudes regarding the difficulty and relevancy of economics, what topics within economics interest students the most, how do these things change over time, and so on. It might be argued that effectiveness of both cognitive outcomes and attitudes regarding a course could be enhanced if a course were structured along topics of interest to students. Second, these data can also be used to determine, with respect to ending attitudes and changes in attitudes, whether or not the CAI system impacts in a unique way. This also represents a basis for using the CAI system independent of the system's effect on cognitive achievement. In this context the CAI system may be a preferred instructional element if it leaves the student user with the attitude that economics is a useful discipline or not as difficult a discipline as originally perceived. These types of ending attitudes would be desirable because they may be directly correlated with students taking additional courses in economics. Or, from a less selfish perspective, they may be directly correlated with students being less afraid to address themselves to economic problems in the world around them or even to use economic analysis in examining problems of all sorts.

The third and final attitudinal area concerns student opinions regarding certain economic institutions, problems and policies, or, for purposes of brevity, opinions on economic issues. Again surveys or questionnaires were distributed at the beginning and end of each semester. On these surveys an item or issue–say inflation–is presented, and under it are listed a series of semantic differentials such as "bad-good," "inevitable-controllable," "demand pull–cost push," and so forth. Each semantic differential is viewed as a continuum ranging in numerical terms from 1 to 5, with a 3 representing a middle position. This questionnaire is reproduced as Appendix C.

In this instance we did not collect the data because of its possible use in explaining cognitive achievement. Rather it seems to us that in evaluating either education in a general sense or the effects of an educational innovation, the broadest possible spectrum should be employed. To ignore opinions on issues is to shorten the spectrum and reduce the range of potential insights. We need to know what goes on in terms of student opinions on issues and whether the CAI system operates differentially in this area. This is not to say that greater change of opinion on economic issues is to be preferred to lesser change or that change in one direction is to be preferred to change in another, but it is an argument for a fuller basis of evaluation.

The three areas of attitudinal concern may be compared to what can be called the *continuum of the affective domain.*[2] This continuum, according to one taxonomy, begins with the individual being aware of a phenomenon; that is, the student perceives that he or she is in receipt of a stimulus. At the next level the student not only perceives the stimulus but also responds to it. At some point in the process the student begins to internalize the stimulus leading to the development of a set of attitudes or values. This continuum, is finally marked by the organization of a value system. The correspondence between our three attitudinal areas and the affective-domain continuum just described is neither exact nor complete. Certainly to the extent that the student forms an attitude on an instructional element implies that the student perceives the element and is responding either positively or negatively to it. The results of the questionnaire on economic issues might also be interpreted as the formulation of a value system. Given these types of similarities, there remains a certain lack of correspondence which arises from ambiguities within both our attitudinal instruments and in the affective-domain continuum. For example, is the value system included within the continuum to be interpreted as a consistent set of opinions regarding stimuli, here interpreted as instructional elements or as a consistent set of opinions regarding issues raised by the particular course? Even if we were to assume the latter interpretation, what represents a consistent set of opinions? The instrument used to measure opinions on economic issues was not designed to yield a specific pattern of responses that might be labeled, say, as conservative or liberal or even desirable or undesirable. Even though a full one-to-one correspondence cannot be established, we believe the three areas we address do represent a relatively wide range within the attitudinal domain.

It should also be apparent that these three attitudinal areas are both conventional and unconventional. In the conventional realm many colleges and universities employ devices similar to the University Course Evaluation Form. The results generated through the use of these devices have been used in a variety of ways and have been the subject of some research activity. The determinants of student attitudes or evaluations of their teachers are probably the focal points of this research.[3] In addition the information generated by these course-evaluation questionnaires can and have been used in evaluating educational innovations. Here reactions of students who use the educational innovation are compared with those who do not. As indicated we will use this procedure as well.

Slightly less conventional is the questionnaire dealing with student reactions to economics as a discipline and topics of interest within economics. Much effort has been devoted to devising techniques and approaches to economics that will increase student interest in, and satisfaction with, economics. In evaluating these techniques and procedures, the tendency has been to rely on course-specific questions of the sort mentioned above. Our approach is to supplement the course-specific questions with discipline-specific questions. It is not entirely clear that responses will necessarily be the same and it is entirely possible that the latter types of questions will add new insights into both the effects of educational innovation and the determinants of the responses to the course-specific questions.

The most unconventional attitudinal area is that dealing with student opinion on economic issues. We have already offered a general rationale for the collection of these data. At this point it might be useful to address several questions that might be raised concerning the construction of the questionnaire and the interpretation of results obtained. We can begin with the fact the questionnaire was not designed to yield a particular set of responses that might be labeled as representative of a given political or philosophic position or even as desirable or undesirable.[4] The avoidance of political or philosophic interpretations seemed reasonable given the ambiguity of such labels. For example, should the term "liberal" be interpreted in its current political context or in terms of nineteenth-century connotations? Avoidance of labels with respect to desirable and undesirable is not so easily dismissed. Certainly on a specific semantic differential for a selected issue, a particular response could be described as desirable. For example, an instructor in the 224 course carefully constructs the concept of comparative advantage, indicating the benefits that can be obtained from specialization and and international trade. The logical consequence of this presentation is that free trade is desirable; it is, in terms of one of the semantic differentials on the issue of international trade, "good." Indeed if the student is able to learn the various concepts and arguments as evidenced by his ability to recapitulate them on examinations, but the student remains with the opinion that international trade is "bad," one might question the effectiveness of the course or the methods of instruction. However, the selection of desired outcomes is possible only on relatively few of the semantic differentials. In addition, and perhaps more importantly, the basis for the opinion is not identified. In terms of the trade example, a country can become worse off if it is forced to accept terms of trade below those implied by domestic production conditions. If the student has this perspective in mind, then "bad" can be interpreted as a desirable response. Of course, to supply such conditions as the context for selecting a response for each semantic differential on each issue would turn the questionnaire into an examination. But to admit that there is not necessarily a pattern of responses that is desirable in our mind is not to admit that such information is uninteresting and unimportant.

The usefulness of this information might also be questioned given the current vogue in the social sciences, and particularly in economics, to distinguish between positive and normative aspects of a discipline. Recognizing this distinction has led some individuals to argue that instruction should constrain itself to the introductions and elaborations of positive science.[5] As a consequence the success of a course should be viewed solely in terms of student mastery of positive aspects of the discipline. But even such an approach will not necessarily produce a completely random set of responses to an issue questionnaire. If the basis for the initial responses to the questionnaire was an empty set of economic tools, the ending responses should reflect a nonempty set. It is not entirely clear that giving students the analytic apparatus of economics will generate a systematic evaluation of opinions on economic issues. This represents an open question that should be examined. If an instructor believes that economics is both positive and normative and includes both aspects in a course, then there is all the more reason to measure opinions on issues. In this instance it might be argued that the success of such a course should include both references to the cognitive domain and this attitudinal area, with the latter, perhaps, yielding a better indication of the extent to which normative objectives have been accomplished.

There are several other questions concerning the opinion area, but these will be taken up in the next section where we construct a view of possible determinants of student opinions on economic issues. We can close the current discussion by stating that the three attitudinal areas addressed with the various questionnaires are of interest not because they fully develop an affective-domain continuum. They are of interest because the results may give us a better idea of what goes on in a course; they are, in part, necessary to explain cognitive achievement, and they provide additional grounds for an evaluation of the CAI system.

C. Determinants of Student Opinions on Economic Issues

In this section we will focus on the determinants of student attitudes in only one of the three areas outlined above–student opinions on economic issues. This exclusiveness of focus arises because this is the one area that is most interesting from a research point of view, for it represents basically virgin territory.[6] This is not to say that all the questions regarding the determinants of student attitudes in the other areas have been resolved, but that by directing our attention to this previously ignored area, we can develop a fuller understanding of what goes on during a Principles of Economics sequence. We can begin by examining in a little more detail what it is we hope to explain.

As we have stated, the questionnaire on economic issues was not designed to yield a particular set of responses that could be identified by some particular political, philosophic, or ideological label. Nor did we feel that a particular set of responses should be interpreted as more preferable than another. As a consequence we are not attempting to explain patterns of responses over the entire questionnaire by the various students. Our approach is to look at each semantic differential separately, attempting to isolate factors that are important in explaining the pattern of responses by the various students to that semantic differential. Once this is done for each of the seventy-four semantic differentials, we then can attempt to make broader summary statements; that is, identifying which factors are important in all, many, some, or none of the seventy-four cases.

Given that the issue questionnaire was distributed both at the beginning and end of each semester, there are two major possible specifications of the dependent variable. We may deal either with an opinion as it existed at the end of a semester (postcourse opinion) or we may deal with the change that has occurred over a semester (postcourse opinion less precourse opinion). At this stage it is uncertain as to whether the two alternatives are really different from a conceptual view. For pragmatic reasons, namely, that postcourse attitudes are seemingly less ambiguous than changes per se, we will use the former specification.

But what explains the postcourse opinions of a group of students to a particular semantic differential? Clearly, in arriving at an explanation of a postcourse opinion we should control for the precourse opinion. Beyond this we can argue that several different types of factors may contribute independently to the formulation of opinions. One set of factors might be labeled *other opinions.* These other opinions might induce a consistent type of movement across a group of students. These other opinions include those of the instructors as well as those of the author or authors of textbooks used in a course. With regard to the instructor, try as he might to avoid the rendering of his own opinions, it is likely that students may perceive an attitudinal bias. The same is true of text authors. The argument then is that if there is a difference between the students' initial opinions and those of "experts" with whom he comes in contact, the student is likely to move in the direction of the "experts."

Another set of factors might be considered human-capital elements. Here we would include both human capital as it existed as of the beginning of the semester as well as the amount which was accumulated over the course of the semester. In terms of initial human capital, the argument is that the greater this stock, all other things being equal, the smaller will be the difference between precourse and postcourse opinions. This should be the case because greater stocks of initial human capital imply a more solid foundation for the precourse opinion. At the same time, however, the greater the economic knowledge accumulated over the semester, the greater the expansion of the base of specific economic knowledge and thus the greater the likelihood of a reevaluation of an opinion. In this regard one might even go further. Because the instructor's opinions are rooted at least partially in his knowledge, the greater the student's cognitive achievement, the closer may be the similarity between the instructor's opinion and the student's postcourse opinion. Reworded, establishing a commonality of knowledge may be linked, all other things being equal, to a commonality of opinions. Whatever the specific linkages, it would appear that both dimensions of human capital–as it existed at the beginning of the semester and the amount accumulated during the semester–should be included as potential determinants of postcourse opinion.

The third and final set of factors might be termed the *sociodemographic background of the student*. No one will deny that elements such as the occupational and educational status of parents, age of the student, geographic backgrounds, and so on might be significant determinants of precourse opinions. We are taking the argument one step further by saying that these elements will continue to operate as a student reevaluates his position on an issue as presented by a specific semantic differential. Thus it is entirely possible that various types of backgrounds may be more or less favorable for reevaluation of opinion.

We can restate our position algebraically as:

$$\text{POST} = F(\text{PRE}, \text{OO}, \text{HC}, \text{SD})$$

where

POST = the student's postcourse attitudinal opinion on a semantic differential.

PRE = the student's precourse attitudinal position on that semantic differential.

OO = opinion of other on that semantic differential.

HC = the student's human capital.

SD = the sociodemographic background of the student.

Within this context we cannot predict specifically the nature of the relationship between the various factors and the dependent variable. This inability arises because particular postcourse opinions on a specific semantic differential cannot be labeled—for example, as to conservative or liberal—and because each of the independent variables have not been fully defined. Equation (4.1), therefore, is simply to be understood as an algebraic statement of particular factors that might influence student postcourse attitudinal opinions. That is, the equation represents a crude but conceptual view of the determinants of student postcourse opinions.

In addition, and perhaps more importantly, there are three types of semantic differentials and the effect of the factors shown above may not be consistent as we move from one type to another. In our mind the three types of semantic differentials are political, content or analytic, and value-laden. For example, one issue that included all three types of semantic differentials (Appendix C) is the FEDERAL INCOME TAX, which was defined as follows:

FEDERAL INCOME TAX:

Progressive	1	2	3	4	5	Regressive
Good	1	2	3	4	5	Bad
Democratic	1	2	3	4	5	Republican
Free Enterprise	1	2	3	4	5	Socialism
Too High	1	2	3	4	5	Too Low
Fair	1	2	3	4	5	Unfair

In the context of the 223 course we would contend that the first semantic differential is of the content or analytic type. This is based on the fact that the terms "progressive" and "regressive" have very specific meanings in economics. The students are exposed to these definitions as well as their applications to the federal income tax.[7] The second and the last semantic differential would be categorized as *value-laden.* This is defined as a type that the student will react to personally, reflecting his own value system. The political category is the "Democratic-Republican" semantic differential which appears under almost all of the issues.

Some semantic differentials appear to overlap between categories. For instance the "free enterprise-socialism" semantic differential could well depend on the manner in which the particular lecturer treated the issue and the manner in which the student interprets the discussion. Finally an identical semantic differential is interpreted, hence evaluated, differently by students when it appears under a different issue.

In this view of determinants we would suspect that any time a new educational element is introduced in a course, it may affect the opinion forming process. This can occur in a variety of ways; by affecting cognitive achievement or by interjecting a new attitudinal perspective.

To summarize, we have employed a variety of attitudinal instruments. These instruments are useful in a number of ways, but the two most important ways are the insights they provide as to what goes on in a course and the fact that they can be used as an additional measure of the impact of CAI. The question now is: what did the completed questionnaires reveal?

5

THE ATTITUDINAL RESULTS

A. Introduction

This chapter is the empirical counterpart of the preceding chapter. As such we will begin by examining the responses of the students to the questionnaires distributed in each of the attitudinal areas: attitudes toward instructional elements, attitudes toward economics, and opinions regarding economic issues. In each instance we are interested in determining whether CAI generates a unique impact relative to the discussion classes. In the section dealing with attitudes toward instructional elements, we have omitted a comparison of student evaluations of CAI and the discussion classes. This comparison, because it is rather extensive, is reserved for Chapter VI. In the last section of this chapter, we explore the determinants of student opinions on economic issues. Here we are concerned both with isolating determinants of student's postcourse opinions and whether there is a differential impact for CAI on these opinions.

B. Attitudes toward Instructional Elements

Two survey instruments were employed in this area. The first and most important is the University Course Evaluation Form (Appendix A Part I). The Form was distributed once at the end of each course. For this instrument, a desired outcome can be specified. Higher numerical scores–they can range from 1 to 4–are evidence of a student satisfaction with both the teacher and the course. Aside from wanting to leave students satisfied, this is a desired outcome because the model for cognitive achievement implies that higher numerical scores should be consistent with greater levels of cognitive achievement. Even if there were no positive relationship between the responses to this questionnaire and cognitive achievement, higher numerical scores would still be desirable. In this instance we are simply recognizing the fact that data generated from these kinds of instruments are used by administrators to evaluate teachers. As a consequence an instructor might want to use an educational innovation even if it has no effect on cognitive achievement if it will raise his average scores. Regardless of the reasons underlying the desirability of higher numerical responses, the question is: whether the use of CAI has a systematic and significant effect on the University Course Evaluation Form (UCEF).

Table 5.1 presents information which can be used to answer this question. Here we have recorded the average responses to each of the items on the UCEF by the two groups of students in each section of each course. To facilitate the discussion, we will define a positive (negative) effect as an instance where the mean response for the experimentals on an item is greater (less) than the mean for the controls. With this in mind, we will summarize the results for each section and then attempt to generalize across all four sections.

Section 61. There are four positive effects and thirteen negative effects. Only in the latter group were any of the differences in means statistically significant[1] at the 5-percent level, for items 3, 5, and 10. Within this section, then, CAI appears to have an undesirable impact on the UCEF, although the overall effect seems fairly weak.

Section 62. Positive effects are obtained on nine of the eighteen items, with seven negative effects. For the sixteen items in which there were differences in the mean responses, none were significant. The overall effect for CAI in this section might be labeled favorable but very weak.

Section 63. Seven positive effects and ten negative effects are recorded for this section. In all of these seventeen cases, the differences in means were not significant, implying a generally unfavorable but very weak impact for CAI.

Section 64. Here we observe twelve positive effects and five negative effects. One of the positive effects, on item 14, is statistically significant. Overall then this section indicates a favorable CAI impact, but it too is fairly weak.

Summarizing the evidence across the four sections, we conclude that there is no consistent CAI impact, either upward or downward, on the UCEF. The two alternative approaches, CAI or the discussion classes, seem to yield approximately equivalent numerical scores on the various items for a given section.

The second attitudinal instrument employed in this area was distributed at the beginning and end of each course (Appendix A Part II). This questionnaire should probably be considered as a supplement to the UCEF, yielding more specific information on student reactions to large lectures, objective tests, and textbooks. For each of these instructional elements students were given several statements and were asked to indicate whether they agreed or disagreed with the statement (a "1" indicating strong disagreement, a "5"

TABLE 5.1

Attitudes on Instructional Elements
University Course Evaluation Form
(Standard Deviations in Parentheses)

Item	Economics 223				Economics 224			
	Section 61		Section 62		Section 63		Section 64	
	Controls	Experimentals	Controls	Experimentals	Controls	Experimentals	Controls	Experimentals
1. Teacher's knowledge of subject matter	3.82 (0.419)	3.86 (0.365)	3.93 (0.252)	3.92 (0.275)	3.41 (0.589)	3.36 (0.628)	3.81 (0.459)	3.82 (0.388)
2. Teacher's enthusiasm for subject	3.50 (0.619)	3.51 (0.561)	3.87 (0.343)	3.85 (0.357)	3.34 (0.615)	3.34 (0.628)	3.82 (0.431)	3.86 (0.348)
3. Effectiveness of class teaching or direction	3.14 (0.679)	2.96 (0.732)	3.42 (0.552)	3.46 (0.583)	2.75 (0.688)	2.56 (0.726)	3.30 (0.655)	3.38 (0.696)
4. Ability to stimulate student interest in subject	3.00 (0.688)	2.83 (0.771)	3.07 (0.679)	3.14 (0.625)	2.53 (0.814)	2.40 (0.812)	3.10 (0.706)	3.11 (0.672)
5. Interest in students, e.g. availability, helpfulness	2.99 (0.808)	2.72 (0.777)	2.89 (0.767)	2.94 (0.735)	3.12 (0.793)	3.19 (0.846)	3.32 (0.807)	3.28 (0.795)
6. Fairness in dealing with students	3.23 (0.698)	3.09 (0.733)	3.32 (0.688)	3.25 (0.682)	3.16 (0.749)	3.04 (0.742)	3.38 (0.713)	3.46 (0.699)
7. Respect for students' viewpoints	3.20 (0.749)	3.12 (0.725)	3.08 (0.686)	3.25 (0.656)	3.38 (0.700)	3.24 (0.676)	3.46 (0.662)	3.40 (0.651)
8. Organization and management of course	3.27 (0.737)	3.30 (0.738)	3.54 (0.590)	3.56 (0.556)	3.18 (0.671)	3.10 (0.777)	3.44 (0.723)	3.51 (0.568)
9. Overall rating of teachers compared with other teachers at Notre Dame	3.27 (0.678)	3.24 (0.699)	3.57 (0.517)	3.55 (0.570)	2.90 (0.672)	2.68 (0.747)	3.59 (0.595)	3.59 (0.561)

10. Teacher's ability to lecture in a clear, interesting manner	3.46 (0.733)	3.17 (0.841)	3.68 (0.508)	3.68 (0.608)	2.69 (0.880)	2.64 (0.856)	3.62 (0.633)	3.61 (0.671)
11. Teacher's ability to encourage independent thinking	2.88 (0.845)	2.80 (0.786)	3.00 (0.643)	3.00 (0.695)	2.51 (0.775)	2.49 (0.715)	2.90 (0.637)	2.95 (0.632)
12. Teacher's carefulness of preparation for class	3.50 (0.716)	3.41 (0.757)	3.77 (0.446)	3.69 (0.526)	3.23 (0.656)	3.33 (0.746)	3.51 (0.570)	3.56 (0.516)
13. Teacher's promptness in returning student work	3.78 (0.602)	3.72 (0.698)	3.88 (0.387)	3.91 (0.363)	3.77 (0.484)	3.82 (0.391)	3.93 (0.294)	3.84 (0.494)
14. Intellectual level of lectures	3.42 (0.655)	3.29 (0.725)	3.38 (0.702)	3.46 (0.635)	3.06 (0.643)	3.24 (0.682)	3.47 (0.537)	3.62 (0.489)
15. Quality of text	3.40 (0.827)	3.23 (0.925)	3.24 (0.728)	3.22 (0.807)	3.23 (0.746)	3.44 (0.707)	3.39 (0.822)	3.51 (0.692)
16. Personal value of course to you	3.08 (0.818)	3.06 (0.879)	3.30 (0.686)	3.25 (0.750)	2.91 (0.819)	2.86 (0.822)	3.13 (0.702)	3.05 (0.815)
17. Standard for students' performances required for course	3.04 (0.824)	3.18 (0.760)	3.24 (0.704)	3.32 (0.700)	3.22 (0.592)	3.39 (0.662)	3.30 (0.553)	3.38 (0.555)
18. Workload compared with other Notre Dame course loads	2.73 (0.789)	2.73 (0.827)	2.73 (0.616)	2.83 (0.743)	2.74 (0.689)	2.80 (0.666)	2.78 (0.569)	2.85 (0.588)

indicating strong agreement). Given the nature of the statements, higher numerical responses are not always to be desired. Because of this, as well as the fact that responses are available on both a postcourse basis and in terms of changes (postcourse minus precourse), these data are difficult to summarize. For the sake of completeness we have presented both postcourse attitudes and changes in attitudes for each section of each course in Table 5.2. For purposes of brevity we will restrict discussion to a comparison of the average changes for controls and experimentals in each section.

Section 61. For the twenty items, we find instances where the average change for controls and experimentals is in the same direction and also instances of movements in opposite directions. A comparison of the mean changes reveals only one instance of statistical significance. This occurred on item 20. Here we find what might be labeled a positive effect for CAI; that is, in revising their opinions, the experimentals were less inclined to agree with the statement that textbooks are not integrated into lectures, while the controls were more inclined to agree.

Section 62. Again we find instances where the direction of change between the two groups is similar and disimilar. Only in one instance do we have a significant difference in the average change between the two groups, on item 6. Here both controls and experimentals were less inclined to agree with the statement that large lectures were boring, but the extent of the change was larger for the controls.

Section 63. As before we find only one instance where the average change in attitudes between the two student groups is statistically significant, on item 8. This might be considered a favorable CAI effect; that is, in revising their opinions regarding objective tests as a fair measure of knowledge, the experimentals were moving in a direction of greater agreement, while the controls in a direction of greater disagreement.

Section 64. For this section there were no significant differences in the average change in attitudes between the two student groups on any of the twenty items.

Looking across the four sections, we again find no evidence that CAI has any consistent and significant impact on student attitudes regarding instructional elements. This result reinforces, of course, the conclusion generated from the examination of attitudes toward instructional elements as recorded by the UCEF.

C. Attitudes toward Economics

This questionnaire was also given at the beginning and end of each course (Appendix B). In this instance students were given five descriptors of economics (hard, abstract, useful, theoretical, and relevant) and were asked whether they agreed or disagreed (a "1" indicating strong disagreement and a "5" indicating strong agreement) with that descriptor. On this questionnaire we can also specify a desired outcome, at least in part. The discussion of the previous chapter has indicated why we would like to have students consider economics useful and relevant and thus higher numerical scores are to be desired on these two descriptors. CAI would have a favorable impact if it yielded statistically significant higher postcourse scores or generated greater revision in this upward direction. In addition an educational innovation should make a discipline less difficult, and therefore we would like lower scores on the "hard" descriptor. From the standpoint of a CAI proponent, the postcourse score on this descriptor should be lower for the experimentals than that for the controls or the revision in this direction should be greater. On the remaining descriptors there is, a priori, no reason to say that a given result, all other things being equal, should be more or less desirable than any other.

In any event, Table 5.3 indicates both the ending attitudes as well as the change in attitudes on this questionnaire as recorded for the controls and the experimentals in each section of the two courses. We will summarize these on a section by section basis and, for the sake of brevity, concentrate on the average changes in attitudes.

Section 61. Here the controls and the experimentals moved in the same direction on four of the five descriptors, both student groups found economics less hard, less abstract, less theoretical, and less relevant. Comparison of the average change between the two student groups reveals no statistically significant differences. The two groups moved in opposite directions on the useful descriptor. The experimentals revising their attitudes in a downward direction, while the controls moved in an upward direction. This is an undesirable CAI effect, but the difference in average changes was not significant.

Section 62. Here too the direction of change was the same for four of the five descriptors; controls and experimentals found economics less hard, less abstract, less useful, and less relevant. Comparing the average change between the student groups reveals no significant differences. The controls and experimentals moved in opposite directions on the theoretical descriptor, but even here the difference in average change was not significant.

Section 63. Both student groups moved in the same direction on the abstract (downward), useful (upward) theoretical (downward), and relevant (upward) descriptors. The differences in the changes were not significant. In addition, the experimentals found economics harder, while the controls found economics less hard. From a CAI standpoint this is an undesirable effect, but again the difference in the mean change was not significant.

Section 64. Common movement occurred on three of the five descriptors: abstract (downward), useful (upward), and relevant (upward), but again the

TABLE 5.2

Attitudes on Instruction Elements
Supplementary Questionnaire

Higher numerical scores indicate strong agreement with statement
(Standard Deviations in Parentheses)

	Economics 223							
	Section 61				Section 62			
	Controls		Experimentals		Controls		Experimentals	
Item	Post	Change	Post	Change	Post	Change	Post	Change
LARGE LECTURES ARE:								
1. good teaching methods	2.63	-0.247	2.41	-0.1216	2.5556	-0.1429	2.6899	-0.3876
	(1.051)	(0.950)	(1.093)	(1.298)	(1.028)	(1.134)	(1.067)	(1.113)
2. good ways to present	3.48	-0.1296	3.18	-0.2432	3.4194	-0.1774	3.3411	-0.3438
information	(0.906)	(0.953)	(1.117)	(1.199)	(0.984)	(1.167)	(1.121)	(1.276)
3. useful for presenting	2.96	-0.1852	2.64	0.0676	3.1270	-0.3810	2.8837	-0.2403
policy	(1.045)	(1.083)	(1.076)	(1.188)	(0.992)	(1.184)	(1.043)	(1.279)
4. useful for presenting	3.30	-0.2407	2.99	0.0135	3.1746	-0.905	3.0465	-0.0388
theory	(1.05)	(1.080)	(1.149)	(1.189)	(1.056)	(1.203)	(1.131)	(1.331)
5. well related to text	3.17	-0.222	2.80	0.0203	3.0159	-0.0952	2.9225	0.0543
	(0.986)	(1.192)	(1.125)	(1.097)	(1.055)	(1.434)	(1.072)	(1.233)
6. boring	3.23	0.0943	3.49	0.0405	3.0645	-0.4032	3.2188	-0.0078
	(1.120)	(1.458)	(1.122)	(1.288)	(1.099)	(1.286)	(1.064)	(1.187)
7. stifling to creative	3.00	0.1667	3.34	0.0270	3.3548	-0.2623	3.3047	-0.0469
thought	(1.116)	(1.384)	(1.111)	(1.380)	(0.889)	(1.031)	(1.098)	(1.362)

OBJECTIVE TESTS ARE:								
8. fair measures of knowledge	3.59	0.1111	3.55	0.2297	3.5079	0.0476	3.7287	-0.1085
	(0.981)	(1.110)	(0.964)	(1.089)	(1.148)	(0.941)	(0.882)	(1.048)
9. good if limited to specifics	3.76	0.0741	3.77	-0.0473	3.7460	-0.0317	3.6899	0.1163
	(0.751)	(0.949)	(0.701)	(0.794)	(0.822)	(1.015)	(0.716)	(0.949)
10. superior to essay tests	3.35	-0.0926	3.33	-0.0135	3.2222	-0.2698	3.2481	-0.0930
	(1.102)	(1.137)	(1.090)	(1.149)	(1.069)	(1.035)	(1.053)	(1.086)
11. such as to require	2.78	0.1111	2.86	-0.0541	3.0476	0.0328	2.7364	0.1395
memorization	(1.076)	(1.284)	(1.079)	(1.130)	(1.084)	(1.390)	(1.115)	(1.171)
12. useful for testing theory	3.0926	0.0	3.2027	-0.0612	3.1905	-0.3226	3.2713	-0.3101
	(0.976)	(1.082)	(0.954)	(1.130)	(1.014)	(1.184)	(0.933)	(1.103)
13. useful for testing policy	3.4815	-0.0556	3.5135	-0.0541	3.3016	-0.0484	3.6512	-0.2248
	(0.863)	(1.188)	(0.821)	(1.142)	(0.873)	(1.286)	(0.757)	(1.010)
TEXTBOOKS ARE:								
14. good teaching devices	4.0741	0.0	3.9459	-0.0816	3.7937	0.1905	3.8915	-0.0155
	(0.669)	(0.752)	(0.717)	(0.856)	(0.864)	(0.780)	(0.721)	(0.838)
15. useful for presenting policy	3.9259	-0.2037	3.8514	-0.1216	3.8065	-0.0667	3.7829	-0.0930
	(0.696)	(0.833)	(0.643)	(0.888)	(0.807)	(0.936)	(0.739)	(0.988)
16. useful for presenting theory	3.9259	0.0	3.9527	-0.1973	3.9524	0.0635	3.8217	0.0233
	(0.843)	(0.824)	(0.693)	(0.782)	(0.682)	(0.693)	(0.755)	(0.939)
17. always dull	2.2222	-0.0556	2.2838	0.0748	2.3651	-0.1587	2.3411	-0.0930
	(1.003)	(0.979)	(0.825)	(0.930)	(0.921)	(0.846)	(0.897)	(0.897)
18. not relevant to class goals	2.1667	0.02264	2.0811	-0.0338	2.2581	-0.1452	2.0078	0.0543
	(0.765)	(0.776)	(0.714)	(0.795)	(0.767)	(0.786)	(0.619)	(0.794)
19. not suitable to class goals	2.2222	0.0926	2.3401	0.0680	2.5556	-0.0952	2.3387	0.1371
	(0.769)	(0.759)	(0.781)	(1.083)	(0.857)	(0.962)	(0.764)	(0.940)
20. not integrated into lecture	2.1111	0.2778	2.4324	-0.0743	2.1452	0.2459	2.1484	0.2500
	(0.664)	(0.656)	(1.044)	(0.656)	(0.721)	(1.043)	(0.888)	(0.980)
N	54	54	148	148	63	63	129	129

TABLE 5.2
(continued)

Attitudes on Instruction Elements
Supplementary Questionnaire

Higher numerical scores indicate strong agreement with statement
(Standard Deviations in Parentheses)

	Economics 224							
	Section 63				Section 64			
	Controls		Experimentals		Controls		Experimentals	
Item	Post	Change	Post	Change	Post	Change	Post	Change
LARGE LECTURES ARE:								
1. good teaching methods	2.6522	0.0580	2.7541	-0.2459	2.5568	-0.1818	2.7368	-0.0947
	(1.027)	(0.998)	(1.105)	(1.386)	(1.027)	(1.109)	(1.074)	(1.001)
2. good ways to present	3.4058	-0.0145	3.5410	-0.1803	3.3068	-0.0682	3.3895	-0.9632
information	(1.062)	(0.899)	(0.976)	(1.118)	(1.097)	(1.294)	(1.034)	(1.090)
3. useful for presenting policy	2.8696	0.0145	3.1811	-0.3279	2.7614	-0.0805	2.9263	-0.0532
	(1.097)	(1.207)	(0.991)	(1.060)	(1.145)	(1.260)	(0.970)	(0.999)
4. useful for presenting theory	3.1739	-0.0290	3.1311	0.0820	2.9886	0.2159	3.1789	0.0316
	(1.137)	(1.1084)	(1.118)	(1.159)	(1.119)	(1.326)	(1.031)	(1.026)
5. well related to text	3.0870	-0.0145	3.0492	0.0	2.8851	-0.1149	3.1158	-0.3053
	(1.222)	(1.289)	(1.040	(1.140)	(1.094)	(1.261)	(1.030)	(1.092)
6. boring	3.6522	-0.5652	3.3770	-0.1833	3.1136	0.3721	3.1579	0.1789
	(0.983)	(1.131)	(1.098)	(1.308)	(1.139)	(1.338)	(1.123)	(1.203)
7. stifling to creative thought	3.3768	-0.1884	3.2951	0.0492	3.1705	0.1818	3.2737	-0.1053
	(1.045)	(1.287)	(0.972)	(1.203)	(1.147)	(1.394)	(1.143)	(1.242)

OBJECTIVE TESTS ARE:								
8. fair measures of knowledge	3.7391	-0.0145	3.2787	0.4333	3.6023	-0.0455	3.6737	-0.1368
	(0.885)	(0.106)	(1.051)	(1.031)	(0.929)	(1.071)	(0.983)	(0.974)
9. good if limited to specifics	3.7536	-0.9290	3.8689	-0.1311	3.8409	0.0227	3.6421	0.1158
	(0.755)	(0.822)	(0.645)	(0.785)	(0.676)	(0.830)	(0.824)	(1.071)
10. superior to essay tests	3.333	0.1014	2.9344	0.2459	3.2955	0.0341	3.1579	0.1368
	(1.053)	(0.877)	(1.031)	(1.075)	(1.052)	(1.098)	(1.123)	(1.068)
11. such as to require memorization	2.695	0.0580	3.1639	-0.3167	2.8864	-0.0682	2.7340	0.1489
	(0.975)	(1.259)	(1.128)	(1.228)	(1.087)	(1.230)	(1.069)	(1.116)
12. useful for testing theory	3.2609	0.2029	3.2295	-0.9667	3.3068	-0.0909	3.4632	-0.2000
	(0.949)	(1.119)	(0.956)	(1.133)	(0.939)	(1.121)	(0.909)	(1.107)
13. useful for testing policy	3.3913	0.3188	3.2951	0.2667	3.4773	0.1364	3.4526	0.0
	(0.826)	(0.931)	(0.823)	(0.989)	(0.857)	(1.030)	(0.884)	(1.031)
TEXTBOOKS ARE:								
14. good teaching devices	3.9130	0.0145	4.0328	-0.0164	3.9318	-0.0568	3.9684	0.0105
	(0.853)	(0.831)	(0.605)	(0.764)	(0.944)	(0.963)	(0.750)	(0.881)
15. useful for presenting policy	3.7971	-0.0435	3.6721	0.0	3.7273	0.0568	3.6000	0.2842
	(0.778)	(0.930)	(0.724)	(1.017)	(1.003)	(1.010)	(0.830)	(0.883)
16. useful for presenting theory	3.9275	0.0145	3.9180	0.0820	3.8068	0.0227	3.7789	0.2211
	(0.734)	(0.915)	(0.690)	(0.690)	(0.819)	(1.039)	(0.788)	(0.788)
17. always dull	2.2609	0.1304	2.1311	0.2131	2.1364	0.1250	2.2211	0.0737
	(0.816)	(0.984)	(0.670)	(0.933)	(0.819)	(0.814)	(0.746)	(0.878)
18. not relevant to class goals	1.9420	0.1014	2.0656	0.0492	2.0909	-0.0227	1.9474	0.1474
	(0.591)	(0.789)	(0.574)	(0.805)	(0.797)	(0.909)	(0.513)	(0.635)
19. not suitable to class goals	2.1884	0.0870	2.4754	0.0	2.3409	-0.9227	2.3298	-0.0213
	(0.845)	(1.095)	(0.788)	(1.000)	(0.908)	(1.072)	(0.753)	(0.950)
20. not integrated into lecture	2.0145	0.0145	2.1311	0.2131	2.2159	0.1591	2.0105	0.3158
	(0.757)	(0.866)	(0.741)	(1.097)	(0.928)	(1.240)	(0.574)	(0.937)
N	69	69	61	61	88	88	94	94

TABLE 5.3

Attitudes toward Economics

Higher numerical scores indicate strong agreement with the statement.

Student Classification	HARD Ending Position	HARD Change	ABSTRACT Ending Position	ABSTRACT Change	USEFUL Ending Position	USEFUL Change	THEORETICAL Ending Position	THEORETICAL Change	RELEVANT Ending Position	RELEVANT Change	N
Economics 223, Section 61											
Controls	3.7308 (0.976)	-0.4872 (0.879)	2.9615 (1.025)	-0.2436 (0.914)	4.2436 (0.563)	0.0641 (0.690)	3.5641 (0.934)	-0.1667 (0.986)	4.4103 (0.568)	-0.0256 (0.702)	78
Experimentals	3.5500 (1.033)	-0.2200 (1.104)	2.9565 (1.109)	-0.1933 (1.185)	4.2813 (0.574)	-0.1333 (0.783)	3.7875 (0.788)	-0.3299 (0.826)	4.3062 (0.572)	-0.0133 (0.786)	160
Section 62											
Controls	3.5096 (1.043)	-0.3465 (1.195)	2.8738 (1.035)	-0.0990 (1.054)	4.4327 (0.553)	-0.2178 (0.832)	3.7981 (0.768)	-0.1980 (1.058)	4.5192 (0.539)	-0.2475 (0.793)	104
Experimentals	3.6917 (0.939)	-0.5000 (1.136)	3.0451 (1.007)	-0.1705 (1.276)	4.2256 (0.724)	-0.0077 (0.858)	3.5802 (0.885)	0.0698 (0.978)	4.2879 (0.636)	-0.0465 (0.943)	133
Economics 224, Section 63											
Controls	3.4810 (1.108)	-0.1884 (0.959)	3.1266 (1.102)	-3.3478 (1.148)	4.2250 (0.675)	0.1884 (0.753)	3.9114 (0.737)	-0.1594 (0.933)	4.3291 (0.571)	0.1449 (0.692)	79
Experimentals	3.7260 (0.990)	0.0645 (0.939)	3.0833 (1.071)	-0.3226 (1.113)	4.0959 (0.785)	0.1290 (0.820)	3.8028 (0.749)	-0.1803 (0.904)	4.2857 (0.684)	0.0164 (0.866)	73
Section 64											
Controls	3.7117 (0.928)	0.0440 (1.010)	3.3333 (1.021)	-0.4286 (1.212)	4.0901 (0.769)	0.2857 (0.750)	3.9640 (0.738)	-0.3297 (0.895)	4.2342 (0.687)	0.1209 (0.680)	111
Experimentals	3.6552 (0.970)	-0.0309 (1.122)	3.2609 (1.018)	-0.2708 (1.165)	4.0517 (0.767)	0.1753 (0.764)	3.9569 (0.703)	0.1856 (0.982)	4.1638 (0.745)	0.1753 (0.662)	116

differences in the extent of these common movements were not significant. Opposite movements were observed on the hard and theoretical descriptors. For the former, experimentals moved downward, while the controls moved up. This is a desirable CAI effect. On the latter the controls moved downward while the experimentals moved up. In both cases, the differences in average change were not significant.

Generalizing across all four sections it would appear that CAI does not exert a unique impact on attitudes toward economics. By and large both controls and experimentals tend to change such attitudes in the same direction but by varying amounts that are not statistically significant. Even in those instances where the attitudinal changes are in opposite directions, the magnitudes are not sufficiently large to be significant.

Aside from these essential points it is interesting to observe some additional insights revealed by Table 5.3. For example, it is often remarked that students find macroeconomics more useful and relevant than microeconomics. This assertion is contradicted by our results on changes in attitudes. In Table 5.3 the general tendency is for both controls and experimentals to revise their opinions downward on these two descriptors during the 223, or macroeconomics course but to revise them upwards during the 224, or microeconomics course. It is also frequently asserted that in order to make economics useful and relevant, instructors must reduce the amount of abstraction and theoretical content of the course. We obtain no consistent evidence on this assertion. For the 223 course it would appear that as students revised their opinions in a downward direction on the abstract and theoretical descriptors, they also revised their attitudes on usefulness and relevancy of economics in the same direction. On the other hand, the 224 results tend to support the assertion; both student groups in each section of this course, in general, move downward on the theoretical and abstract descriptors and upward on the useful and relevant descriptors. These and other points are worthy of future investigation.

D. Attitudes toward Economic Issues

This questionnaire was also distributed at the beginning and end of each course (Appendix C). The questionnaire listed the thirteen economic issues with a number of semantic differentials under each issue. Summing over the thirteen issues, there were seventy-four semantic differentials. In this instance we cannot posit a desirable outcome, the reasons for this inability were cited in the previous chapter. The central point of the current discussion is to determine whether or not CAI operates uniquely on these attitudes or opinions.

To facilitate discussion of the mass of data we will concentrate on changes in opinion or more correctly average changes on the semantic differentials of the two student groups in each section of the two courses. These results are presented in Appendix I.

Section 61. In general the controls and the experimentals moved in the same direction (on 56 of the semantic differentials), but there are a substantial number of cases where they moved in opposite directions. However, of the seventy-four cases there were only two instances of statistical significance. Oddly enough both occur when the two groups are moving in the same directrion, the "desirable-undesirable" semantic differential for FREE TRADE and the "efficient-inefficient" differential for CAPITALISM.

Section 62. The two student groups move in the same direction on 51 of the semantic differentials. None of these average changes are statistically significant. Of the remaining differentials we find two instances of statistical significance. These occurred on the "should be free-should be controlled" differential for FOREIGN TRADE and the same differential for BIG BUSINESS.

Section 63. Again in the majority of cases the controls and experimentals moved in the same direction (on 42). In each of these cases the magnitude of the change was not statistically significant. The same was true for the cases where the two student groups moved in opposite directions.

Section 64. Here again common direction of movement was observed in a majority of cases (44). Of these only one yielded a statistically significant difference in magnitude of common direction of change: the "abstract-concrete" differential for MARKET MECHANISMS. For the remaining cases where the direction of change was not common we find significant differences in average changes on three semantic differentials: "random-political" for DECISION-MAKING FOR NATIONAL ECONOMIC POLICY; "inevitable-controllable" for INFLATION; and "good-bad" for BIG BUSINESS.

Looking across all four sections, the evidence again appears to support the assertion of no unique CAI impact. For the most part both student groups in each section move in the same direction and by magnitudes that are not significantly different. Even in those instances where the groups move in opposite directions the differences in the average changes are not significant. Indeed the evidence across all three attitudinal areas is the same—whether the student was exposed to CAI or discussion classes made no difference on attitudes toward instruction elements, attitudes toward economics as a discipline, or his opinions on economic issues.

E. Interpretation of the Regression Results on Economic Issues

1) THE MODEL

This section will consider specifically the determinants of student opinions on economic issues. The analytic approach, discussed below, has an explicit model, which takes the following form:

$$\text{POST} = F(\text{PRE}, \text{OO}, \text{HC}, \text{SD}) \qquad (4.1)$$

where

POST = the student's postcourse attitudinal opinion on a semantic differential.

PRE = student's precourse attitudinal position on that semantic differential.

OO = opinion of others on that semantic differential.

HC = student's human capital.

SD = the sociodemographic background of the student.

The purpose of the model is to attempt to explain the student's attitudes on the economic issues as of the end of the semester. It is clear that the totality of the students' attitudes on any set of issues would not be entirely dependent on the occurrences in the course itself. Particularly on economic issues, it seems clear that two possible alternative sources of information could affect student opinions on the economic issues.

The first point concerns the sum total of the student opinion on the economic issues at the beginning of the course. This would be the result of the student's home environment, public or private elementary and high schools attended, basic intelligence (human capital), the general overall exposure to public information, reading popular or professional journals, previous exposure to economics, and the like. In short many students will have opinions on economic issues before they enroll in an economics course where the issues will be discussed systematically.

The second element that would enter into the students' opinions about economic issues at the end of the semester would be the magnitude of publicity releases about specific issues over the semester itself while the class is in session. For instance, in the instant experiment, President Nixon had initiated the price and wage freeze in November 1971, with consequent publicity about the freeze (Phase 1) and the following Phase 2. The impact of this would be incorporated into the students' precourse opinions. However, during the fall 1973 semester, the president initiated Phase 3 of the overall program, with its resultant widespread publicity. There is no way that we can isolate this phenomenon from the student attitude changes resulting (perhaps on the same issues) from the course itself. Thus any major publicity or news concerning economic issues, unless actually occurring during a given semester, would be incorporated in the students' precourse attitudes on the issue. The students' attitudes at the end of the course on any issue would be conditioned, in fact perhaps determined, by their opinion on the issue at the beginning of the course. All of these variables, although operating on precourse attitudes, may continue to be important as a student revises his or her opinions.

A third specific factor that would probably affect student opinions on economic issues are the opinions held by the teacher. We would hypothesize that the teacher's attitudes on specific economic issues, whether given explicitly or implicitly, are probably major stimuli that cause students to change their opinions of economic issues.

The human capital variables that are a familiar and important aspect of a cognitive achievement model, including VSAT, MSAT and the improvement on the Test on Understanding College Economics, are useful in the regression model as a control.

The overall point of the experiment was to test the impact of computer-assisted-instruction (CAI) as a teaching method in all aspects of instruction. Thus the EXPCODE, or experimental code indicating whether the student was in the discussion class group (control) or used CAI (experimental), is entered as a variable in the equation. From the sum total of our analysis to this point we would hypothesize that the EXPCODE would not be a significant variable on determining student attitudes on economic issues.

Thus the regression model that we intend to use in analyzing the potential influences on student opinions about economic issues is shown below. The major purpose of the regression analysis is to determine whether or not the differential attitudinal results found from the surveys could be attributed to the course-related variables, or to the sociodemographic variables, or whether exogenous factors exert a major influence. The regression analysis will permit us to control for the simultaneous variation of all of the variables included in the equation for all students to determine which variables appear to be most significant in explaining the student attitudes at the end of the semester. The general form of the regression model is:

$$\begin{aligned} \text{ATTITUDE}_{\text{Post}} = {} & a + b_1\,(\text{PRE}) + b_2\,(\text{AGE}) + b_3\,(\text{HS}) + b_4\,(\text{VSAT}) + \\ & b_5\,(\text{MSAT}) + b_6\,(\text{SEX}) + b_7\,(\text{EXPCODE}) + b_8 \\ & (\text{RELIGION}) + b_9\,(\text{TUCEIMP}) + b_{10}\,(\text{SWAT}) + b_{11} \\ & (\text{CHILD}) + b_{12}\,(\text{FAGE}) + b_{13}\,(\text{MAGE}) + b_{14}\,(\text{FED}) \\ & + b_{15}\,(\text{MED}) + u \qquad (5.1) \end{aligned}$$

The variables are defined as follows:

- a = constant term
- PRE = the student's opinion on each of the semantic differentials at the beginning of the course, on the 5-point scale.
- AGE = age of the student.
- HS = high school of the student—used as a binary variable where a public high school was coded 0 and a private high school was coded as a 1.
- VSAT = the score attained in the verbal portion of the student's Scholastic Aptitude Test.
- MSAT = the score attained by the student on the mathematics portion of the Scholastic Aptitude Test.
- SEX = a binary variable where males are coded as 0 and females as 1.
- EXPCODE = a binary variable used to indicate whether the student was a control student attending a discussion class or was an experimental student using the CAI system. Controls were coded 0 and experimentals 1.
- RELIGION = students indicated whether they were Catholic or other religion. Catholics were coded 0 and all other religions as 1.
- TUCEIMP = measured the student's improvement on the TUCE examination, calculated as TUCE precourse score subtracted from the TUCE postcourse score.
- SWAT = measures the attitude of the instructor at the beginning of the course—taken from same semantic differential attitude survey as the students used. Coded 1 if student moves toward instructor during the semester and 0 if the student moves away from instructor's position.[2]
- CHILD = the number of children in the family—entered as a 0 for no children or a number representing the number of children in the family.
- FAGE = father's age—the student marked the father's age in age classes of 5 years each. The information was coded using the median age of each age group.
- MAGE = mother's age—using the same age group category discussed for father's age.
- FED = father's education. A series of questions were posed asking the student to indicate the amount of education of the father from 0 years or no schooling of any kind, through the number of years necessary to obtain a Ph.D. or M.D. degree. This item was coded from 0 to 20 years.
- MED = mother's education—same basic grouping as used for father's education.
- u = stochastic error term.

An attempt was made to obtain information on the occupations of the father. However, it was not possible to code the information in a way to incorporate it into the regression as a single variable, and it was felt that twelve variables entered into the regression in binary form would not be useful. Further, an attempt to obtain income information for the family was not successful. Finally, five variables (CHILD, FAGE, MAGE, FED, and MED) are not used in Economics 223 regressions as they were not available for that semester. With the exception of these five variables, the model used for Economics 223 is identical to that used for Economics 224.

The first variable included within equation (5.1) is the students' precourse position on that semantic differential. Recall that each semantic differential represents a five-point spectrum. It is possible that there is no difference between the precourse and postcourse opinions. This, of course, does not imply that nothing has happened. What may have occurred is a change in the basis underlying a particular response. Such an event is most likely in regard to a semantic differential that is a 3 on both the precourse and postcourse attitudinal surveys. The former is more likely to be interpreted as a "no opinion" and the latter as a "middle of the road" position. In any event, the questionnaire does not reflect in any way the basis for such a position.

Turning to the remaining factors shown in equation (5.1) consider SWAT opinions of the teacher. On a given semantic differential an instructor can have only one opinion. While student postcourse opinion on that semantic differential can range from 1 to 5. Constructing a diagram for this relationship would yield the line presented in Figure 1. We will always obtain such lines—perpendicular to the horizontal axis—with the line shifting along the instructor axis as we move between semantic differentials. To avoid this problem we must somehow transform the instructor's opinion so that it is variable between students.

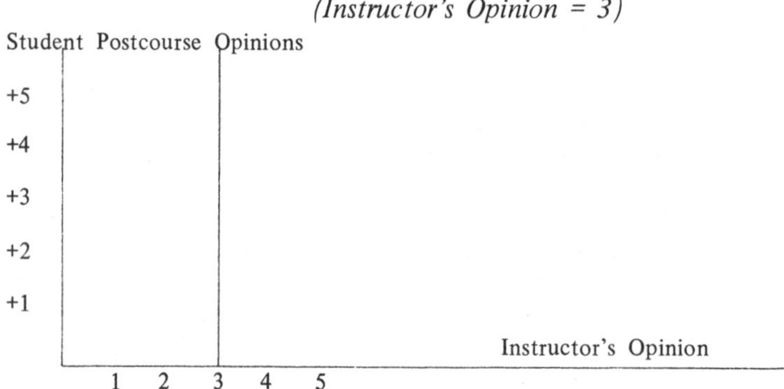

Figure 1. Relationship Between Instructor's Opinion and Changes in Student Opinions

If we assume that students tend to move toward the instructor, then a possible transformation is to use the instructor's opinion in conjunction with the students' initial opinions; that is the difference between the instructor's opinion and the students' initial opinions.[2] Simply, one would expect that if a student's initial opinion were below (above) that of the instructor's, the student would tend to revise his opinion in an upward (downward) direction. Thus a positive (negative) change in student opinion should be associated with a positive (negative) difference between the instructor's opinion and the student's initial position. This is not to say that the student will adjust perfectly to the difference, he may adjust by less than or more than the difference, but at least the implied direction of change is unambiguous. Likewise, we may determine the relationship between the instructor's position and the student's position at the end of the semester. We would anticipate that some students would be closer to the instructor at the end of the semester than at the beginning. Other students would move away from the instructor's position and be farther from the instructor at the end of the semester. By coding the instructor's position as a binary variable we can determine the impact of the instructor's position on the students' postcourse attitude positions on the economic issues.

Turning to the human-capital elements we can employ several different variables here. For purposes of this study we will utilize MSAT, VSAT, and improvement on the TUCE (postcourse test score on the Test of Understanding College Economics minus the precourse test score denoted TUCEIMP). The first two variables may be considered as a measure of the initial stock of human capital, while the TUCE improvement represents a measure of the amount of specific economic knowledge accumulated during the semester.

Turning to the sociodemographic variables, we have a variety to choose from. Unfortunately the majority of these are available on a systematic basis only for students in the two sections of the 224 course especially those concerning family background. At this time we will specify the elements to be included within this set of factors as though the data were available for students in both courses. Student-specific characteristics include age (AGE), type of high school (HS = 0 for public, HS = 1 for private), and race (R, 0 = white, 1 = nonwhite). Family background data include occupation of father and mother, educational attainment of father and mother, and the number of children in the family.

Finally we seek to determine whether or not the CAI system operates differentially upon student opinions on economic issues. Here again we can employ the same technique used in the regression analysis for cognitive achievement: utilize a dummy variable EXPCODE which sets controls equal to 0 and experimentals equal to 1. In this instance, although we did attempt to anticipate the impact of several of the independent variables, it is unclear as to what the relationship will be between the majority of the variables and the dependent variable.

A major point to remember concerning the regression model is that each semantic differential on each issue was considered separately, since each semantic differential was in fact a separate aspect of each overall issue. No aggregation was done over economic issues. There were, therefore, a total of seventy-four separate regressions for each section of Economics 223 and for each section of Economics 224. The basic difference between the two sections of Economics 223 and the two sections of Economics 224 is that the last five indicated independent variables in the model (equation [5.2]) were not available for Economics 223. The tabulated results for the output of the regressions are shown in the Appendices as follows:

Economics 223:

Section 61	Appendix D
Section 62	Appendix E

Economics 224:

Section 63	Appendix F
Section 64	Appendix G

Our approach to the analysis of the regression results is as follows. First, we will present an overall description and evaluation of the regression results and of the model as capable of predicting student end-of-course attitudes. Second, we knew when we made up the attitude surveys that there were a number of different types of questions or semantic differentials for each issue, that is, thirteen issues including seventy-four semantic differentials or descriptors. Some of the semantic differentials reflect political choices, some reflect value oriented or subjective positions, and others reflect economic content or analysis. By noting the manner in which different independent variables become significant in explaining the student attitudes on specific semantic differentials (descriptors), we can, perhaps, identify the nature of the descriptors themselves. Third, we hypothesize that the two most significant variables ought to be the instructor's attitude and the students' precourse attitudes on the issues. It is clear that the instructor's position ought to dominate on the content or analytic descriptors.

2) ECONOMICS 223, SECTION 61

The minimum F-ratio obtained from any of the regressions was 7.09, and we can conclude that the overall regressions are significant.[3] The coefficient of determination (R^2) varied from a low of .27 to a high of .69 over the seventy-four regression equations.[4] Thus our next step is to determine if there is some pattern to the variation of the coefficient of determination.

Let us note first exactly what the regression equation does indicate. What we are trying to explain is the level (on a five-point scale) of student opinions on economic issues at the end of a semester of study. From Appendix D, we do obtain a considerably lower set of coefficients of determination for the macroeconomic issues than we do for the microeconomic issues. This arbitrary value, which we select, is a coefficient of determination of .40:

macroeconomic issues	R^2	:	.27 to .69 (Range) N = 40 12 values under .40
microeconomic issues	R^2	:	.35 to .69 (Range) N = 34 1 value under .40

Table 5.4 below shows the semantic differentials that had a coefficient of determination of less than .40 as well as those that had a coefficient of determination of greater than .55.

A couple of points come to mind immediately. The model did less well at predicting student outcome on the broad political issues and the value-oriented issues than it did in predicting student reaction to the more specific or content or analytic semantic differentials. The descriptor "Democratic-Republican"—clearly a political descriptor or one with political overtones—had the lowest predictability of all of the semantic differentials. The second point is that the microeconomic issues had fewer regressions with the very low coefficients of determination and relatively more of the highest coefficients of determination. The conclusion is that the model is a better predictor for student attitudes on microeconomic issues than it is for student attitudes on macroeconomic issues.[5] We see two possible reasons for this. First, the student could well have been familiar with the types of issues suggested by the microeconomic area such as labor unions, big business, and the like. The Russian wheat deal in 1972, with the consequent impact on consumer prices for foods, was given wide publicity. The publicity on this issue, much of which occurred during the course itself, could have had a significant impact on the students. Second, it is possible that the type of semantic-differential descriptor chosen for the microeconomic issues was more specific, and because of this the student was more able to relate to this type of descriptor. A student may well not understand the implications (for himself) of the term INFLATION even after a course in macroeconomics. However the student at the same time may be perfectly well able to understand that MARKET MECHANISM in the United States does or does not allocate goods and simultaneously provide for high or low prices—for example, cost of tuition at the University, room and board, or books.

In any event, from Table 5.4 there were eight macroeconomic semantic differentials that had coefficients of determination that were high, arbitrarily set as over .55. The information in the table is not completely unam-

TABLE 5.4

Regression Analysis: Distribution of R^2's
(Economics 223: Section 61)

Coefficient of Determination under .40		Coefficient of Determination over .55	
MACROECONOMIC ISSUES	R^2	MACROECONOMIC ISSUES	R^2
Decision-making for National Economic Policy:		Decision-making for National Economic Policy:	
Simple–Complex	.38	Important to me–Irrelevant to me	.55
Political–Apolitical	.32		
Government Spending Deficit:		Government Spending Deficit:	
Desirable–Undesirable	.36	Decreases Demand–Increases Demand	.59
Democratic–Republican	.35	Government Controls such as Wage-Price Freeze:	
Promotes Inflation–Promotes Depression	.38	Ineffective–Effective	.61
Poverty:		Poverty:	
Unimportant–Serious	.37	Laziness–Lack of Opportunity	.66
		No Skills–No Jobs	.58
Inflation:		Inflation:	
Democratic–Republican	.34	Bad–Good	.69
High Unemployment:		High Unemployment:	
Democratic–Republican	.37	Bad–Good	.60
Not Controllable–Controllable	.37		
Federal Income Tax:		Federal Income Tax:	
Democratic–Republican	.27	Unfair–Fair	.57
Increasing Money Supply:			
More Paper–More Gold	.30		
Democratic–Republican	.38		
MICROECONOMIC ISSUES		MICROECONOMIC ISSUES	
Big Business:		Labor Unions:	
Competitive–Monopolistic	.35	Bad–Good	.62
		Important–Unimportant	.60
		Unfair–Fair	.63
		Irresponsible–Responsible	.64
		Unnecessary–Necessary	.58
		Capitalism:	
		Reality–Nonreality	.56
		Desirable–Undesirable	.69
		Declining–Growing	.60
		Monopolistic–Competitive	.64
		Market Mechanism:	
		Practical–Theoretical	.57
		Abstract–Concrete	.57

biguous, but the model seems to predict more accurately opinions on those issues that the student can immediately relate to himself and on which he can express a value judgment. This suggests the significance of the student's precourse opinions in the prediction of postcourse opinions on economic issues.[6]

The instructor's position and the students' precourse positions were statistically significant in all of the regression equations for all four of the lecture sections. In fact it is the interaction of these two variables that appear to be most important in predicting the student opinion on the various economic issues. Appendix J indicates the relative and absolute explanatory power of these two variables in predicting the students' postcourse attitudes on each of the seventy-four issues. For instance, in the table under the issue DECISION-MAKING FOR NATIONAL ECONOMIC POLICY, descriptor "Simple-Complex," column 3, row 1, the students' precourse opinions were most important providing .24 of the overall R^2 with the instructor's position contributing .04. Thus the two variables together provided .28 of the overall coefficient of determination for the equation.

There are a number of significant points to be made from Appendix J. First, the students' precourse opinions dominated all of the other variables including the instructor's opinion on twenty-nine of the forty macroeconomic issues and on twenty-nine of the thirty-four microeconomic issues. Since the precourse attitude dominated the explanatory or predictive capability of the model on so many of the regressions, let us list those semantic differentials that were dominated by the instructor's position in explaining the R^2. We may be able to isolate a pattern to explain the influence of the two variables. Here, we note that the instructor's attitude dominated on none of the microeconomic issues that were not included in the lectures the first semester. The MARKET MECHANISM was discussed systematically the first semester, which explains the instructor's influence on that issue. This has nothing per se to do with whether the student was moving toward the instructor or away from him, a point discussed extensively above. This simply means that the student's precourse attitude had more to do with predicting the position of the student's postcourse attitudes than did any other variable in the equation.

The second point while not completely unambiguous, is that the instructor's position tended to dominate on the so-called content or analytic issues. These are summarized in Table 5.5 These issues are specifically discussed in the course as a part of the subject matter. For instance, the question of "cost push" or "demand pull" as causes of inflation normally constitutes a part of the analysis of inflation.

Before leaving this section let us examine the question of the significance of the "other variables," that is, other than the student's precourse opinion

TABLE 5.5

Regressions Dominated by Predictive Power of Teacher's Attitude on Student Opinions (Economics 223, Section 61)

ISSUES	Contributed to R^2	R^2
Decision-Making for National Economic Policy:		
Important to society–Irrelevant to society	.42	.54
Government Spending Deficit:		
Desirable–Undesirable	.20	.36
Inflationary–Recessionary	.24	.38
Decreases Aggregate Demand–Increases Aggregate Demand	.33	.59
Government Controls: Wage-Price Freeze		
Socialism–Free enterprise	.22	.41
Poverty:		
Market Determined–Discrimination	.30	.48
Inflation:		
Cost Push–Demand Pull	.23	.49
High Unemployment:		
Recession–Prosperity	.22	.40
Federal Income Tax:		
Democratic-Republican	.14	.27
Socialism–Free Enterprise	.43	.51
Increasing the Money Supply:		
Inflation–Recession	.24	.44
Democratic–Republican	.19	.38
Free Enterprise–Socialism	.21	.45
Market Mechanism:		
Efficient–Inefficient	.30	.54
Practical–Theoretical	.27	.57
Workable–Unworkable	.32	.53
Desirable–Undesirable	.29	.49

and the teacher's position. Column 14 of Appendix D shows which of the "other" variables were statistically significant in each regression. Essentially the "other" variables were significant to some extent, but they lack power in explaining the student postcourse attitudes on the economics issues. While generalizations are dangerous, it is relatively rare for any of the other variables to contribute more than .005 to the R^2 for any of the regressions. The instances where the "other variables" were statistically significant included all three types of issues, with no pattern observable–analytic or content, moral or value-oriented, and political issues. The human capital variables –VSAT, MSAT and TUCEIMP–were the most important of these other variables.

One of the specific questions that we asked concerned the importance of the experimental code, EXPCODE, as an explanatory or predictive variable. It was statistically significant in eight of the seventy-four cases, and in two of those cases it was for semantic differentials not covered either by the instructor or by the CAI programs–for example, on microeconomic descriptors. There is no consistency in sign or explanatory power for this variable. This variable contributed more than .01 of the R^2 only three times. We would conclude that CAI does not exert a systematic and significant influence on student postcourse opinions on economic issues.

3) ECONOMICS 223, SECTION 62

The minimum F-Ratio obtained from any of the regressions was 6.95.[7] The R^2 varied from a low of .27 to a high of .69 over the seventy-four regression equations. Thus our next step is to determine if there is some pattern to the variations noted in the R^2. Appendix E, the basic data for the seventy-four regressions for Section 62 of Economics 223, indicates that the R^2 values for the macroeconomic issues are a good deal lower than those obtained for the microeconomic issues. The arbitrary value which we select is an R^2 of .40:

macroeconomic issues	R^2	:	.27 to .69 (Range) N = 40 10 under .40
microeconomic issues	R^2	:	.36 to .65 (Range) N = 34 2 under .40

Table 5.6 below shows the semantic differentials that had an R^2 of less than .40 as well as those semantic differentials that had an R^2 of greater than .55.

The model, in the instance of Economics 223 Section 62, appears to have done better at predicting value-oriented issues than it did at predicting either content issues or political issues. Again, the evidence is not completely un-

TABLE 5.6

Distribution of R^2's
Economics 223: Section 62

Coefficient of Determination under .40

ISSUE	
MACROECONOMIC ISSUES	R^2
Decision-Making for National Economic Policy:	
Simple–Complex	.34
Political–Apolitical	.27
Government Deficit Spending:	
Undesirable–Desirable	.35
Poverty:	
Serious–Unimportant	.34
Inflation:	
Recession–Prosperity	.35
High Unemployment:	
Controllable–Not Controllable	.35
Federal Income Tax:	
Progressive–Regressive	.36
Democratic–Republican	.27
Increasing Money Supply:	
More Gold–More Paper	.39
Democratic–Republican	.40
MICROECONOMIC ISSUES	
Big Business:	
Monopolistic–Competitive	.36
Market Mechanism:	
Efficient–Inefficient	.38

Coefficient of Determination over .55

ISSUE	
MACROECONOMIC ISSUES	R^2
Decision-Making for National Economic Policy:	
Important to me–Irrelevant to me	.59
Important to Society–Irrelevant	.58
Government Deficit Spending:	
Increases Aggregate Demand–Decreases Agg. Demand	.60
Government Controls: Wage-Price Freeze:	
Undesirable–Desirable	.55
Democratic–Republican	.59
Effective–Ineffective	.62
Poverty:	
Lazy–Lack of Opportunity	.66
No Jobs–No Skills	.58
Inflation:	
Bad–Good	.62
High Unemployment:	
Bad–Good	.61
Federal Income Tax:	
Too High –Too Low	.69
Fair–Unfair	.61
MICROECONOMIC ISSUES	
Foreign Trade:	
Desirable–Undesirable	.63
Should be Encouraged–Discouraged	.64
Unimportant–Important	.64
Political–Apolitical	.56

TABLE 5.6
(Continued)

Labor Unions:	
Bad–Good	.63
Important–Unimportant	.63
Fair–Unfair	.65
Responsible–Irresponsible	.64
Necessary–Unnecessary	.57
Capitalistic–Socialistic	.56
Big Business:	
Bad–Good	.62
Capitalism:	
Reality–Nonreality	.56
Declining–Growing	.61
Superior–Inferior to Socialism	.64
Politically Involved–Uninvolved	.60
Market Mechanism:	
Theoretical–Practical	.56

ambiguous, and the reader may wish to examine the evidence and decide for himself. However, from Table 5.7, let us look at the question on FEDERAL INCOME TAX. Here, the model did a poor job at predicting two semantic differentials and did a good job at predicting two others. The model did a poor job at predicting the student opinions on the semantic differentials "progressive-regressive" and "Democratic-Republican," while it did a good job in predicting student opinion on "too high-too low" and "fair-unfair."

The concept that a tax is "progressive or regressive" is in fact a complex issue. The federal income tax is nominally progressive. However, the myriad of loopholes and explicit deletions of income from the tax base suggests that perhaps the income tax is in fact regressive—for example, taxing the lower income groups relatively more heavily than higher income groups. It is in fact a complex academic or content issue in economics. The "Democratic-Republican" is clearly an issue with political overtones. The model did a poor job of predicting student opinions on these two issues. On the other hand, the model did a good job of predicting student opinion on the semantic differentials "too high-too low" and "fair-unfair"—which are issues to which the student apparently could directly relate and state a value position. Our conclusion, after examining these issues, is that the model best predicted the value-oriented issues of the student and did not predict as well on those semantic differentials dealing with the political area or the content area. Further, from Appendix J, the higher R^2 obtained for these last two issues is primarily the result of student precourse attitudes.

Finally, the model did a better job of predicting the outcomes on the microeconomic issues than it did on the macroeconomic issues, even though the microeconomic issues were not discussed during the Economics 223 semester and the general results are similar to those from Economics 223, Section 61. *First*, since the professor did not discuss the microeconomic issues, the student did not understand the economic (content) aspects (if any) in the microeconomic issues. The student simply reacted to each semantic differential as if it were a value question, which could explain the high predictive capability of the model and the importance of the student's precourse attitudes. *Second*, the type of semantic differential used for the microeconomic issues could have been worded such that the student could relate more directly to them. Perhaps this is the type of question that the model really does predict the best.

The instructor's position and the students' own pre-course opinions were again statistically significant in all of the regression equations for Economics 223, Section 62. In fact it is the interaction of these two variables that are most important in predicting the student opinion on the postcourse attitude survey. Appendix K is a summary of the regression equations for Economics 223, Section 62. The summary includes the R^2, the contribution to the R^2 of each of the two indicated variables, and the beta weights for the two variables.

There are a number of significant points to be made from the table. The students' precourse opinions dominated all of the other variables including the instructor's opinion on twenty-nine of the forty regressions involving the macroeconomic issues and on twenty-eight of the thirty-four microeconomic issues. Since the students' precourse opinions dominated the predictive power of the model on so many of the regressions, Table 5.7 shows the regressions that were dominated by the instructor's position.

The first point is that the instructor's position dominated on none of the microeconomic issues that were not included in the lectures, as might be expected. The MARKET MECHANISM was discussed systematically in the first semester, which explains the instructor's dominance there. The point is, this course was probably the first time that the students had encountered a systematic discussion of the market mechanism as such.

The second point, while not completely unambiguous, is that the instructor's position tended to dominate on the so-called content issues. A content issue would be some issue that would require considerable discussion of the theory as well as practicality to permit understanding. An example is whether the FEDERAL INCOME TAX is progressive or regressive. Appendix K does indicate a few of the issues that could be considered as political, although those issues that are worded as "socialism–free enterprise" are often handled as analytic considerations in the classroom. Thus Table 5.7 indicates a very high percentage of the so-called analytic or content issues. There is a notable absence of the "personal" or value-oriented issues. The tentative conclusion is that either the teachers do not spend much time on the personal, political, and/or value-oriented aspects of economic issues, or the students do not pay much attention to them if they do.

Before leaving this discussion let us examine the significance of the "other variables" in the equation—that is, other than the teacher's position and the students' precourse opinions. Again, it is rare for any other variable to contribute significantly to the predictive power of the equation, as shown in Appendix E. Column 14 of this appendix indicates which of the "other" variables were statistically significant in each regression.

While none of the other variables were significant in contributing much to the predictive power of the equations, there is an interesting pattern observable for Section 62 students that was not apparent for Section 61. For Section 61, the other variables were statistically significant in only thirty-four of the seventy-four regressions, and there was no particular pattern to their appearance. However, for Section 62 students, the other variables were significant on *sixty* of the seventy-four equations, many times with two or more of the other variables for a single regression equation. An interesting implication that appears is that some professors appear able to present information on a subject to students in a manner such that the students' learning processes require the students to incorporate previously learned or encountered information. The consideration of Economics 223, Sections 61 and 62, clearly indicates that professors do approach their lecture materials differently. The Section 62 lecturer apparently provided an environment where the human capital variables were statistically significant in the formation of student attitudes. In fact, the human-capital variables VSAT, MSAT, TUCEIMP, accounted for thirty-eight of the seventy-four times that the other variables appeared as significant in the regressions.

Clearly, we are not offering evidence that would permit acceptance or rejection of this argument but simply suggesting that the evidence thus far indicates that different lecture approaches to a subject provide an environment for the "learning process" where that process can proceed relatively in abstraction from other phenomena. Other lecturers can proceed in a manner to incorporate other phenomena in that "learning process." All of this is not to say that the other variables provided much explanatory power in the equation. As in Section 61, the great majority of the predictive "power" of the regression model was in the students' precourse attitudes and the

TABLE 5.7

Regressions Dominated by Predictive Power of Teacher's Attitude on Student Opinions (Economics 223, Section 62)

ISSUES	Contributed to R^2	R^2
Decision-Making for National Economic Policy:		
Important to Me–Irrelevant to Me	.28	.58
Important to Society–Irrelevant to Society	.47	.58
Government Spending Deficit:		
Desirable–Undesirable	.18	.35
Government Controls: Wage Price Freeze		
Democratic–Republican	.32	.59
Poverty:		
Market Determined–Discrimination	.24	.44
Inflation:		
Cost Push–Demand Pull	.26	.47
High Unemployment:		
Recession–Prosperity	.31	.46
Bad–Good	.31	.61
Federal Income Tax:		
Progressive–Regressive	.19	.36
Socialism–Free Enterprise	.41	.45
Increasing the Money Supply:		
Free Enterprise–Socialism	.21	.42
Foreign Trade:		
Important–Unimportant	.31	.64
Should be Apolitical–Political	.26	.56
Market Mechanism:		
Efficient–Inefficient	.22	.39
Practical–Theoretical	.28	.56
Workable–Unworkable	.30	.47
High Prices–Low Prices	.20	.43

teacher's opinion. However, in the Section 62 course the other variables were systematically statistically significant in most of the regressions. There is no clear pattern, however, indicating the types of semantic differentials or types of issues in which the other variables will be statistically significant. They appear, variously on all three types of issues—content or analytic issues, political issues, and value-oriented issues.

The Experimental Code (EXPCODE) was statistically significant in ten of the seventy-four issues. It contributed little to the explanatory power of the equation with a maximum contribution to the R^2 in one equation of .018. Again it would appear that CAI does not operate on student opinions in any consistent and significant manner.

4) ECONOMICS 224; SECTION 63

The minimum F-Ratio obtained from any of the regressions was 3.36,[8] and we can therefore conclude that the overall equation was significant. Appendix F, the basic regression data for the seventy-four equations for Economics 224, Section 63, indicate that the R^2 values for the micro-economic and macroeconomic attitudinal questions are much closer together than they were for the Economics 223 semester. Furthermore the overall R^2 values for Economics 224 are higher than they were for Economics 223. The reader must remember that we have added variables 11-15 to the model as defined for Economics 223. Thus the specification for the model for Economics 224 is as shown below:

$$\text{ATTITUDE} = a + b_1 \text{ (PRE)} + b_2 \text{ (AGE)} + b_3 \text{ (HS)} + b_4 \text{ (VSAT)} + b_5 \text{ (MSAT)} + b_6 \text{ (SEX)} + b_7 \text{ (EXPCODE)} + b_8 \text{ (RELIGION)} + b_9 \text{ (TUCEIMP)} + b_{10} \text{ (SWAT)} + b_{11} \text{ (CHILD)} + b_{12} \text{ (FAGE)} + b_{13} \text{ (MAGE)} + b_{14} \text{ (FED)} + b_{15} \text{ (MED)} + u$$

The arbitrary value that we select is an R^2 of .40 or less as being considered low and regressions with an R^2 of .55 or greater as considered high. The lowest R^2 value for any of the seventy-four equations is .39 and the highest R^2 value is .778.

macroeconomic issues	R^2	:	.39 to .72 (Range) N = 40
microeconomic issues	R^2	:	.395 to .778 (Range) N = 34

There was only one macroeconomic descriptor (equation) and one micro-economic descriptor with an R^2 of under .40. The macroeconomic issue (descriptor) was INFLATION, "demand pull-cost push," with an R^2 of .39. The microeconomic issue (descriptor) was FOREIGN TRADE, "unimportant-important," with an R^2 of .395. There were a total of fifty-three (of the remaining seventy-two descriptors) with an R^2 greater than .55 as shown on Table 5.8 below. As is indicated, there is no pattern to the issues. The model predicted well on all three types of issues—value-oriented, political issues and content or analytic issues.

TABLE 5.8

Distribution of R^2's
Economics 224: Section 63

ISSUE	COEFFICIENT OF DETERMINATION
Macroeconomic Issues with R^2 Over .55	
Decision-Making:	
Simple-Complex	.57
Random-Rational	.58
Important to me-Irrelevant to me	.72
Important to Society-Irrelevant to Society	.62
Government Spending Deficit:	
Undesirable-Desirable	.65
Inflationary-Recessionary	.70
Increase-Decrease (Aggregate Demand)	.60
Government Controls:	
Undesirable-Desirable	.59
Free Enterprise-Socialism	.71
Facilitates-Distorts (Market Operations)	.58
Poverty:	
Lazy-Lack of Opportunity	.72
Serious-Unimportant	.65
Market Determined-Discrimination	.70
No Jobs-No Skills	.57
Inevitable-Can be Eliminated	.65
Individual-Social Responsibility	.63
Inflation:	
Bad-Good	.72
Inevitable-Controllable	.56
Democratic-Republican	.68
High Unemployment:	
Democratic-Republican	.59
Inflation-Deflation	.570
Bad-Good	.657
Federal Income Tax:	
Progressive-Regressive	.648
Good-Bad	.581
Too High-Too Low	.639
Fair-Unfair	.559

TABLE 5.8
(continued)

Increasing Money Supply:	
More Gold-More Paper	.653
Free Enterprise-Socialism	.598
Microeconomic Issues with R^2 Over .55	
Foreign Trade:	
Should be Political-Apolitical	.634
Labor Unions:	
Good-Bad	.653
Important-Unimportant	.651
Fair-Unfair	.772
Responsible-Irresponsible	.726
Capitalistic-Socialistic	.622
Greedy-Selfless	.650
Necessary-Unnecessary	.609
Big Business:	
Good-Bad	.725
Growing-Declining	.566
Should be Controlled-Free	.788
Pays its Share-Gets Free Ride	.641
Socially Responsible-Irresponsible	.690
Monopolistic-Competitive	.666
Politically Involved-Uninvolved	-------
Capitalism:	
Reality-Nonreality	.740
Desirable-Undesirable	.650
Declining-Growing	.673
Superior-Inferior (to socialism)	.578
Socially Responsible-Irresponsible	.678
Monopolistic-Competitive	.597
Politically Involved-Uninvolved	.666
Market Mechanism:	
Theoretical-Practical	.557
Desirable-Undesirable	.597
High Prices-Low Prices	.560
Allocates-Does not Allocate	.628

The beta weights, shown in Appendix L, show that when the variables are adjusted from their raw score to standard scores, the standard partial regression coefficients become much more even. The approximately equal beta weights for the instructor's opinion and the students' precourse opinions in this section are consistent with the results obtained in both sections of 223.

The regression equation used for Economics 224 (with the five additional sociodemographic variables) yielded better predictive ability than did the equation for Economics 223. There are two possible reasons for this. The first and most obvious is that there are five additional variables that had some explanatory power in the Economics 224 equation. The second reason is that 95 percent of the students have just previously had Economics 223, which would serve to act as a stability or control factor with regard to students' familiarity with economics. That is, the opinion change of the first semester is incorporated into the students' precourse opinions for the second semester. Thus the precourse attitudes at the beginning of the second semester should be more important in explaining postcourse attitudes than the first semester precourse attitudes. Partial evidence of this is the fact that the contribution of R^2 of student precourse opinion is higher in 224 than it was in 223.

In Economics 224 the instructor's position and the student's precourse attitude were statistically significant in all of the regression equations. In fact, again, it is the interaction of these two variables that provide the greatest importance in predicting the student opinion on the post-course survey. The first entry in Appendix L is DECISION-MAKING FOR NATIONAL ECONOMIC POLICY, and the first specific semantic differential descriptor under that issue is "simple-complex." The overall R^2 for the equation is .577 and the contribution to that R^2 for the teacher's position and the students' precourse opinions are .04 and .41 (respectively), accounting for a total of .45 of the overall R^2 of .57. As before these two variables are most important in explaining student postcourse opinions on this semantic differential as well as on the other semantic differentials. But the R^2 for the regression equation for this semantic differential of this issue is nearly twice as high as the R^2 for this same issue in the previous semester. Now, what has caused this? The students' changes of attitude on this issue that occurred in the previous semester are now incorporated in the students' precourse attitudes as of the start of the second semester. We would expect that there would be little further change over the second semester, and that, therefore, the students' precourse attitudes for the second semester are better predictors of the final opinions for the second semester. This is, in fact, seen from Appendix L. The instructor's position remains at about .04 contribution toward the R^2, as it was the first semester on the first semantic differential for the first issue. The students' precourse opinions for Economics 224 were, however, nearly two times as high during the second semester as it was during the first. Thus the predictive capability of the overall equation was increased because of what occurred during the first semester of the course. This comment is generally appropriate to all of the regression results seen in Economics 224, Section 63, as contrasted with Economics 223. The overall R^2 for each equation has increased rather substantially.

As seen in Appendix L, the instructor's position dominated in nineteen of the seventy-four regression euqations, and these are summarized on Table 5.9. It seems clear that except for the three issues with clear political overtones the instructor's position dominated on the content or analytic issues. This is a trend that we have noticed in Economics 223.

It is rare for any other variable to contribute significantly to the predictive power of the equations for Economics 224, Section 63. Column 19 of Appendix F indicates which of the "other" variables were statistically significant in each regression. In fact the other variables were statistically significant in forty-six of the seventy-four regressions.

Of the total number of appearances of the other variables, the human-capital variables appeared twenty-four times, or 26 percent of the total number of significant appearances of any of the other variables. The five new variables appear to be widely varying in their significance in the regressions. They account for thirty-five of the ninety appearances, or one-third, of the appearances of other variables as statistically significant. Typically they contribute very little to the R^2 of the equation, aggregating about .01 to .02. However, for some of the regressions these five variables contribute about one-sixth of the overall R^2. The following instances are illustrative only, and the reader may consult Appendix F. For the issue GOVERNMENT SPENDING DEFICIT, for the semantic differential "Desirable–Undesirable," the overall R^2 is .62. The last five sociodemographic variables account for .06 of the overall R^2, with the bulk of that coming from variable CHILD which is the number of children in the family. In short, the larger the number of children in the family, the more undesirable is government spending. For the issue GOVERNMENT CONTROLS, for the descriptor "Undesirable–Desirable," the overall R^2 for the equation is .59. The five new sociodemographic variables account for .05 of this, with the power being approximately evenly divided between the father's age and the mother's age. That is, the older were the father and the mother, the more desirable were GOVERNMENT CONTROLS such as the wage-price freeze (which is not a surprising result). Finally, for the issue INFLATION, and the semantic differential "inevitable–controllable," the five new variables accounted for .09 of the R^2 with the variable number of children accounting for .055 of the R^2.

In short the majority of the equations indicated that the explanatory (predictive) power of the last five variables was relatively small. However, for some of the descriptors, particularly those that could be classified as "value-oriented" issues, the sociodemographic variables appeared to contri-

TABLE 5.9

Issues Dominated by Predictive Power of Instructor's Attitudes (Economics 224, Section 63)

ISSUES	Contributed to R^2	R^2
Decision-Making for National Economic Policy:		
Important to Society-Irrelevant to Society	.40	.62
Government Spending Deficit:		
Democratic-Republican	.19	.52
Government Controls: Wage-Price Freeze		
Democratic-Republican	.19	.52
Distorts-Facilitates Market Operations	.23	.58
Inflation:		
Cost Push-Demand Pull	.16	.39
High Unemployment:		
Recession-Prosperity	.22	.52
Bad-Good	.32	.65
Federal Income Tax:		
Progressive-Regressive	.36	.64
Increasing Money Supply:		
More Paper-More Gold	.25	.65
Democratic-Republican	.21	.40
Free Enterprise-Socialism	.23	.59
Labor Unions:		
Important-Unimportant	.31	.65
Big Business:		
Declining-Growing	.23	.56
Market Mechanism:		
Efficient-Inefficient	.28	.50
Practical-Theoretical	.37	.55
Workable-Unworkable	.32	.52
Desirable-Undesirable	.31	.59
Abstract-Concrete	.22	.49
Allocates-Does Not Allocate	.29	.62

bute somewhat more to the R^2 relative to the content semantic differentials, as shown in Appendix F, Column 19. Our conclusion is that these other variables, particularly the sociodemographic variables become important in identifying influences that affect student opinions on the value-oriented issues independently of the influence of these variables on precourse opinion. Finally, the Experimental Code was statistically significant on nine of the seventy-four issues but with little contribution to the explanatory power (R^2) of the regressions.

5) ECONOMICS 224: SECTION 64

The minimum F-Ratio obtained from any of the regressions was 3.4, and we can therefore conclude that all seventy-four regressions were significant.[9] From Appendix G we note that the R^2 values for the regressions are quite high, considerably higher than they were for the Economics 223 sections. The lowest R^2 is .286 and the highest R^2 for Economics 224, Section 64, is .72. For the breakdown between microeconomic issues and macroeconomic issues, the following summary may be useful:

macroeconomic issues	R^2	:	.286 to .72 (Range) N = 40
microeconomic issues	R^2	:	.39 to .72 (Range) N = 34

Assuming arbitrarily that any R^2 under .40 is low, there were five regressions with the R^2 under .40 and only one in the microeconomic area. Table 5.10 lists the regressions that had an R^2 of less than .40 or over .55.

There were a total of forty-four semantic differentials, bracketing all of the issues, with an R^2 greater than .55. In short, the model seems to predict relatively well on all three types of issues for Section 64 of Economics 224. The two most important variables, instructor's opinion and the students' precourse opinions, are of comparable beta weight. This result is, of course, consistent with the results for the previous sections.

In the Economics 224, Section 64, the instructor's position and the students' precourse attitudes were statistically significant in all of the regressions. In fact, again, it is the interaction of these two variables that provide the greatest importance in predicting the student opinions on the postcourse survey. The detail for the regressions is shown in Appendix G, with a summary shown in Appendix M. For instance, for the first issue which is DECISION-MAKING FOR NATIONAL ECONOMIC POLICY, for the descriptor "simple-complex," the overall R^2 for the equation was .56 with the students' precourse attitudes contributing .41 toward the overall R^2 and the instructor's position contributing .04. The two variables, instructor's opinion and student precourse opinions, together contributed .45 toward the overall R^2

TABLE 5.10

Economics 224: Section 64
Coefficient of Determination Under .40

Macroeconomic Issues with Low R (Below .40)		*Microeconomic Issues with Low R (Below .40)*	
Inflation:		Labor Unions:	
Demand Pull-Cost Push	.39	Effective-Ineffective	.39
High Unemployment:			
Controllable-Not Controllable	.36		
Federal Income Tax:			
Democratic-Republican	.306		
Increasing Money Supply:			
Helps-Hurts People	.375		
Democratic-Republican	.286		

TABLE 5.11

Distribution of R^2's
Economics 224: Section 64
Coefficient of Determination Over .55

ISSUE	
Macroeconomic Issues in R^2 Over .55	
Decision-Making for National Economic Policy:	
Simple-Complex	.56
Random-Rational	.637
Important to Me-Irrelevant to Me	.685
Important to Society-Irrelevant to Society	.612
Government Spending Deficit:	
Undesirable-Desirable	.607
Increase-Decrease Aggregate Demand	.63
Government Controls:	
Undesirable-Desirable	.63
Democratic-Republican	.675

TABLE 5.11
(continued)

Free Enterprise-Socialism	.617
Effective-Ineffective	.583
Facilitates Market Opinions-Distorts Market Opinions	.63
Poverty:	
Lazy-Lack of Opportunity	.685
Serious-Unimportant	.667
Market Determined-Discrimination	.57
No Jobs-No Skills	.60
Inevitable-Can be Eliminated	.72
Individual-Social Responsibility	.66
Inflation:	
Bad-Good	.655
High Unemployment:	
Democratic-Republican	.695
Recession-Prosperity	.60
Federal Income Tax:	
Progressive-Regressive	.609
Too High-Too Low	.565
Increasing Money Supply:	
Inflation-Recession	.58
More Gold-More Paper	.61
Microeconomic Issues with R^2 Over .55	
Labor Unions:	
Good-Bad	.59
Fair-Unfair	.65
Responsible-Irresponsible	.64
Capitalistic-Socialistic	.60
Greedy-Selfless	.627
Necessary-Unnecessary	.657
Big Business:	
Good-Bad	.648
Growing-Declining	.55
Should be Controlled-Should be Free	.61
Pays Its Share-Gets Free Ride	.63
Socially Responsible-Socially Irresponsible	.665

TABLE 5.11
(continued)

Capitalism:	
Reality-Nonreality	.68
Desirable-Undesirable	.61
Declining-Growing	.71
Superior to Socialism-Inferior to Socialism	.688
Monopolistic-Competitive	.60
Politically Involved-Uninvolved	.665
Market Mechanisms:	
Efficient-Inefficient	.626
Theoretical-Practical	.615
Workable-Unworkable	.641

of the equation of .56. Thus the remaining thirteen variables contributed .11 toward the overall R^2, with half of that amount coming from the human-capital variables. The variable that has significantly increased (relative to 223) in predictive capability is the students' precourse opinions. It is approximately doubled over its contribution to R^2 for the first semester in 223 regressions. These comparisons may be made from Appendices J and K for Economics 223, and Appendices L and M for Economics 224. A large measure of the increased predictive power of the equation comes from the variable that we have defined as the students' precourse attitude.

Table 5.12 shows the issues and descriptors where the instructor's position dominated the predictive power of the regression. Again, on the seventeen descriptors (regressions) that were dominated by the instructor's attitudes, they seem very clearly to be the type of issue that we would suggest as content or analytic. As such, these semantic differentials constitute an element or component of the discussion of economic theory and policy. It is surprising, for both Sections 63 and 64 of Economics 224, that while the semester deals with microeconomic topics and issues, the instructor apparently had a more significant impact on the macroeconomic issues than he did on the microeconomic issues. This point has been apparent throughout the discussion. That is, the instructor has had a significant impact on student opinions of both microeconomic and macroeconomic semantic differentials regardless of the semester involved. One possible conclusion would be that economics is essentially a subject where all of the topics and issues are interrelated. An alternative interpretation is that both microeconomic and macroeconomic events are taking place in the real world, and they exert an independent influence on student opinions while they are taking the courses.

One overall conclusion seems appropriate at this point, and that concerns the manner in which the instructor's position has related to the student post-course opinions for all sections of Economics 223 and 224. That is, the instructor's opinion has seemed to dominate clearly only on the content or analytic semantic differentials of the various issues. This would suggest first that the instructors as such are not attempting to polemicize their students with regard to values or suggested attitudes (see Table 5.12). The lecturers are in fact following a type of positivist approach to economics in discussing economics as a treatise in theory and policy. In this sense the student attitudes on noncontent issues would simply reflect the students' own ideas on those issues or their own conclusions about those issues as derived from the theory and policy discussions in class. Whether this is a desirable result or not would, we suppose, depend on whether one took a normativist or positivist approach to economics.

Again, it is relatively rare for the other variables in the equations to contribute significantly to the predictive power of the equation.

TABLE 5.12

Economics 224: Section 64
Issues Dominated by Predictive Power
of Instructor's Attitudes

ISSUES	Contribution to R^2	R^2
Decision-Making for National Economic Policy:		
Important to Me-Irrelevant to Me	.32	.68
Important to Society-Irrelevant to Society	.41	.61
Government Spending Deficit:		
Desirable-Undesirable	.25	.60
Poverty:		
Market Determined-Discrimination	.29	.57
Inflation:		
Cost Push-Demand Pull	.21	.39
High Unemployment:		
Recession-Prosperity	.44	.60
Bad-Good	.28	.47
Federal Income Tax:		
Progressive-Regressive	.34	.61

TABLE 5.12
(continued)

Increasing Money Supply:		
Inflation-Recession	.34	.58
More Paper-More Gold	.27	.61
Democratic-Republican	.14	.28
Big Business:		
Good-Bad	.30	.64
Capitalism:		
Desirable-Undesirable	.45	.61
Market Mechanism:		
Efficient-Inefficient	.47	.62
Workable-Unworkable	.46	.64
Desirable-Undesirable	.25	.45
Allocates-Does Not Allocate	.22	.51

Column 9 of Appendix G shows the other variables that were statistically significant in each regression. Of the total of 111 appearances of the other variables as significant, the human capital variables were significant 30 times, or 27 percent of the total occurrences.

The EXPCODE (Experimental Code) was statistically significant in eleven of the seventy-four equations. It contributed a maximum of .02 toward the overall R^2 of the equation in only two instances, with decreasing importance in the other equations where it was statistically significant. As before, we would conclude that CAI exerts no systematic or significant effect on student post-course opinions.

Section 64 of Economics 224 did have one type of development with the other variables that was not apparent in the other sections. In a total of fourteen regressions, three or more of the "other variables" were significant in each of the regressions as summarized in Table 5.13.

TABLE 5.13

Economics 224: Section 64
Other Variables

Decision-Making for National Economic Policy

Important to Me-Irrelevant to Me
Important to Society-Irrelevant to Society

TABLE 5.13
(continued)

Government Spending Deficit

Desirable-Undesirable
Democratic-Republican

Government Controls: Wage-Price Freeze

Socialism-Free Enterprise
Distorts-Facilitates Market Operations

Poverty

Market Determined-Discrimination
No Skills-No Jobs

Inflation:

Bad-Good
Inevitable-Controllable

High Unemployment

Bad-Good

Increasing Money Supply

Free Enterprise-Socialism

Labor Unions

Not Necessary-Necessary

Market Mechanism

Desirable-Undesirable

Clearly (even though here the evidence is not completely unambiguous), these descriptors tend to reflect the value-oriented semantic differentials.

Having examined the evidence on determinants of student postcourse opinions on economic issues on a section-by-section basis we can now attempt to summarize across sections. First, it appears that CAI did not exert an unique independent influence on students' postcourse opinions on economic issues. Second, the two most important variables in explaining postcourse opinions are the students' precourse opinion and the instructor's opinion. Third, the instructor's opinion was relatively most important in explaining postcourse opinion on the content or analytical issues as opposed to the value-oriented and political issues. Fourth, the absolute importance of the students' precourse opinions in explaining postcourse opinions increased during the second semester, reflecting the leveling impact of a first course (the first semester) in economics. Fifth, and finally, it appears that the process by which lecture materials are presented can contribute to the manner in which student opinions are formed. Here we are specifically referring to Economics 223, where we noted that in Section 61 the human capital variables are not important in any sense in the formulations of student postcourse opinions while in Section 62 these variables are important.

6

ATTITUDES TOWARD CAI & THE DISCUSSION CLASSES

A. Introduction

Although the previous chapter presented an extensive empirical analysis of the effect of CAI on student attitudes, the question of student reaction to CAI and its alternative, the discussion class, was not raised. This question is the theme of the current chapter. In addressing this question, we begin with what might be labeled a general analysis, comparing the overall reactions of the control students to the discussion classes, with the reactions of the experimental students to CAI. Because the questionnaires used to generate the relevant data were not the same during both semesters, we present separate analyses for each of the two courses. We then proceed to a more disaggregated investigation. This is necessary because eight different graduate teaching assistants were responsible for the discussion classes during each semester. Consequently, we would expect that the reactions of the controls would vary depending in large measure on the abilities of the teaching assistant who presided over their particular discussion class. Again separate analyses will be presented for each course. Finally, we will summarize information obtained from a series of student interviews conducted during each semester. The interviews are important in several respects, but primarily because they can be used to isolate the strengths and weakness of both CAI and the discussion classes as perceived by the student.

B. A General Comparison

1. ECONOMICS 223

During the first semester, the experimentals were asked a series of questions regarding CAI, while the controls were asked a somewhat similar set of questions about the discussion classes. The questionnaire was distributed to both student groups at the beginning and the end of each semester. In

TABLE 6.1

CAI vs. Discussion Classes
Comparison of Instructional Methods
Economics 223

	Section 61					
	Controls		Experimentals		Forced Experimentals	
Item	Post	Change	Post	Change	Post	Change
CAI is:						
A good teaching method			3.4241	-0.1258	3.6829	0.1538
Useful for presenting Policy			3.1013	-0.0066	3.2561	0.1154
Useful for presenting Theory			3.0063	0.0530	3.0732	0.1410
A good review			4.1266	0.5364	4.4024	0.9103
Stimulating			3.1019	-0.4901	3.3457	-0.1923
Dehumanizing			2.5063	0.0733	2.3293	-0.1026
The discussion class is:						
A good teaching method	4.1169	-0.0260				
Useful for presenting Policy	3.9091	-0.1169				
Useful for presenting Theory	3.8182	-0.0390				
Helpful for promoting discussions	4.1688	-0.0909				
Useful for resolving questions	4.3377	-0.0130				
Better than a third lecture	4.1948	-0.1169				

each instance the students were given a series of statements and were asked whether they agreed or disagreed with the statement (a "1" indicating strong disagreement and a "5" indicating strong agreement). Table 6.1 presents the results of the postcourse questionnaire as well as the change (post minus pre) that was recorded over the semester.

The postcourse attitudinal data for Section 61 indicates that the controls thought more highly of the discussion classes than the experimentals thought of CAI; that is, the average postcourse attitudes of the controls ranges from 3.8 to 4.3, while the average postcourse attitudes of the experimentals ranges from 3.0 to 4.1 (we have ignored the last item on CAI because this statement is phrased so that a higher numerical score is an unfavorable attitude toward

TABLE 6.1
(continued)

		Section 62							
Free Experimentals		Controls		Experimentals		Forced Experimentals		Free Experimentals	
Post	Change	Post	Change	Post	Change	Post	Change	Post	Change
3.1447	-0.4247			3.5926	0.0889	3.7381	0.1667	3.5269	0.0538
2.9342	0.1370			3.3556	0.2889	3.4524	0.2619	3.3118	0.3011
2.9342	-0.0411			3.0074	0.1259	3.1905	0.3810	2.9247	0.0108
3.8289	0.1370			4.3037	0.8148	4.4524	1.0476	4.2366	0.7097
2.8421	-0.8082			3.2015	0.2388	3.2857	0.1905	3.1630	0.4348
2.6974	0.2639			2.4222	0.0370	2.4048	-0.0476	2.4301	0.0753
		3.6863	-0.3600						
		3.5728	-0.1386						
		3.3981	-0.2673						
		3.5049	-0.7030						
		3.8350	-0.5842						
		3.8447	-0.2772						

CAI). As might be expected, the most favorable aspect of CAI is its review function, while the fact that the discussion classes can be used for resolving questions represents the most desirable aspect of this alternative. The separate data for the free and forced experimentals reveals that of these two types of experimentals, the forced were more favorably disposed toward CAI. On each of the six statements regarding CAI, the average postcourse attitudes are more favorable for the forced experimentals. This suggests that the way in which CAI is implemented can affect a student's attitude toward it, with a structured approach yielding a more favorable outcome.

Also interesting are the changes in attitudes that occurred over the semester in Section 61. The controls revised their attitudes toward the discussion classes in a downward direction, indicating that their expectations regarding this alternative were not met. For the experimentals, movement in an unfavorable direction occurred on four of the six statements about CAI (now including the last item on CAI). It would appear then that the evidence on changes is not so consistently against CAI as the postcourse attitudinal data. Disaggregating the experimental results, the forced group moved in a favorable direction on five of the six statements, while the free experimentals moved in a favorable direction on only one item. The change data, like the postcourse data, suggest that the manner employed for implementing CAI is important.

Turning to the Section 62 results, we can begin by noting that a comparison of postcourse data between controls and experimentals does not reveal a strong difference in the attitudinal reception of CAI and the discussion classes. The average postcourse attitudes range from 3.4 to 3.8 for the controls and 3.0 to 4.3 for the experimentals (again ignoring the last item for CAI). We also find that the most attractive feature of CAI is its review function, while the use of the discussion classes to resolve questions was the most attractive feature of the discussion classes. Disaggregation of the experimentals confirms a Section 61 result, namely, that the forced experimentals are more favorably disposed toward CAI then the free experimentals. Indeed we should point out that the numerical value for the review function by CAI obtained from the forced experimentals in both sections was highest of any of the numerical results obtained.

Focusing on changes in attitudes, we find the controls moving in an unfavorable direction on all six statements regarding the discussion classes. Now, however, the experimentals are moving in a favorable direction on five of the six CAI statements. Thus, not only is there very little difference in postcourse attitudes between the controls and the experimentals, but the changes are in basically opposite directions. The latter outcome implies that CAI is the better alternative. Disaggregation of the experimental students indicates that the forced experimentals moved in a favorable direction on all six items, while the free experimentals moved in a favorable direction on five of the six. Hence, in terms of changes, the distinction between the two types of experimentals is less clear, and movement is similar for both groups.

Summarizing over both sections we may posit the following conclusions: (1) the controls reacted negatively to the reality of the discussion classes, (2) the method of implementing CAI appears to be important in determining student attitudes toward CAI, and (3) there does not appear to be a consistent and strong distinction between the student groups in terms of their final attitudes toward the instruction alternatives.

2. ECONOMICS 224

For the second semester, a questionnaire was distributed to both student groups, controls and experimentals, only once at the end of the semester. This questionnaire raises a number of points concerning each of the educational alternatives, CAI and the discussion classes. The results of this questionnaire are presented in Tables 6.2 and 6.3.

In Table 6.2 we have attempted to isolate those elements on the questionnaire which allow a direct comparison of the control students' reactions to the discussion classes with the experimental students' reactions to CAI. First we asked both student groups whether they were satisfied and the degree of their satisfaction with their educational alternative. As Table 6.2 indicates, we obtained what appear to be section-specific results. That is, for Section 63, 38.9 percent of the seventy-five responding controls said that they were very satisfied with the discussion classes, while 31.3 percent of the sixty-nine responding experimentals were similarly disposed toward CAI. For Section 64, however, the results favor CAI; only 22.6 percent of the controls were very satisfied, while 33.6 percent of the experimentals were so disposed toward CAI. Second, we asked each student group three questions regarding each alternative (again, a "1" indicates strong disagreement with the statement while a "5" indicates strong agreement). On these three items we also obtained what appear to be section-specific results. The average responses to the three statements were higher for the controls in Section 63, while they were lower on two of the three statements in Section 64. Simply, the results presented in Table 6.2 do not indicate that one student group consistently favored one alternative over the other.

Table 6.3 contains the remaining information generated from this questionnaire, which does not however allow for a direct comparison between the two student groups. Of the data obtained from the controls, the responses on item 4 are the most important; approximately half of the controls in each of the sections had frequent access to the computer printouts. This, of course, implies that there was a substantial breakdown in the experimental design. This result was probably predictable, given that the experiment was being conducted over an academic year, that students were switching status between semesters (some experimentals becoming controls and so on), and that most students at Notre Dame live in dormitories, so there is extensive interaction both in and out of the classroom. Interview data to be presented later in this chapter indicates that this breakdown was not nearly as severe during the first semester. The question then is: what are the consequences of this breakdown?

Presumably the only advantages to be gained by having a computer print-

TABLE 6.2

Attitudes toward CAI and Discussion Classes
Economics 224

	In Percent			
	Section 63		Section 64	
Item	Controls	Experi-mentals	Controls	Experi-mentals
1. Are you satisfied with the discussion class (CAI System)?				
Very Satisfied	38.9	31.3	22.6	33.6
Slightly Satisfied	26.4	37.3	42.2	45.5
Unsatisfied	29.2	24.4	24.5	13.6
Very Unsatisfied	5.5	9.0	10.8	7.3
2. Are you satisfied with the discussion class (CAI System)?				
Complemented the course well	3.71	3.42	3.52	3.66
Is an effective way to review	3.87	3.53	3.76	3.77
Increased the value of the course	3.68	3.16	3.53	3.45
N	75	69	106	110

The items were phrased specifically in terms of the discussion class for the controls and specifically in terms of CAI for the experimentals.

out is that the control student would have the explanation of right answers as interpreted by the writer of the questions for the review routines and an idea of what the demonstrations and simulations were like. The fact that the controls would go to the trouble to obtain this information can be interpreted in two ways. First, it might indicate that the logic for right answers as supplied by the graduate teaching assistants in the discussion classes was not considered adequate by the control students. Alternatively, the answers may have been adequate, but the controls were risk-averters; they wanted to double-check the answers and explanations supplied by the graduate teaching assistant with those contained in the review routines. In any event, we must admit that the breakdown did occur, and the results we have presented thus far and will continue to present must be interpreted accordingly.

The additional information contained in Table 6.3 underscores a point previously made with regard to the CAI system. As far as the experimentals were concerned, the essential element of the system was the review routines; the use of the system was concentrated here because the students perceived that these routines were the most useful. This data also implies that if stu-

TABLE 6.3

Attitudes and Use of CAI and the Discussion Classes
Economics 224

Student Classification and Question	In Percent Section 63	Section 64
Controls	N = 75	N = 106
1. The personal element of the discussion class was important to me.	3.85*	3.80*
2. How often did you attend the discussion class?		
Every Week	41.3	31.1
Fairly regularly	33.3	31.1
Only a few times	18.7	24.5
Never	6.7	13.2
3. Did you have access to a computer terminal?		
Yes	29.2	45.6
No	70.8	54.4
4. Did you have frequent access to computer printouts?		
Yes	46.6	49.5
No	53.4	50.5
Experimentals	N = 68	N = 110
1. The CAI system was available at convenient times.	3.33*	3.82*
2. The CAI system depersonalized the course too much.	2.60*	2.52*
3. How often did you use the computer?		
Every week	14.5	20.0
Fairly regularly	31.9	33.6
Only a few times	47.8	41.8
Never	5.8	4.6
4. How many review routines did you run?		
All 23	32.4	36.7
18–22	17.7	15.6
13–17	14.7	16.5
8–12	10.3	13.8
3–7	11.8	10.1
0–2	13.2	7.3
5. How many demonstration routines did you run?		
All 5	17.7	10.1
2–4	20.6	40.4
Less than 2	61.8	49.5
6. Did you run the simulation?		
Yes	32.2	51.9
No	61.8	48.1
7. Which type of routine helped you learn the most?		
Review routines	93.4	92.2
Demonstration routines	3.3	5.8
The simulation	3.3	1.9
8. Which type of routine was most useful in preparing for exams?		
Review routines	100	98.0
Demonstration routines	0	1.0
The simulation	0	1.0

*These entries reflect the average response to the statement with a 1 indicating strong disagreement and a 5 indicating strong agreement.

dents are to use demonstrations and simulations and to find them useful, they must be integrated into a course. We made no attempt to accomplish such an integration, and student reactions to these types of routines indicate as much.

C. Influence of Individual Graduate Teaching Assistants

1. ECONOMICS 223

The previous discussion has ignored the fact that eight different graduate teaching assistants were involved with the teaching of the discussion classes during each semester. Recognition of this raises two interesting questions: (1) What was the extent of the variation in the quality of the discussion classes as taught by each of these assistants? and (2) How does CAI compare with the discussion classes, when account is taken of the impact of the individual assistants?

With respect to the first question, Table 6.4 presents the results for the 223 course. Here we have disaggregated the data from the questionnaires completed by the controls regarding the discussion classes according to graduate teaching assistants. Using any criteria, there is little doubt that we obtain substantial variation between the assistants. On the basis of the average post-course attitudes on the six items, GTA8 appears to be superior ($\overline{X} = 4.26$),

TABLE 6.4

Reaction to Discussion Classes
According to Graduate Teaching Assistants
Economics 223

Item	GTA1		GTA2		GTA3	
	Post	Change	Post	Change	Post	Change
Discussion Classes are:						
1. a good teaching method	3.867	-.466	4.000	-.167	3.765	-.291
2. useful for presenting policy	3.867	-.333	3.833	+.166	3.333	-.667
3. useful for presenting theory	3.867	-.200	4.000	.000	3.278	-.278
4. useful for promoting discussion	4.333	-.134	3.833	-.666	3.389	-.944
5. useful for resolving questions	4.133	-.534	4.167	-.333	3.833	-.778
6. better than a third lecture	4.133	-.534	4.000	-.500	3.889	-.389
$\overline{X}$	4.02	-.36	3.97	-.25	3.58	-.56
Number of controls responding to both pre and post questionnaires	15		6		18	

$\overline{X}$ is a simple average across the preceding six items

while GTA5 is decidedly inferior ($\bar{X} = 3.17$). Shifting the basis of comparison to the average change on all six items, GTA 8 again would be ranked first ($\bar{X} = +.20$), while GTA6 would be ranked last ($\bar{X} = -.60$). Changing criteria may lead to changes in ranking, but the evidence on variation and substantial variation remains.

Having established that there is variation, we can now proceed to the second question, which can be rephrased as follows: If we want to rank the teaching assistants and CAI, what order in the ranking would CAI take? Clearly the result will depend in part on the criteria used for the ranking. Because of this, we have chosen to use several different criteria. All of these are shown in Table 6.5.

The first ordering is obtained by averaging the postcourse attitudes of the controls on all six items pertaining to the discussion classs. These are taken directly from Table 6.4. To determine the corresponding value for CAI and, consequently, its ranking, we have used the postcourse attitudes of the experimentals on the first five statements regarding CAI shown in Table 6.1. (Again, the last CAI statement was omitted because higher numerical scores on this item are indicative of an unfavorable attitude toward CAI.) With this ordering we find that CAI assumes the second-last position.

The second ordering is obtained by using the average change in attitudes of the controls on all six items pertaining to the discussion class, also shown in Table 6.4. For the CAI value we used the average change on the first five items regarding CAI. With this criterion CAI takes the second-highest position.

TABLE 6.4
(continued)

GTA4		GTA5		GTA6		GTA7		GTA8	
Post	Change	Post	Change	Post	Change	Post	Change	Post	Change
4.000	.000	3.286	-.857	3.528	-.528	4.114	+.057	4.333	+.190
4.000	+.375	3.000	-.571	3.500	-.222	3.771	-.229	4.190	+.190
3.844	+.156	2.786	-.500	3.306	-.555	3.657	-.229	4.000	+.381
3.844	-.437	3.071	-.786	3.389	-.805	4.057	-.029	4.333	+.047
4.125	-.250	3.429	-.542	3.722	-.750	4.400	+.086	4.476	+.333
4.281	.000	3.429	-.214	3.639	-.417	4.200	.000	4.238	+.048
4.02	-.03	3.17	-.58	3.51	-.60	4.00	-.06	4.26	+.20
32		14		36		35		21	

TABLE 6.5

Rank Ordering of CAI and Discussion Classes
Taught by Individual Graduate Teaching Assistants
Economics 223

Criteria							
Average postcourse attitude on all six statements regarding discussion classes		Average change in attitude on all six statements regarding discussion classes		Average postcourse attitude on the usefulness of the discussion class for resolving questions		Average change in attitude on the usefulness of the discussion class for resolving questions	
Order	Value	Order	Value	Order	Value	Order	Value
GTA8	4.26	GTA8	+.20	GTA8	4.48	CAI	+.67
GTA1	4.02	CAI	+.10	GTA7	4.40	GTA8	+.33
GTA4	4.02	GTA4	-.03	CAI	4.21	GTA7	+.09
GTA7	4.00	GTA7	-.06	GTA2	4.17	GTA4	-.25
GTA2	3.97	GTA2	-.25	GTA1	4.13	GTA2	-.33
GTA3	3.58	GTA1	-.36	GTA4	4.13	GTA1	-.53
GTA6	3.51	GTA3	-.56	GTA3	3.83	GTA5	-.54
CAI	3.42	GTA5	-.58	GTA6	3.72	GTA6	-.75
GTA5	3.17	GTA6	-.60	GTA5	3.43	GTA3	-.79

The remaining two orderings are based on the most important aspect of the discussion classes. As revealed in the previous section, the controls were most impressed with the fact that discussion classes allowed a resolution of questions. The postcourse scores obtained, and the changes that occurred are again taken from Table 6.4. For the corresponding values of CAI, we have used its most favorable aspect, its usefulness as a review devise. Thus these last two rank orderings are based on the most desirable features of the two educational alternatives. For postcourse attitudes, CAI takes third place, while it assumes the top position when the change in attitude criterion is employed.

The 223 results in total indicate that there was indeed variation in the quality of the discussion classes as taught by the individual assistants, regardless of the criteria used to measure quality. At the same time the results indicate that CAI, on at least three of the four criteria here employed, can outperform all but the best assistants. This implies that if one desires to eliminate the variation that almost always accompanies the use of several assistants, CAI can be an effective alternative. The question now is: Are the 224 results consistent with these conclusions?

2. ECONOMICS 224

For the 224 course we again used four criteria to generate rank orderings.

The results are shown in Table 6.6. First, we ranked CAI and individual assistants in terms of the percentage of students who said they were very satisfied. Under this criterion CAI outperforms all but two of the assistants. With the second ordering we added together the percentage of students who were very satisfied and satisfied, and CAI assumed the top rank. The third criterion measures the response of students to the statement that the educational alternative complemented the course well ("1" indicates strong disagreement while a "5" indicates strong agreement). Here CAI does less well; it is outperformed by four of the assistants. With the last criterion the students were commenting on the usefulness of the alternative as a review devise (same numerical interpretation as the complementary statement). CAI in this instance is outperformed by five of the eight assistants.

On the whole, then, the 224 results are consistent with the conclusion generated from the evidence for 223–CAI tends to outperform all but the best teaching assistants. As we have indicated, this result might be expected, given the usual variation in the quality of assistants and given the fact that the CAI system was prepared by faculty members who had taught the course a number of times in the past. Although the results suggest that substitution of CAI for discussion classes may resolve the problem of variation in teaching assistant quality, we must admit that there is another solution. Here we have in mind the preparation of the assistants for their teaching duties.[1] The assistants used during the year had no formal preparation, and some of the variations observed may reflect the fact that some of the assistants had previous experience, while others did not. The point we wish to make is that by more formal preparation, the quality of the discussion classes could be improved and the variation in results between assistants may be reduced. Note, however, that this alternative solution has its own additional costs which would then have to be included in any cost comparisons.[2] At the same time the CAI system could be improved as well. Indeed, the above attitudinal results and the interview data which are to follow suggest a number of ways in which the CAI system could be improved.

D. Student Interviews

1. ECONOMICS 223

Approximately midway through the 223 course, a series of interviews were carried out with thirty-six students by a trained interviewer, a professional sociologist. The students were drawn from both sections of the course.[3] The stratified sample represents students that were classified as forced experimentals, free experimentals, and controls. In addition the sample was drawn to insure that students with various grades (from the first midterm examination) were represented in the sample. The purpose of these inter-

TABLE 6.6

Ranking of CAI and Discussion Classes as Taught by Individual Graduate Teaching Assistants Economics 224

Criteria							
Percent Very Satisfied		Percent Very Satisfied and Satisfied		Complemented the Course Well		A Good Review Device	
Order	Value (in Percent)	Order	Value (in Percent)	Order	Value	Order	Value
GTA4	42	CAI	77	GTA4	4.1	GTA4	4.1
GTA1	40	GTA8	72	GTA8	3.8	GTA8	4.0
CAI	36	GTA2	66	GTA1	3.7	GTA1	3.7
GTA8	35	GTA4	65	GTA5	3.7	GTA5	3.6
GTA2	33	GTA5	62	CAI	3.6	GTA2	3.5
GTA5	28	GTA6	62	GTA2	3.5	CAI	3.4
GTA3	25	GTA1	60	GTA6	3.3	GTA7	3.2
GTA6	16	GTA7	52	GTA7	3.2	GTA6	3.2
GTA7	14	GTA3	50	GTA3	3.1	GTA3	2.9

views was to examine further and more intensively the student reaction to the course generally as well as to the CAI and discussion class alternatives. The interviews were seen as a way of both broadening and reinforcing the information developed through the written surveys.

The one continuing concern is with the student reaction to a course of the size of 223 or 224; thus this was the theme of our initial question to the students in the interview. A typical response to the question was: "You just don't get to know a professor in a class of 300." This did not seem to influence the students particularly in their response to other aspects of the course, as students do not expect much teacher contact in a class of this size and thus the aggregate disappointment appeared to be minimal. It was clear from the interviews that the students did not like large classes, but they seemed to accept them as a fact of university life.

The students maintained that the teaching assistant, acting through the discussion class, is not an adequate substitute for the lecturer. The interviews also made clear that the student is looking for a type of personal relationship with the lecturer, perhaps somewhat beyond a normal lecturer-student relationship found in a small class. The student appears to desire a situation where he can approach the instructor at any time (in class, immediately after class, or any time the student encounters a question or problem) with questions and/or can discuss related materials. The students in the interviews widely agreed that they were not comfortable asking questions in a class of 300. In addition, if the student delayed asking the question, either it would be forgotten or the importance and context of the question would be lost. Presumably, in a smaller class the student would be more willing to ask questions leading to some kind of class discussion.

This student concern about questions and the discussion of content materials was critical in the view of students interviewed. They suggested that the instructor should have some type of review session in which the students could ask him, rather than the teaching assistant, questions. A majority of the students interviewed (in the control group) felt that the teaching assistant either could not or would not answer their questions adequately or did not answer their questions as the "professor would." Furthermore, a majority of the control students interviewed felt that the primary value of the discussion class was to obtain the sheet of review questions handed out—that is, the questions from the CAI programs.

Another point was repeatedly raised by the students from the control group. These students generally agreed that the discussion class with a teaching assistant was conceptually better than the CAI approach because a student could get his own questions answered. Unfortunately, all of the students interviewed were also agreed in their disappointment with the reality of their particular discussion class. A typical quotation from the interviews states: "The tutorial is a waste of time. The idea is great, but the teaching assistant does not give the guidance and knowledge needed."[4]

The reactions of the experimental students (CAI group) to the 223 course are quite interesting and can be summarized as follows:

1. The students felt that the active involvement inherent in using the CAI programs was superior to the passive involvement typical of the discussion classes. They felt that being an active participant enhanced the learning experience by offering the student an opportunity to learn why the answers were right or wrong according to the instructor in the course.

2. The students found that CAI was a good drill and sharpened their ability to handle multiple-choice tests. The CAI review programs provided a record of the correct and incorrect answers and why the answers were correct or incorrect. Some students said that they would think they knew an answer, but later (when they discovered they did not know the answer) the printout served as an instant review.

3. Other students were critical of the "relative ease" of the CAI questions as compared with the questions on the examinations. These students said they would often run the CAI review routines without reading the textbook, and they would do well on the CAI reviews. This lulled them into a sense of

security that was shattered when the questions on the first midterm examination were "relatively harder" than those on the CAI reviews. They said the CAI reviews concentrated more on recognition and understanding questions, while the examination questions concentrated more on applications. This caused some of the students to become disillusioned with the CAI reviews during the first semester. The students left the interviewer with the impression that the CAI questions should be at least as hard as those found on the examinations.

4. A few students mentioned an aversion to the use of the computer per se. One student said that he felt pressured to answer the questions quickly even though he knew that he did not have to.

5. Many of the experimental students interviewed said that there should be some coercion to use the computer, just as many of the control students said that there should be compulsion to attend the discussion classes. The students said that it was the instructor's responsibility to force them (students) to attend class and/or use the CAI materials. This perhaps explains why the attitudes of the forced experimentals were more positive to CAI than than those of the free experimentals, as revealed by the survey data.

6. The interviews uncovered a number of student comments regarding the mechanics of computer use:

   a. the user should be able to enter the middle of a program or should be able to select specific questions from the review program to execute;
   b. the computer should print the output more rapidly; and
   c. there should be the capability of delaying the move to the next question until the student has had the opportunity of exploring all of the alternatives of a given question.

It should be noted that the students regard the Economics 223–224 course sequence as one more required course sequence that must be taken in a large lecture format. As of the time of this initial interview, the students did not know what the other students were doing. The experimental students did not know that the control students received the same questions. This awareness, however, began to change, partially as a result of the interviews and partially as a result of the fact that students began to become acquainted with one another. This awareness did change and by the spring semester there was a great deal of exchange of information between the controls and experimentals, as we have already indicated.

2. ECONOMICS 224

In the interview conducted during Economics 224, the starting point, as in Economics 223, concerned the size of the courses. All of the students interviewed were concerned about large lecture classes. They did not like them. They felt that discussion was almost impossible in this environment. As one student indicated: "You sort of feel inhibited to ask questions, and I like to ask a question right on the spot when the teacher is there when I'm learning."

When the controls were asked if they were satisfied with their discussion classes, those who responded "yes" gave the reason that they could ask questions and get them answered. One of the students indicated that this was the only reason why a student would go to the discussion class. Many of the control students being interviewed expressed concern over the quality of the teaching assistants. They were in agreement that a good teaching assistant would respond to and answer questions and could adequately explain difficult topics. Thus, in the second semester, as in the first, the need to ask questions and get immediate response was of primary concern to both the control students and the experimental students. Both groups of students interviewed agreed that the ideal solution was a smaller lecture class.

When the students were subsequently asked which group, experimental or control, would do better on examinations, most students being interviewed responded that they felt the experimental students (using CAI) would do better. For those students who responded that they felt the control students would do better, they qualified the answer by saying that the discussion class would be an advantage only if the teaching assistant were good. The students felt that if the teaching assistant were "poor," then the CAI would be an advantage.

An interesting comment concerning the advantage of a discussion class was that the discussion class was better for those students who did attend it. One student noted: "If you can get a situation where you get one tutor to five guys, have a pretty good setup." An obvious conclusion, and one documented elsewhere, is that the low attendance at the discussion classes made individual attention possible to those who attended. The counterpoint to this is that a "poor" teaching assistant would have a bad impact on all or perhaps many of his students.

Students who chose the computer group as likely to do the best on examinations indicated that they thought the CAI was more consistent and flexible than the discussion-class approach. One point developed by the students interviewed was that there was an increased need for the CAI user students to have questions answered. One experimental student indicated that he did not like to use the computer because he had to answer questions asked by others and he could not ask his own questions. Yet the same student admitted that the CAI programs covered most of the material and that he did not attend the office hours of the professor or the teaching assistant although he knew he could.

The final aspect of the interviews during the Economics 224 course was a series of student comments on the CAI programs. These comments are summarized below:

1. The students felt that the computer was like a "private tutor." it enabled them to see where they should concentrate their study time. The programs helped the students to see if they "really understood the materials."

2. The programs in the CAI group put down "in black and white" why an answer was wrong, and this output was available for later study.

3. During the second semester the students found a more consistent relationship between the CAI materials and the examination questions. Both the computer questions and the examination questions placed emphasis on application. The students were able to practice their applications of the theory on the CAI materials and were better prepared for the application questions that appeared on the examinations.

4. Some students enjoyed the computer and the CAI approach as learning techniques. One student responded: "You are a captive audience–can't help but read and try to learn."

5. A common comment concerned the flexibility of CAI. Students were satisfied with the ability to work on their own. Unlike a discussion class that met at a specific time, some students found the computer available at times convenient to them.

6. Students who were dissatisfied with CAI indicated that the programs took too much time. One student termed the procedure: "effective but not efficient."

7. Many of the experimental students interviewed stated that there should be some coercion to use the computer. They also felt it was necessary to force students to attend the discussion class.

8. The experimentals frequently indicated that they did not use CAI weekly. These students preferred to run the programs before examinations. One student commented: "I'd get two terminals going at once, and I got four programs done in one hour, so I got all of the programs done in one day. I don't think it's really that important to keep up with it all along as long as you get it done before the test, like a week or so before, so you can go over it [the output list] a couple of times."

During the interviews carried out the second semester, it became evident that the students were aware of the procedures being used for both the discussion classes and for the CAI students. The control students indicated that they received computer printouts from friends who were in the experimental group or used their friends' computer numbers.[5] In general, student interest in the course did not depend upon the students' participation in discussion class or CAI. The class size, the individual lecturer, and the textbook were the largest factors of student concern.

The final impression from the interviews is that the students made two very important points with regard to the instructional procedures. First, they felt that in order to do well on the examinations, it is important to have a good review device. When asked which group (controls or experimentals) would do better on examinations, students in both groups felt that experimentals would perform better. The reason was that CAI covered most of the material and written printouts could be used as a study guide. Using the printout, the students could find out why the answers were wrong. Second, the students felt a need for discussion and for having questions answered. CAI did not satisfy this need. Students indicated, however, that the tutorial or discussion class fulfilled this need only if the student happened to get a good teaching assistant.

To summarize, over both the written questionnaires and the interviews, it is obvious that a number of things could be done to improve both the CAI system and the discussion classes. It is also clear that the students would like to have both CAI and the discussion classes available. Each alternative has valuable and unique characteristics to which the students are sensitive. It would be possible to substitute smaller lectures for the discussion class. However, the role of CAI, as a review technique, would still be useful regardless of lecture size.

7

THE COST OF COMPUTER-ASSISTED INSTRUCTION

A. Introduction

Costs enter into economically efficient choices, and the costs of CAI should, therefore, be an important part of an evaluation of this new educational element as well as any decision to use it in the classroom. The costs associated with CAI may be divided into two major categories: development costs, which represent outlays for the construction of a system, and operational costs, or the expenses incurred as students use the system. This chapter contains separate discussions of each of these cost categories. But to make these cost determinations meaningful, they must be compared to alternative teaching arrangements. Thus in the third section of this chapter the operational costs of CAI are compared to the costs associated with discussion classes. We begin with a discussion of development costs.

B. Development Costs

Development of a CAI system involves three distinct activities: (1) specification of the objectives of a course, (2) design of an overall plan or series of procedures to achieve these objectives, and (3) preparation of CAI programs in a manner consistent with (1) and (2). Of these activities only the last is usually considered as an explicit cost associated with the introduction of CAI. This is the case because the first two activities are, presumably, undertaken each time a course is taught. All too often, however, only cursory attention is given to these first two activities. To the extent that consideration is given to the development of a CAI system or to the acquisition of some existing system, instructors may be forced to undertake these activities in a more careful and systematic way. If this is indeed true, then not only should the first two activities be excluded as a part of development costs, but they should be considered as benefits. Although we fully accept these arguments, we will not attempt to adjust the development cost data accordingly—mainly, because these adjustments would be somewhat arbitrary.

The CAI system employed in the Economics 223-224 sequence was constructed over the course of a summer and involved the efforts of two groups of people. Three of the four faculty members who were to teach in the sequence constituted one group. Each of these faculty members had extensive experience with his particular course, and the group as a whole was responsible for the preparation of the various programs to be included in the system. As is obvious from the composition of the system, with its heavy emphasis on review routines, the faculty effort was concentrated on the writing of multiple-choice questions and the appropriate prompts for correct and incorrect answers. As a faculty member completed the writing of a routine, it was passed to a member of the second group, student programmers. A programmer would convert the written routine into a computer routine and enter it into the computer. This was usually accomplished as a single step. Actually two types of programmers were employed. One type was less advanced and processed the review routines. Advanced programmers were necessary for the preparation of the demonstration and game simulation routines. Another individual was employed who does not fit into either of these two groups. This individual was an economics graduate student; his assignment was to execute each program after it had been entered into the computer to see that it ran properly and to check for errors of various sorts. Expenditures for each of these labor components are detailed in Table 7.1.

TABLE 7.1

Costs for the Development of the CAI System

Labor Costs	
1. Content Development	$9,000
Three faculty members full-time for two months	
2. Programming	7,000
Five programmers full-time for two months ($5,000)	
Two advanced programmers full-time for one month ($2,000)	
3. Review	1,000
One graduate student full-time for two months	
Computer Charges	3,434
Total Development Costs	$20,434

In addition to the labor expenses, charges were also incurred for using the computer. These charges are also shown in Table 7.1. Adding the labor expenses and the computer charges yields the total development cost of

$20,434 for the system. As indicated in Chapter I the completed system contained forty-two review routines, ten demonstrations, and five game simulations.

This cost of course pertains to a specific system, but our experience indicates the cost of any system will depend uniquely on several different factors. To allow for a generalization of development costs, it is useful to review these factors. One such factor, rather obviously, is the size of the CAI system. As the size of the system increases, greater effort will be required of both faculty members and programmers, and the greater will be the computer charges. We believe our system can be described as a large system with a large development cost. Such a large expenditure was justified in terms of both achieving an adequate test of CAI and the number of students who might eventually use the system.

Another factor that will influence the cost of developing a system is its composition—that is, the kinds of programs to be included within it. The cheaper kind of program is the review routine; it generally requires less faculty time to prepare as well as less time to program using individuals with lesser skills. Associated computer charges will usually be lower as well. Game simulations represent the other end of the cost spectrum. These kinds of programs require extensive time in terms of content development or faculty time and the use of programmers with more advanced skills. Computer charges for the completion of a routine of this kind, because it normally is larger and necessitates substantial debugging and alteration, will also be higher.

In any event it would appear that development of a system implies substantial costs. A teacher interested in using CAI recognizing this has an option. Rather than developing his own system, he may acquire an existing one. Such an acquisition, as an alternative to developing a new system, usually appears to be highly advantageous, for the necessary expenditure for acquisition is typically quite small. As an example we can cite the cost of obtaining our system. The entire system is available for the cost of preparing a tape according to the specification of the user. We have distributed over forty copies of the system in this way, and the mean charge has been in the neighborhood of $30.00.

But obtaining an existing system and using it are two different things, for an acquired system will never match exactly what the purchaser would like in terms of a CAI system for his course. Given this imperfect matching one must now consider adjustment activities and their subsequent costs. There are two extreme types of adjustment activities; (1) changing the course to match the system or (2) modifying the system to match the course. With the first technique an instructor may be forced to change textbooks, alter the content and sequence of lectures, and so on. Such activities, although they do not normally involve out-of-pocket expenditures, do impose a substantial burden in terms of opportunity cost. Under the second technique, routines may be added or deleted, changes in, say, notation made in others, and so on. In this instance the adjustment costs may involve some out-of-pocket expenditures, if a programmer must be hired to make the changes. But even with this technique, there is still a substantial opportunity cost for the instructor must decide on what changes are to be made. We should also mention that under this second technique the adjustment costs can vary with the type of system acquired. If the system consists of a number of short and independent routines, then necessary adjustments can usually be made by additions and deletions and the consequent costs will be farily small. Feedback from some of the users of our system indicates a very simple adjustment. The teacher provides students with a listing of our programs with a notation to his own text and lecture outline. The student then uses the appropriate CAI routines as they were originally developed but with the new chapter references. This procedure appears to yield minimal adjustment costs. If, on the other hand, the system contains a number of large and interdependent routines, a modification in one section may require a number of changes in both that section and in the other segments and involve substantial time and money.

The point, however, remains that the acquisition of an existing system involves both acquisition costs and adjustment costs. Any attempt to employ an acquired system without some adjustment activities is almost sure to result in an unsatisfactory experience with CAI. In the construction of CAI systems, as with nearly everything else, no one does anything exactly the way someone else would like it done. But once a system is available, a new set of costs are generated, and these must be considered in detail.

C. Operating Costs

Student user charges, or the costs incurred when students use a CAI system, are relatively unique among the category of educational costs. This uniqueness stems from the fact that these operational costs, at least in terms of their allocation among departments of an academic institution, are variable, increasing in amount as student use increases. Compare this to, say, library charges, which can be characterized as fixed. Presumably a student pays some portion of his tuition to cover the costs of maintaining the library as well as the instructional activities of the computer. In terms of the Notre Dame accounting system, a department's charges will not vary with the intensity of library use by students in the department's courses, but these charges will increase as the intensity of instructional computing increases. It is not clear that the costs of maintaining a library are independent of student use, while those costs related to instructional computing are directly linked with such use. Even though one might argue that these distinctions are simply a quirk of budgeting procedures (computer costs are simpler to allocate than library costs), they do represent a problem for determining cost effectiveness. We will return to this problem in some detail in the next section of this chapter. For our present discussion we will assume that the user charges were incurred on the basis that they were allocated to the department during the experimental year.

Table 7.2 indicates the various cost and use items for each section of the two courses. Aggregating across all four sections, total operational costs for the experimental year amounted to $16,361.33. Having arrived at this figure it is necessary to discuss the elements that influence this total.

Rather obviously, costs are influenced by the number of students using the system, the number of times each of the students used the system, and the amount of time the student users spend on the system. These elements are represented by the total number of experimentals, the total number of logons, and total connect time respectively. Increases in any of these elements individually will increase total operational costs, but the three elements may not be systematically related. For example, compare the two sections of the 224 course. Here Section 64 had fewer student users, fewer experimentals, but each used the system more frequently and for longer periods of time than the Section 63 experimentals.

In addition to these elements, total operational costs will be influenced by the cost algorithm employed by the computer center. According to the Notre Dame Computing Center cost algorithm, an hour of connect time, unlike a rose, is not an hour of connect time. More specifically, as indicated in Table 7.2 the cost per unit of connect time varies between the four sections. This variation arises because actual charges per hour of connect time depend on such things as the number of logons needed to generate that hour of connect time and, more importantly, on the number of lines of data transmitted between the computer and the computer terminal during the hour.[1] The number of lines of data transmitted depends, in turn, on the type of routine being executed and the manner of its execution. Generally, a specific amount of time with a demonstration or a game simulation will require more lines of transmission than the same amount of time spent with a review routine. Even in executing a review routine, a student who responds by guessing without studying the questions and their corresponding choices will generate more lines of transmission in an hour of connect time than a student who carefully examines each question and selects the correct answer on his first response. Note that these alternative approaches may require the same length of time to complete a particular review routine.

To remove the influence of the number of students who used the system,

TABLE 7.2

Operational Costs by Section
Economics 223 and 224

Item	Economics 223		Economics 224	
	Section 61	Section 62	Section 63	Section 64
Total Operational Costs	$4,811.57	$4,427.08	$3,087.29	$4,035.39
Number of Experimental Students	219	172	152	146
Total Number of Logons	1,801	1,583	820	1,186
Total Connect Time (hours)	1,222.69	1,078.19	680.41	933.07
Cost per hour of Connect Time	$3.94	$4.11	$4.53	$4.32
Number of Logons per Experimental Student	8.22	9.20	5.40	8.12
Connect Time per Experimental (hours)	5.58	6.27	4.48	6.39
Cost per Experimental	$21.97	$25.74	$20.31	$27.64
Number of Logons per Experimental Student*	9.79	10.08	9.32	11.74
Connect Time per Experimental (hours)*	6.65	6.87	7.73	9.24
Cost per Experimental*	$26.15	$28.20	$35.08	$39.95

*These calculations omit those students who were classified as experimentals but who never logged on. These students numbered 35 in section 61, 15 in section 62, 64 in section 63, and 45 in section 64.

Table 7.2 presents data on a per-student or per-experimental basis. In one case all experimentals are used as the base in calculating these ratios, but data are also presented in terms of those experimentals who used or logged onto the system at least once. Because the latter group is smaller, this adjustment raises all the corresponding ratios. Regardless of the base for these ratios we observe variations between sections. For example cost per experimental (all) ranged from a low of $20.31 in Section 63 to a high of $27.64 in Section 64. This difference arises because of the greater frequency of use (logons per experimental) and greater intensity of use (connect time per experimental) and in spite of a lower cost per hour of connect time in Section 64.

It is also useful to compare the cost data to our expectations of how the system would be used. The system was designed as a potential substitute for the discussion class. Thus the size of the system was constrained in part by this consideration. In addition, some preliminary testing indicated that an appropriate scheduling of weekly CAI assignments would involve approximately an hour per week for eleven weeks (there were no assignments for two weeks when the discussion classes would be used simply to hand back examinations). Obviously this approximation depended on a number of assumptions. These assumptions included: (1) students would run the CAI assignments on a weekly basis as scheduled, and students would never rerun a routine; (2) with the review routines, students would try to get right answers on their initial attempt and miss about 25 percent of the questions on their first response but would always get the correct response on their second attempt; (3) demonstrations would usually involve only two reactions to data inputed by the student; (4) game simulations would involve only two sets of policy variations by the students. If these assumptions were correct and the corresponding semester time on the system were accurate, then the cost for a student using the system in the way we had expected would have been $45.98. This figure is simply the multiple of the eleven semester hours of connect time estimated as necessary to run the system as we had envisioned it and the average cost per hour of connect time over the year [11 x ($16,361.33/3,914.36)].

The expected cost per student differs substantially from the actual cost per student for several reasons. Primarily it is because a number of students each semester did not use the system at all, and those that did did not use it as extensively as we had expected. The most obvious case of the latter is that the students did not use, for the most part, the demonstrations or the game simulations. In any event it is quite clear that the total costs and the cost per student user were substantially less than they could have been. Having established what the operating costs could have been and what they actually were, we can now compare the costs of CAI with the cost associated with the discussion classes.

D. Cost Comparison: CAI versus Discussion Classes

In the chapters evaluating the impact of CAI on cognitive and attitudinal outcomes, the experimentals, those who used the CAI system, were compared to the controls, those who did not, For the sake of consistency, we would like to maintain this comparative basis for an evaluation of costs—that is, compare the operational costs of CAI as developed in the preceding section with the expense involved with the processing of students through discussion classes. As necessary background we need to describe the nature of the expenses generated by the discussion classes.

Normally, and during the experimental year, the discussion classes are manned (or should we say personed) by graduate teaching assistants from the Economics Department. In exchange for their services, graduate teaching assistants receive a cash stipend as well as a remission of tuition for their own education activities during the year of the assistantship. Over time the cash stipend has been gradually increasing, but during the experimental year it amounted to \$2,400. The value of the tuition remission depends upon the number of credit hours taken by the individual graduate student (either formal course work or research credits) and the prevailing tuition levy. The latter also has been increasing over time, in this instance rather steadily. For graduate students taking between nine and twelve credit hours each semester, the normal load for graduate teaching assistants, the cash value of the tuition remission during the 1973–74 academic year was \$2,416. Thus the cost to the Economics Department of allocating a graduate assistant to the 223–224 sequence during the experimental year was \$4,816.[2]

As a general departmental rule, all graduate assistants, including graduate teacing assistants, are expected to devote twelve hours each week to their assistantship duties. For a graduate teaching assistant attached to the 223–224 sequence, these twelve hours have been historically divided as follows: four hours spent in the discussion classes themselves (four discussion classes each week), four hours when the graduate teaching assistant is available to his or her students (four office hours each week), and four hours of preparation and miscellaneous duties (attending lectures, reading the text, grading examinations, and so on). Thus only one-third of the twelve weekly hours are actually devoted to formal classroom activity. An experienced graduate teaching assistant who has no students come to him during his office hours may indeed come close to rendering only this minimum (ideal from his standpoint) to his assistantship duties.

With this background in mind we can begin to compare the costs associated with discussion classes and the operational costs of CAI. First it appears that the two types of costs are truly different. A graduate teaching assistant is paid the same if all of his students attend his classes and he has students lined up for his office hours or if no one attends either his classes or his office hours. In economic terms the teaching assistant is a fixed factor and his renumeration a fixed cost, an expenditure that does not vary with student use. Reworded, availability of the graduate teaching assistant and not the number of students taught or advised is the basis of his pay. CAI charges, on the other hand, are not fixed. If no students use the CAI system, there are no charges allocated to the department. If one student uses the system and another does not, the former incurs or generates such a charge, while the second does not. Furthermore, the student user is charged on the basis of time spent with the system and the way in which it is used. Again to employ economic terms, the CAI system appears to be a variable factor in the educational process, and the charges generated from its use represent a variable cost.

This distinction between fixed and variable factors and their corresponding costs not only makes cost comparisons difficult, it also raises several interesting questions. Perhaps the most obvious one is: Is the distinction really correct? Our answer to this question is a conditional "yes"—that is, it depends on an institution's budgeting process and one's perspective in examining that budget. Thus our conditional answer is positive, given the budgeting system here at Notre Dame and the department's view of the budget. If neither of these conditions hold, then the distinction may no longer be correct. For example, take a broader university view. From this perspective, both the costs of instructional computing and graduate teaching assistants for a certain academic year may represent fixed costs. Simply, given a computer facility, the actual expenditures involved with maintaining that facility and its various systems may be independent of the number of students who use it as well as the way in which they use it. Thus the charges made against a department for students using the computer may simply be an efficient manner of allocating this fixed cost to different departments within the university. Our suspicion is that this is indeed the case.[3]

But even from a department's view, what is fixed is the number of graduate assistantships and the cash value of each. A department, again within the Notre Dame context, appears to be free to use these assistants in any manner it wishes. If this is the case, then the total costs associated with the discussion classes depend strictly on the number of graduate assistants assigned such teaching responsibilities. This departmental decision depends, in turn, on two other considerations: the class teaching load of the graduate teaching assistant (the number of discussion classes taught each week by an assistant) and the size of the discussion classes. By increasing either or both of these elements, a given number of students can be processed through the discussion classes handled by fewer graduate teaching assistants and, therefore, at a lower total cost.[4] Rephrased, the discussion class costs are fixed for the duration of an academic year, but the level at which they are fixed is at the discretion of the department. Also note that this decision is also influenced by the demand for graduate assistants for other purposes, such as teaching their own courses and working as research assistants. In this context graduate assistants are scarce resources that must be allocated efficiently among competing uses.

Given all these considerations, the problem is still to compare the costs of CAI with the costs of discussion classes. Because both of these costs are affected by the number of students involved (admittedly CAI costs are more sensitive to this element than discussion class costs), it is useful to deal with a fixed number of students. Here we will assume that 640 students take each of the two courses and that they are equally divided into each section—that is, 320 students in each section of 223 and 320 students in each section of 224. We want to know what the costs would be if all these students used CAI without any discussion classes and, alternatively, what the cost would be if all students were processed through discussion classes without any CAI.

To estimate the costs of CAI for our fixed number of students we must make assumptions concerning both the use of the CAI system and the associated charges as billed by the computer center. We can use the data presented in Table 7.2 to generate these assumptions. Aggregating over both semesters, 689 students used the system with a total connect time of 3,914.36 hours. Thus the average connect time per experimental (note we have included all students who were so classified but never used the system) was 5.68 hours (3,914.36/689). This last figure is based on the entire academic year. Table 7.2 also indicates that the average cost per hour of connect time was $4.18 ($16,381.33/3,914.36). Applying these data to the assumed number of students, we have total costs for the entire academic year of $30,390.17–1280 experimentals, total connect time of 7,270.4 hours (1,280 x 5.68) and total costs of $30,390.27 (7,270.4 x $4.18).

To establish the costs of processing the fixed number of students through the discussion classes we must make assumptions regarding the class teaching load and pay of the graduate teaching assistant and the size of the discussion classes. Historically (1968-69 through 1973-74) a graduate teaching assistant taught four discussion classes per week with the size of the discussion classes set at approximately twenty students. Under these conditions eight graduate teaching assistants are needed over the academic year to handle the fixed number of students. As for the rate of pay of the graduate teaching assistant we can use the figure already cited for the 1973-74 academic year of $4,816. Thus the cost of using discussion classes exclusively would be $38,528 ($4,816 x 8). Under these assumptions CAI appears to be the less expensive alternative. If the cognitive and attitudinal outcomes were comparable under the two alternatives (as Chapters III and V indicate), then CAI would be the more cost effective approach.

But, one may argue, this type of comparison is biased in favor of CAI, indeed, biased for several different reasons. First of all the derived cost estimate for CAI is lower because there were no charges for students who did not use the system. More specifically the $30,390.27 of CAI operational costs provide 5.68 hours of instruction per experimental over the academic year, while the $38,528 of discussion class costs provide about 13 hours of discussion class instruction per control. Note here that the assumption now is that when the discussion-class approach is used, all the students go to all the discussion classes. We have evidence again from the 1973–74 academic year to examine the validity of this assumption. Table 7.3 reveals that attendance at the discussion classes, at least as they were structured during that year, was no where near what it could have been. Aggregating across all four sections and all the weeks of the academic year, we have 523 controls and 3,107 total student hours spent in discussion classes (we have assumed the fifty minute discussion classes are one hour time periods). Thus on the average the time spent in discussion class was 5.94 hours (3,107/523). If this pattern of discussion class attendance obtained with our fixed number of students, there would be 7,603.2 total student hours spent in discussion classes. To repeat, the assumptions imply that for the fixed number of students the CAI operational costs of $30,390.27 would generate almost the same number of hours of instruction as would an expenditure of $38,528 for discussion classes (total hours of 7270.4 versus 7603.2, or average hours of 5.68 versus 5.94).

Within this context we should raise an additional point. The CAI approach involves hours that are spent in a one-to-one relationship—the student interacting individually with the CAI system. The discussion class does not allow for this possibility. The graduate teaching assistant is interacting not with an individual student during the class for the entire class but with an entire class. This fact, it seems to us, biases the above comparison in favor of the discussion classes—that is, the 7,603.2 total hours of discussion classes is a group activity, while the 7,270.4 hours of CAI time are on an individual basis. We think that this difference is very important but will leave it to the reader to make any adjustments he feels are appropriate.

Returning to our initial cost comparison, there is another bias in favor of CAI. In this instance we must recognize that, presumably, only one-third of the graduate teaching assistants' weekly responsibilities are the formal classroom activities. Thus if the discussion classes were eliminated, students would not only lose the instruction provided by the graduate teaching assistant but also the possibility of seeing the graduate teaching assistant during his office hours. In addition the loss of the assistant for grading and other purposes would also have to be borne. In this regard we can make several comments. First, the normal case is that students during the experimental year, regardless of whether they were controls or experimentals, did not make use of the office-hour privilege. If this is viewed as an essential ingredient, rather than have a graduate assistant both teach and hold office hours, it might be

TABLE 7.3

Attendance at Discussion Classes

(Figures in parentheses indicate percentage of total number of controls attending discussion classes that week.)

	Economics 223		Economics 224	
Week	Section 61	Section 62	Section 63	Section 64
1	101 (92.7)	127 (94.8)	123 (89.8)	108 (75.5)
2	58 (53.2)	80 (59.7)	65 (47.4)	67 (46.9)
3	46 (42.2)	71 (53.0)	61 (44.5)	57 (39.9)
4	64 (58.7)	106 (79.1)	63 (46.0)	61 (42.7)
5	75 (68.8)	63 (47.0)	67 (48.9)	60 (42.0)
6	48 (44.0)	65 (48.5)	95 (69.3)	38 (26.6)
7	47 (43.1)	69 (51.5)	18 (13.1)	18 (12.6)
8	44 (40.4)	67 (50.0)	51 (36.2)	58 (40.6)
9	69 (63.3)	91 (67.9)	54 (39.4)	58 (40:6)
10	46 (42.2)	61 (45.5)	79 (54.7)	72 (50.3)
11	40 (36.7)	56 (41.8)	48 (35.0)	22 (15.4)
12	51 (46.8)	61 (45.5)	35 (25.5)	32 (22.4)
13	-----	-----	49 (35.8)	42 (29.4)
Total	689	917	808	693
N	109	134	137	143

more efficient to simply have graduate assistants hold office hours. For example, in the above description, eight assistants would provide thirty-two office hours each week. If the CAI alternative were used two assistants could be retained with each devoting his or her time exclusively to office hours. Under such conditions the number of office hours held each week would fall from thirty-two to twenty-four (a reduction that would indeed be justified given the historical use of office hours by students), but the cost of CAI would rise to $40,022.27 [$30,390.27 + (2 x $4,816)].

We could continue to make a series of cost comparisons, but let us hope that this discussion has made clear the difficulties of cost comparisons and at the same time provided sufficient data for the reader to develop his own, particularly if he rejects some of the comparisons we have made.

E. Additional Considerations

At this point it might be useful to mention several additional cost considerations that should be made when CAI is considered. Of these, hardware acquisitions may be important. We have neglected these in our discussion of both development costs and operational costs because such expenditures were not necessary. At Notre Dame the hardware facilities both in terms of the basic computer installation and the terminal facilities were judged as adequate. The only time when this judgment became suspect was during examination periods. Here we encountered something similar to the peak-load problem. Any time an examination was to be given the number of experimentals using the system increased, as did the amount of time spent with the system. This behavior is reflected by the data in Table 7.4. This problem was compounded when other university classes also using CAI would face an examination at about the same time. At these times access to terminals during particular hours was difficult. Over the course of the semester, however, access did not appear to be a problem—forty terminals available eighteen hours a day, seven days a week.

Another point to consider is the cost per hour of connect time. This cost was, as we have stated, determined by the cost algorithm employed by the computer center as well as the way in which students use the system. Our computer facility, an IBM 370/158, is a research computer and may not be the most efficient machine for CAI or instructional computing. Thus the type of computer facility may have a bearing on the cost algorithm.

Another point to consider is the future direction of alternative costs. In terms of CAI these costs probably will rise less rapidly than the costs of discussion classes and indeed might be falling. For example, the latest information from the Notre Dame Computing Center is that there has been "a substantial computer-rate reduction." The costs of discussion classes, on the

TABLE 7.4

Computer Use by Week

Week	Economics 223				Economics 224			
	Section 61		Section 62		Section 63		Section 64	
	Number of students who logged on	Total number of logons	Number of students who logged on	Total number of logons	Number of students who logged on	Total number of logons	Number of students who logged on	Total number of logons
1	133	144	123	192	43	122	73	173
2	97	172	84	183	33	81	43	95
3	73	139	76	155	24	69	36	81
4	94	275	76	147	38	84	70	212
5	61	172	43	84	36	97	24	57
6	20	76	23	71	2	3	18	35
7	52	64	42	69	3	10	4	4
8	54	82	51	122	8	11	8	16
9	66	149	65	161	29	70	44	116
10	63	199	45	110	37	90	42	135
11	4	19	7	24	9	13	9	19
12	23	29	8	13	5	13	6	10
13	51	106	38	91	12	20	13	24
14	69	152	48	137	18	47	20	55
15	13	23	16	24	32	75	47	143
16	--	--	--	--	6	15	5	11
Σ		1801		1583		820		1186

other hand, are rising both because of an increase in the value of the tuition remission as well as the increase in cash stipend received by graduate students. In this area an additional problem is a diminishing level of support for graduate students. Thus, as the total amount available for assistantships falls while tuition and cash stipends increase, the number of graduate students supported must decrease. As a department finds itself with fewer assistants, it must begin to reexamine its allocation of assistants. If CAI is an effective substitute, as it seems to be in our case, then perhaps the use of assistants for the handling of discussion classes may be abandoned altogether and the assistants reassigned to "more productive" activities.

As noted above in Chapter 6, it is possible to improve the effectiveness of both the discussion classes and the CAI system. Either alternative would increase the cost associated with each. For the former, the graduate teaching assistants would be formally prepared (via formal coursework, as suggested by Lewis and Orvis).[5]

We suspect that this chapter, like its predecessors on evaluation of cognitive and attitudinal outcomes, does not provide simple and direct answers. We have shown that given the use pattern of CAI, it may represent an effective cost alternative to the traditional approaches of discussion classes. But even so, we must admit that such a conclusion can only be advanced provisionally. We hope the nature of these provisions is clear and that sufficient data are available that will allow the reader to make his own evaluation if he finds ours deficient.

8

AN ALTERNATIVE TEST OF THE CAI SYSTEM

A. Introduction

The analysis presented in the preceding chapters pertains exclusively to the experiment conducted during the 1973-74 academic year. As we approached the 1974-75 academic year, we decided that further evidence on the effects of CAI would be worthwhile particularly if CAI were used in a somewhat different way. Because of resource limitations, the breath and depth of this new inquiry had to be reduced significantly. As a consequence, we eliminated a large part of our activity within the attitudinal area and concerned ourselves with only one section of each course in the Economics 223-224 sequence. Again each section had approximately 300 students. Before examining the effects of CAI during this academic year on cognitive achievement, student attitudes, and educational costs, it is necessary to begin with a discussion of some of the changes which occurred between the two academic years.

B. Changes during the 1974-75 Academic Year

Only minor modifications were made in the CAI system. These modifications consisted of the addition of five new routines, two to be used in conjunction with the 223 course and three to be used with the 224 course. These new routines were the locally generated midsemester examinations used in the previous year. These routines can be classified in the review category (as opposed to demonstration or game simulations) but were somewhat different from the usual reviews. Specifically the five new routines did not contain prompts with regard to either correct or incorrect answers, and, as a consequence, the student could not return at the end of the routine to examine a question. Simply, the student would call a new routine, proceed to answer each question, and then obtain an overall evaluation of his performance with a listing of the question numbers, the student's responses, and the correct answers. As with any of the other CAI programs, the student was able to keep a printout of these proceedings. What we tried to do was make these new routines serve as practice examinations for the students.

As far as the courses themselves are concerned, the section of 223 examined in this chapter corresponds to Section 62 of 223 discussed in the previous chapters, while the section of 224 of this chapter corresponds to Section 64 of 224 of the previous chapters. This matching yields identical lecturers and text. The course outlines and text assignments were subject to only minor modifications. Grades were also determined in a similar manner, based solely on two one-hour midsemester examinations and a two-hour final examination.

The more significant changes concerned the structure of the discussion classes and the implementation of the CAI system. For both courses, each student was assigned to a discussion class and was expected to attend it. In the discussion class students were free to ask any questions they had concerning the lectures, the text, or even the CAI materials. But during the 1974–75 academic year the 223 discussion classes had an additional responsibility to discuss the Brookings Institution publication *Setting National Priorities: The 1975 Budget*. This book became an auxiliary text, and coverage of it was restricted to the discussion classes. Questions, obviously of the locally generated variety, on this material was included on each of the three examinations given in 223. In the 224 course no auxiliary text was used, and the discussion classes provided the students with an opportunity to raise questions and to obtain further information on various topics. Once again the discussion classes were manned exclusively by graduate teaching assistants.

For this academic year all students were also given a computer user number and shown how to use the CAI system. Thus, during this second year we decided that the CAI system should be treated in the same way as any of the other instructural elements. Students were free to attend or not attend the lectures and the discussion classes and to read or not read the text, so they should also be free to use or not use the CAI system. From this four-pronged configuration of instructional elements, the student must decide which elements to use and how frequently he will use them. It is to be hoped that he attains an efficient allocation of time that yields whatever outcomes he desires. To this end the only forced contact with the discussion class or the CAI system came at the beginning of each semester where attendance at the first two discussion classes was mandatory. The first of these two classes was used for precourse testing of students, while the second was devoted to a demonstration of how to use the CAI system and the distribution of student user numbers. From that point on, the student using his course outline—detailing lecture topics, text assignments, and CAI assignments—was on his own. The question then is what effects did these new arrangements have on the cognitive achievement of the students, their attitudes, and educational costs.

C. Cognitive Achievement

1) COMPARISON OF AVERAGES

The above description of the arrangements for the 1974-75 academic year implies that students cannot be formally divided into control (non-CAI users) and experimental (CAI users) groups. However, relying on data compiled by the Computer Center students can be arbitrarily divided into groups on the basis of the intensity of their use of the CAI system. Using total connect time over the semester, students were divided into three approximately equal groups. These groups are labeled controls (that third of the students that used the CAI system least), experimental (the middle third), and intensive experimentals (the upper third). Giving this arbitrary division of students, we can make comparisons between them. The data for the three groups in the 223 course are presented in Table 8.1, while Table 8.2 contains the data for the 224 students.

Beginning with the 223 students we find no significant differences (at the 5-percent level) in human-capital characteristics when the controls are compared with either the experimentals or the intensive experimentals. This fact is important not only in evaluating the other data in Table 8.1 but also important because it suggests that the use of CAI by students is independent of their human capital characteristics. Thus, for example, it is not true that only students with high MSAT scores are attracted to CAI. In connection with the human-capital characteristics, we should mention that Part I, Form A, of the TUCE was used as a precourse test while Part II, Form B, was used as a postcourse test. Both forms contain thirty-three multiple-choice questions, with an equal division of these questions among the three objective categories.

With regard to the TUCE, Table 8.1 indicates student performances on the postcourse test as well as improvement (postcourse test minus precourse test). Focusing on improvement we find no significant differences between controls and experimentals and controls and intensive experimentals. If the three groups did in fact attend lectures and discussion classes with the same frequency and studied (exclusive of CAI time) to identical degrees, then this would be a negative result for CAI. This conclusion simply argues that, assuming all other things constant, greater utilization of the CAI did not yield significantly higher levels of TUCE improvement.

This same conclusion cannot be made about the locally generated examinations. Although there were no significant differences between the controls

TABLE 8.1

Human-Capital and Test Performances of Various Groups of Students in Economics 223

	Controls (N=104)		Experimentals (N=105)		Intensive Experimentals (N=109)	
	$\bar{X}$	Standard Deviation	$\bar{X}$	Standard Deviation	$\bar{X}$	Standard Deviation
Human-Capital Characteristics						
MSAT	592.31	71.156	594.67	66.034	606.45	69.931
VSAT	535.19	70.662	541.18	67.781	536.89	80.373
TUCEPRE Total	13.57	4.101	13.63	3.794	14.47	4.231
Recognition and Understanding	5.37	1.833	5.54	1.893	5.65	1.976
Simple Application	4.56	1.592	4.32	1.752	4.88	1.459
Complex Application	3.71	1.808	3.81	1.621	4.06	2.019
TUCE Postcourse Test Performance						
Total	23.65	4.304	24.07	4.470	24.69	4.209
Recognition and Understanding	8.20	1.717	8.26	1.647	8.31	1.678
Simple Application	7.46	1.696	7.72	1.766	7.98*	1.623
Complex Application	7.99	1.855	8.09	2.052	8.39	1.745
TUCE Improvement						
Total	10.13	4.986	10.30	4.319	10.32	4.250
Recognition and Understanding	2.82	2.320	2.70	2.074	2.66	1.974
Simple Application	2.96	2.178	3.33	2.049	3.13	1.921
Complex Application	4.29	2.093	4.23	2.114	4.46	2.265
Locally Generated Examination Performance						
First Midsemester Examination	22.89	3.573	23.34	3.435	23.98*	3.595
Second Midsemester Examination	18.88	4.662	19.50	4.958	21.34*	4.202
Non-TUCE Final Examination	10.37	2.389	11.04	2.520	11.87*	2.292

*Indicates significantly different from controls at the 5-percent level

TABLE 8.2

Human-Capital and Test Performances of Various Groups of Students in Economics 224

	Controls (N=90)		Experimentals (N=90)		Intensive Experimentals (N=91)	
	$\bar{X}$	Standard Deviation	$\bar{X}$	Standard Deviation	$\bar{X}$	Standard Deviation
Human-Capital Characteristics						
MSAT	600.44	68.243	584.27	66.134	596.39	68.578
VSAT	537.22	72.074	525.51	68.118	541.59	77.035
TUCEPRE Total	14.79	3.484	16.03*	3.462	16.42*	3.591
Recognition and Understanding	4.92	1.742	5.38	1.840	5.40	1.514
Simple Application	5.53	1.597	6.01*	1.505	6.06*	1.819
Complex Application	4.35	1.586	4.65	1.590	5.02	1.695
TUCE Postcourse Test Performance						
Total	23.51	4.055	23.26	4.384	24.60	3.506
Recognition and Understanding	7.33	1.919	7.48	1.966	7.72	1.790
Simple Application	7.79	1.573	7.60	1.444	8.13	1.391
Complex Application	8.40	1.868	8.18	2.070	8.74	1.46
TUCE Improvement						
Total	8.62	4.033	7.31*	4.216	8.04	3.291
Recognition and Understanding	2.39	2.310	2.11	2.132	2.39	1.931
Simple Application	2.23	1.840	1.60*	1.864	2.03	1.935
Complex Application	4.00	2.133	3.60	2.259	3.62	1.807
Locally Generated Examination Performance						
First Midsemester Examination	17.78	3.652	18.06	3.303	19.36*	3.192
Second Midsemester Examination	18.44	3.454	18.41	3.600	19.96*	2.954
Non TUCE Final Examination	13.38	2.460	12.87	2.776	14.09*	2.244

*Indicates significantly different from controls at the 5-percent level

and the experimentals on the three locally generated measures of cognitive achievement, the intensive experimentals performed significantly better than the controls on all three. In this area then, again assuming all other things constant, greater use of the CAI system did yield positive benefits in the form of significantly higher levels of cognitive achievement.

To some extent the same conclusions hold for the 224 course. On the human-capital characteristics the data in Table 8.2 indicate that there were no significant differences between controls and experimentals and controls and intensive experimentals on the MSAT and the VSAT. But both the experimentals and the intensive experimentals scored significantly better than the controls on the TUCE precourse test. This in turn is the result of a significantly better performance on the simple application questions. In short, there was a difference in the human capital of the groups in the area of economic knowledge at the beginning of the semester. We do not believe, however, that one can argue on the basis of this evidence that greater prior economic knowledge causes a greater use of the CAI system.

We should also mention that Part II, Form A, of the TUCE was used as a precourse test, while Part II, Form B, was used for the postcourse test. Although both forms contain thirty-three questions, they are not divided in the same way among the objective categories. Form A contains twelve recognition and understanding questions, eleven simple applications, and ten complex applications, while Form B has eleven, ten, and twelve questions in each category, respectively. This difference bears evenly on all three groups of students and should not invalidate any pairwise comparisons.

Table 8.2 presents data for both TUCE postcourse test performance and TUCE improvement, and we will concentrate on the latter. In a comparison of the controls and the experimentals, we find that the latter group of students had significantly less improvement on the examination as a whole, with this primarily accounted for by significantly less improvement in the simple application category. This is, of course, negative evidence against CAI—that is, greater use of CAI assuming all other things constant led to significantly lower levels of improvement. In the comparison of controls with the intensive experimentals, we find no significant difference in improvement either on the whole TUCE or any of the objective categories. This too, assuming all other things constant, is negative evidence against CAI, for even with greater use of the CAI system the intensive experimentals were not able to achieve significantly higher levels of improvement.

To some degree these negative results are mitigated by the results on the three locally generated measures of cognitive achievement. Here we find, as in 223, that there were no significant differences between the controls and the experimentals, but that the intensive experimentals performed significantly better than the controls on all three examinations. In this case, however, the results must be interpreted with caution—that is, the intensive experimentals may have outperformed the controls not because of greater use of the CAI system but because of greater economic knowledge as of the beginning of the course.

These alternative implications for CAI generated from the two courses may be the result of the function of the discussion classes during the year. For Economics 223 the discussion classes were responsible for coverage of the auxiliary text, and thus coverage of lecture and text material rested primarily on the CAI system. Because the discussion class and CAI were not substitutes, the use of CAI by the 223 students should have elevated test scores. For Economics 224 the discussion classes had no unique responsibility and, therefore, all this time was devoted to a reexamination of lecture and text material. Thus, in this course the discussion classes and CAI are substitutes, and even if a student did not use the CAI system, he could maintain his level of examination performance by attending the discussion class. Recognizing these kinds of differences suggest that we need to control for the allocation of time between instructional elements. To do this we again must resort to multiple-regression analysis.

2) REGRESSION RESULTS

For the 1974–75 regression analysis, the empirical version of the learning model appears as:

$$\begin{aligned} CA = a + b_1\ MSAT + b_2\ VSAT + b_3\ BGPA + b_4\ TUCEPRE \\ + b_5\ AWLA + b_6\ AWDCA + b_7\ AWST + b_8\ AWCAIT + u \end{aligned} \quad (8.1)$$

where a, MSAT, VSAT, BGPA, TUCEPRE, and u are as

defined in Chapter III,
AWLA = average weekly lecture attendance,
AWDCA = average weekly discussion class attendance,
AWST = average weekly study time, and
AWCAIT = average weekly CAI time.

In comparing this regression equation with the one employed in Chapter 3, the following should be noted: (1) we have retained the same human-capital variables (MSAT, VSAT, BGPA, and TUCEPRE), (2) we have substituted four specific utilization rates for the overall utilization rate (replaced OUR with AWLA, AWDCA, AWST, and AWCAIT), and (3) we have eliminated all the efficiency variables (dropped LE, TE, and SEX). The elimination of the efficiency elements was required because of the reduction in attitudinal surveys—that is, resource constraints prevented the collection and, therefore, the use of these data.

A word or two is in order about the new utilization-rate variables. The data for AWLA, AWDCA, and AWST were all obtained from a single survey distributed to the students approximately one week from the end of the semester. This survey raised one question on each of these activities (questions 5, 6, and 8 in Appendix H). These questions were not open-ended questions and with the exception of the question on study time were not phrased in average weekly terms. Thus students, when responding to the question on lecture attendance could respond in only five different ways and could only respond in four different ways to the question on discussion-class attendance. These responses were then converted into average weekly equivalents. As a consequence, AWLA could only assume five different values (2.00, 1.75, 1.50, 1.25, and 1.00; with 2.00 representing the maximum), and AWDCA could only assume four different values (1.00, .90, .80 and .60; with 1.00 representing the maximum). The study-time question was phrased in average weekly terms, but only four options were possible; AWST could assume only four values (4.00, 3.00, 2.00, and 1.00; with 4.00 being the maximum). These data, then, are not all we would like them to be: (1) they are limited in range which is important in the lower limit for AWLA and AWDCA and in the upper limit for AWST, and (2) the rates are not subject to variation as we move between segments of a semester.

As far as AWCAIT is concerned, connect time for each student was available on a weekly basis from the Computer Center. Here we broke down the semester into three components corresponding to the three examination periods (beginning of the semester to the first midsemester examination, first midsemester examination to the second midsemester examination, and second midsemester to the final examination), aggregated CAI time for the weeks in the component, and then divided by the number of weeks in the component. Thus, unlike the other utilization rates, AWCAIT does change as we move between measures of cognitive achievement.

In terms of evaluating the impact of CAI on cognitive achievement, the critical elements are the sign and significance of the regression coefficient for AWCAIT. All other things being equal, the greater the use of the CAI system as evidenced by higher value of AWCAIT, the greater should be the student's cognitive achievement. More specifically, the regression coefficient for AWCAIT should be greater than zero and statistically significant.

Table 8.3 contains the regression results for the four measures of cognitive achievement deployed in each of the two courses. We find that the sign for AWCAIT is positive in four of these eight regressions. In these four cases, as well as the four negative cases, the regression coefficient is not statistically significant. Controlling for human capital, time spent in lecture, time spent in discussion class, and time spent studying, we must reject the hypothesis that greater use of the CAI system will result in significantly higher levels of

TABLE 8.3

Regression Results Economics 223 and 224

	Economics 223				Economics 224			
Variable	First Midsemester Examination	Second Midsemester Examination	Non-TUCE Position of Final Exam	TUCE Posttest	First Midsemester Examination	Second Midsemester Examination	Non-TUCE Portion of Final Exam	TUCE Posttest
Constant	2.89221	-7.60202	-1.73044	2.87374	9.43902	3.37494	6.49682	12.34370
MSAT	0.01650*	0.01471	0.00486	0.01089*	0.01195*	0.00613	0.00081	-0.00430
	(4.148)	(3.120)	(1.848)	(2.181)	(2.473)	(1.256)	(0.210)	(0.802)
VSAT	0.01182*	0.00476	0.00782*	0.00845	-0.00920*	-0.00263	0.00252	0.01093*
	(2.902)	(0.981)	(2.895)	(1.647)	(2.083)	(0.611)	(0.706)	(2.224)
TUCEPRE	0.19059*	0.27413*	0.01098	0.25004*	-0.01947	-0.02971	0.03599	0.24169*
	(2.624)	(3.183)	(0.228)	(2.745)	(0.200)	(0.310)	(0.469)	(2.286)
BGPA	0.14548	0.96393*	0.53619*	0.65127	2.81024*	3.41499*	2.41522*	2.22908*
	(0.519)	(2.886)	(2.891)	(1.848)	(4.004)	(4.949)	(4.334)	(2.901)
AWLA	0.15075	3.90881*	0.90852	1.43119	-0.17989	1.70939	-1.20595	0.49315
	(0.095)	(2.120)	(0.885)	(0.734)	(0.095)	(0.927)	(0.804)	(0.239)
AWDCA	-1.20269	0.13148	1.91691	1.95324	0.53706	-0.69648	-1.80205	-1.46169
	(0.486)	(0.045)	(1.171)	(0.628)	(0.235)	(0.310)	(0.971)	(0.571)
AWST	0.68097*	0.91417*	0.41654	0.38389	-0.17695	0.28007	0.30635	-0.48125
	(2.102)	(2.374)	(1.952)	(0.948)	(0.501)	(0.799)	(1.072)	(1.221)
AWCAIT	0.27766	-0.51827	-0.05314	-0.34327	0.12388	1.04535	0.54609	-0.038033
	(0.748)	(1.148)	(0.307)	(1.042)	(0.316)	(1.695)	(1.495)	(0.755)
R^2	0.33998	0.37556	0.28404	0.26377	0.33364	0.43554	0.36288	0.34696
$\bar{R}^2$	.30524	0.34270	0.24636	0.22503	0.27227	0.38355	0.30420	0.28681
F ratio	8.49908	9.92385	6.54591	5.99160	4.69400	7.23372	5.33965	4.98092
N	141	141	141	141	84	84	84	84

t-ratio shown in parenthesis
*significance at the 5-percent level

cognitive achievement. This is, of course, an unfavorable result as far as a CAI proponent is concerned.

This rather pessimistic result is somewhat mitigated when we compare the results for AWCAIT to the results obtained for the other utilization rates. Consider first AWDCA. The results here are identical to the results for AWCAIT: four positive signs and four negative signs with statistical significance lacking in all eight cases. Thus again we find the CAI yields results that are comparable to that of the discussion class; both seem to be equally ineffective in generating higher levels of cognitive achievement. Lecture attendance and study time operate in more consistent fashion, both AWLA and AWST returning positive signs in six of the eight regressions. One instance of significance is isolated for AWLA, and AWST is significant in two cases. Thus, in the larger sense, none of the four utilization rates yield expected results. We suspect that this failure is in part due to the nature of the activities and the way in which they are entered into the regression.

Take CAI as a case in point. A student may not in fact run the routines himself but borrow the printouts from a friend who has. Thus although a positive AWCAIT value is obtained for the lending student, no such use of CAI materials is indicated for the borrowing student even though he is gaining some benefit. The very same case can be made for lecture attendance. Here a student attends regularly but lends his notes to a student who does not. Given such borrowing activity with respect to CAI, lectures, and discussion classes and the method employed for estimating their effects, which excludes the borrowing potential, it is perhaps not surprising that generally insignificant results are obtained.

Regression equation 8.1 was also applied to the student's final grade as well as the three objective categories of the TUCE (see Table 8.4). With respect to grades we again find that the regression equation explains more of the variation among student grades than variations among scores on a particular examination. For example, the highest coefficient of determination (R^2) obtained in the 223 course for any of the four measures of cognitive achievement was .376, while the coefficient of determination for grades in the course was .48. We should also mention that this variant of the learning model tends to yield generally lower co-coefficients of determination than the more complete version used in Chapter 3. Specifically, including a single general utilization rate and three efficiency variables yields better explanation than four specific utilization rates and no efficiency elements. Note that this is a rather cautious conclusion, for none of the measures of cognitive achievement are exactly the same as we move between academic years and regression equations.

The regression results for the objective categories and grades support the earlier conclusion regarding CAI. AWCAIT is statistically insignificant in both grade regressions yielding a negative sign for 223 and a positive sign for 224. In the 223 course, AWCAIT yields a significant negative regression coefficient on the recognition and understanding questions and is insignificant for the other two objective categories. For the 224 course AWCAIT is insignificant for all three

TABLE 8.4

Regression Results for TUCE Objective Categories and Grades
Economics 223 and 224

	Economics 223				Economics 224			
	Grade	Recognition and Understanding	Simple Application	Complex Application	Grade	Recognition and Understanding	Simple Application	Complex Application
Constant	-3.49156	1.26595	-0.85868	2.20905	-0.49658	5.20710	1.77604	6.78739
MSAT	0.00289	0.00342	0.00552*	0.00262	0.00141	-0.00301	0.00039	-0.00115
	(20.002)	(1.700)	(2.788)	(1.118)	(2.022)	(1.108)	(0.152)	(0.396)
VSAT	0.00240	0.00416*	0.00293	0.00320	-0.00067	0.00657*	0.00015	0.00486
	(14.585)	(2.013)	(1.454)	(1.326)	(0.556)	(2.749)	(0.071)	(1.926)
TUCEPRE	0.04994	0.27702*	0.16812	0.13442	0.01800	0.12183	0.15188	0.19895
	(18.070)	(3.537)	(1.806)	(1.511)	(0.834)	(1.185)	(1.411)	(1.668)
BGPA	0.17254	0.08782	0.34075*	0.23260	0.87844	0.61044	1.25961*	0.36846
	(16.463)	(0.623)	(2.461)	(1.408)	(37.681)	(1.555)	(3.682)	(0.998)
AWLA	0.40743	0.06915	0.86514	0.06149	0.11511	-0.14617	-0.43142	-0.16954
	(2.521)	(0.089)	(1.118)	(0.071)	(0.091)	(0.141)	(0.471)	(0.155)
AWDCA	-.79478	0.24809	0.60346	1.48849	-0.30298	-1.51910	1.67581	-2.04350
	(4.539)	(0.202)	(0.477)	(1.030)	(0.421)	(1.185)	(1.473)	(1.499)
AWST	0.16310	0.34366*	0.00109	0.10308	-0.01594	-0.08722	-0.22653	-0.16505
	(9.780)	(2.097)	(0.000)	(0.432)	(0.049)	(0.442)	(1.278)	(0.779)
AWCAIT	-0.00409	-0.41421*	-0.21593	0.00257	0.11035	-0.02091	-0.00206	0.11239
	(0.003)	(2.184)	(1.142)	(0.000)	(0.979)	(0.100)	(0.000)	(0.417)
R^2	0.47950	0.24963	0.24271	0.12854	0.51817	0.21735	0.27843	0.19622
$\bar{R}^2$	0.46042	0.20923	0.20194	0.08162	0.47379	0.14526	0.21197	0.12219
F ratio	21.87924	5.36450	5.16911	2.37852	10.08201	2.60347	3.61749	2.28869
N	199	138	138	138	84	84	84	84

t-ratio shown in parenthesis
*statistically significant at the 5-percent level

objective categories returning two negative signs and one positive sign. Again, AWCAIT does not return the expected result and performance for the course as a whole or the objective categories of the TUCE is largely independent of student use of the CAI system.

D. Attitudinal Results

We have already indicated that there was a substantial reduction in the attitudinal data collected during the 1974-75 academic year. Only one attitudinal survey was distributed during each semester and concerned the students' reactions to the instructional elements, particularly CAI. The responses obtained to this questionnaire in both the 223 and the 224 courses are presented in Table 8.5. Here we have retained the arbitrary classification of students as controls, experimentals, and intensive experimentals.

As indicated in Table 8.5 the first question raised on the survey concerned the students' opinions of the contribution of CAI to their learning experience. As might be expected the intensive experimentals had the highest percentage of respondents who answered "very much." Unexpected, however, is the percentage of responding controls and experimentals who answered "very much," a larger percent is obtained for the former group. This unexpected result, we suspect, may be due to the fact that the controls, although they spent little time on the system, had frequent access to the computer printouts. We have already raised this possibility in discussing the regression results of the previous section, and it would appear that the attitudinal data have the same implication. The percentage of each group who responded "no help" is exactly as expected; the highest percentage is obtained for the controls and the lowest for the intensive experimentals.

The second question focused on what we had previously isolated as the major strength of the CAI system, its review capability. Again as might be expected a larger percentage of responding intensive experimentals answered "very valuable" than responding controls or experimentals. Still, a rather substantial percentage of responding controls also answered "very valuable." Here too we might interpret this as evidence that these students were using printouts obtained from other students in the course. As with the first question, we obtain a greater consistency of actual and expected results in the percentage of each group who responded "of no value"—that is, highest for controls and lowest for the intensive experimentals.

The third question focused on the discussion classes, phrased in such a manner as to make it comparable to the results for the second question. Concentrating on the percentage of each group who responded "of no value," we find that the intensive experimentals not only responded more positively to CAI but also more positively to the discussion classes. This would indicate that the students found CAI and discussion classes as complements rather than alternatives. This

TABLE 8.5

Attitudinal Results: Economics 223 and 224
(Results in Percents)

Item	Economics 223			Economics 224		
	Controls (64)	Experimentals (72)	Intensive Experimentals (93)	Controls (64)	Experimentals (75)	Intensive Experimentals (79)
1. How valuable were the CAI materials in your overall learning experience this semester?						
Very much	12.5	2.8	25.8	10.9	6.7	21.5
Considerably	29.7	34.7	39.8	20.3	29.3	46.8
Some help	32.8	58.3	33.3	46.9	57.3	30.4
No help	25.0	4.2	1.1	21.9	6.7	1.3
2. How valuable were the CAI materials in reviewing the Samuelson materials for a test?						
Very valuable	28.1	27.8	48.4	17.2	16.0	26.6
Moderately valuable	29.7	31.9	33.3	28.1	37.3	41.8
Of some value	20.3	36.1	16.1	34.4	38.7	26.6
Of no value	21.9	4.2	2.2	20.3	8.0	5.1
3. How valuable were the discussion class teaching assistants in reviewing the Samuelson materials for a test?						
Very valuable	9.4	16.7	16.1	3.6	3.0	12.2
Moderately valuable	32.8	37.5	26.9	9.8	9.0	8.1
Of some value	35.9	33.3	44.1	16.3	23.8	29.7
Of no value	21.9	12.5	12.9	70.4	64.2	50.0
4. In terms of your performance on examinations which of the following helped the most?						
CAI materials	8.1	0.0	8.8	6.3	1.3	8.9
Lectures	45.2	63.9	54.9	85.7	81.8	74.7
Discussion classes	1.6	2.8	3.2	0.0	3.9	1.3
Text	45.2	33.3	33.0	7.9	12.9	15.1

indeed should have been the case particularly during the first semester, when the discussion classes were responsible for the auxiliary text. Following this, one might suspect that during the 224 course, where the discussion class had no unique objectives, student dissatisfaction would increase. This certainly appears to be the case, as indicated in Table 8.5. To restate the point, there appears to be no reason to have both CAI and discussion classes unless the discussion classes have some unique contribution to make to the learning experience.

The fourth question asked the student to rank the four instructional elements in terms of the contribution they made to the students performance on the examinations. For the sake of brevity, we have indicated the percentage of each group that rated each alternative as being most helpful. Thus, of the sixty-four controls who responded in 223, 8.1 percent said CAI was most helpful, 45.2 percent said the lectures were most helpful, and so on. Moving across groups and across courses, as one might expect, lecturers are ranked first by more students. This is explained by the fact that the lecturers tend to draw more heavily on their own presentations in construction of the locally generated examinations. Following lectures, the text was rated as more helpful by more students. Note the difference here between the two courses. From the previous argument one might suggest that the lecturer for 224 relied more heavily on his own presentation in constructing examinations then than the 223 lecturer. For what it is worth both lecturers agreed that this was probably a correct assertion. The third most helpful instructional element appears to be the CAI materials—that is, a larger percent of the controls and intensive experimentals in both courses rated this element rather than the discussion class as most helpful. For some reason this pattern was not duplicated by the experimentals. Again we suspect that this anomaly—at least in terms of the difference between controls and experimentals—indicates that the controls had access to the CAI printouts.

Overall the attitudinal responses are, to a large extent, what might be expected. Implementing CAI in this way gave students additional flexibility. A large number of students used CAI and found that it was useful to them. The major attitudinal outcome appears to be that the new (1974-75) implementation reduced student satisfaction with the discussion classes, especially when the discussion classes no longer maintained a unique role (223 versus 224).

E. Costs

As far as costs are concerned, there were very minor additional development costs; the CAI system, with the exception of the five new routines, was the same system that was used during the previous year. The question then is: What happened to operational costs?

The information necessary for answering this question is contained in Table 8.6. To abstract from variation caused by the number of students, we can focus

TABLE 8.6

Operational Costs of CAI
Economics 223 and 224

Item	Economics 223	Economics 224
Total Operational Costs	$9,014.23	$8,761.94
Number of Students	323	271
Total number of logons	2, 507	2,376
Total connect time (hours)	1,879.87	1,838.14
Cost per hour of connect time	$ 4.80	$ 4.77
Number of Logons per Student	7.78	8.77
Connect time per experimentals	5.82	6.78
Cost per student	$ 27.91	$ 32.33
Number of Logons per Student*	9.72	11.82
Connect time per student*	7.29	9.14
Cost per Student*	$ 34.94	$ 43.59

*The calculations omit those students who never logged on time. These students numbered 56 in Economics 223 and 70 in Economics 224.

on cost per hour of connect time and cost per student. With respect to the former, there was a minor variation between the two courses but a relatively large increase between the 1973-74 and the 1974-75 academic years. CAI cost per hour of connect time increased from $4.18 to $4.78. This increase reflects a change in the way the system was used rather than an increase in the basic cost algorithm employed by the Computer Center, with students generating more lines of transmission per hour.

The cost per student was greater during the 224 course, reflecting greater connect time per student. We also find that cost per student was greater during the 1974-75 academic year than it was during the 1973-74 academic year, $29.93 versus $23.75. This difference reflects not only the increase in cost per hour of connect time but also an increase in connect time per student.

We suspect that these comparisons indicate that a precise prediction of operational costs is impossible. Groups of students will react in different ways–using the system to greater or lesser degrees and also altering the way in which it is used. It would appear that the new implementation procedure increased connect time per student simply because for most students using the system it was the only alternative available for obtaining the questions included in the review routines.

To complete this rather brief discussion of costs, we might add that there were also changes in the costs associated with the discussion classes. These changes are the result of two things: (1) a change in discussion-class size and the teaching loads of the graduate teaching assistants and (2) a change in the cash value of a graduate teaching assistantship. With respect to the former, each teaching assistant now was responsible for five discussion classes rather than four, and class size increased so that only six assistants were employed in these activities (six for both sections of 223 and 224 or three for a single section of each course). As far as the cash value of an assistantship is concerned, it increased from $4,816 to $5,100 (tuition scholarship of $2,600 and cash stipend of $2,500). Thus, if four graduate students had been used in each section, then the costs of manning the corresponding discussion classes would have been $20,400 ($5,100 x 4), but given the changes in class size and teaching load the costs were only $15,300 ($5,100 x 3).

F. Summary

Examining the results for the entire academic year, we find that implementing CAI simply as an additional alternative had no systematic and positive impact on cognitive achievement. It did represent an alternative that a number of students used and that they perceived as useful. Costs, of course, were greater than if only the discussion classes or CAI were used. Extrapolating from the evidence presented in this chapter, as well as a more personal feel for what transpired, we would argue that the existence of CAI allows the discussion classes to be used for unique purposes. This in turn would allow on expansion in the breadth of an introductory sequence while maintaining previously achieved levels of depth. Reworded, CAI can handle fairly effectively the more traditional tasks of discussion classes, which then can be used to explore interesting and important topics that may have been previously ignored.

9

ALTERNATIVE USE OF COMPUTERS IN TEACHING ECONOMICS

A. Introduction

It should be realized that the particular approach to instructional computing discussed in earlier chapters is not the only possible approach.[2] Indeed there are many, and we ourselves have experimented with an alternative. This alternative, which is described and analyzed in this chapter, is an integration of statistical programming (computing) as a component of a regular introductory course. In this sense we have converted the purely lecture-and-discussion-class approach to Introductory Economics to a lecture-and-laboratory approach. The computer and the terminals constitute the laboratory equipment, and the census data for 1970 represent the laboratory materials. This new approach required the institution of a new introductory sequence, which is numbered Economics 101-102.

This means, of course, that the Economics Department is in fact offering several different introductory courses. The justification for this apparent duplication of effort is that the department needs to respond to a combination of institutional requirements. The rational department establishes a pattern of offerings that "maximizes" some objective function given institutional requirements and resource constraints.[3] A comparison of the various courses offered at the introductory level requires that the objectives of each alternative introductory course and the techniques of instruction used in each course be carefully specified and measured. Besides providing information regarding the actual outcome of each course, this process allows a department to evaluate the alternative courses in terms of the tradeoffs between them and to determine whether these tradeoffs are acceptable.

In those instances where economics is taught as part of the liberal arts curriculum, the combination of skills, analytical ability, and experience with research provided by our new approach are of considerably greater value than the type of learning that goes on in the traditional principles course.

We have also found from our evaluation of the course that these nontraditional gains can occur with little loss in the learning of the traditional content material.[4]

This chapter begins by describing the new sequence, Economics 101–102. Then the chapter focuses on the first semester of this sequence—Economics 101, the macroeconomic semester—and compares the outcomes generated in this course in both the cognitive and attitudinal areas with the outcomes in two other introductory macroeconomic courses. One of these other courses is the Economics 223 course, which has been examined in detail in the previous chapters. The other course is Economics 121, a freshman macroeconomic course with a policy and issue-oriented approach.

B. Description of the Course

We can begin the description by noting that the students in this new introductory course use the same introductory text used by the traditional course students—Samuelson's *Economics*, 9th edition—with basically the same chapter coverage. In addition, the lecturer who taught Section 62 of the 223 course also taught the new sequence.

Approximately forty students were enrolled in the new course for both semesters of their freshman year. They attend two fifty-minute lectures as well as a two-hour laboratory each week. During the first semester, the lecture deals initially with concepts in philosophy of science and the differences between economics and other sciences. Accompanying these lectures the students read Hempel's *The Philosophy of Natural Science.* The lecture then turns to the content of macroeconomics during the first semester, with microeconomics handled during the second semester. The macroeconomics lectures begin independently of the laboratory assignments, but laboratory assignments of the last four weeks of the semester are generated by the lecture.

The first semester laboratory (macroeconomics) has two components. In the first ten weeks of the semester the student is taught computer programming to permit him to learn: (1) the techniques of data manipulation, transformation, and use, (2) the use of statistical tests for the evaluation of hypotheses, and (3) statistical programming. The students conclude this ten week component with a simple regression test of the consumption function by writing their own linear-regression program according to the algorithm provided. This linear-regression program is the basis for the hypothesis testing done in the last four weeks of the course, where the students test macroeconomic hypotheses suggested by the lectures and the text. Having written the regression program, the students then use either of two prewritten regression programs, each containing fifty variables of data from the U. S. economy, one with annual data and the other with quarterly data from 1948–1972. These last four assignments unify the lecture with the laboratory and provide the students with their first serious exposure to the actual conduct and performance of economic research. Schematically, the relationships indicated below on Figure 9.1 reflect this description for the first semester.

The second semester, microeconomic content, is basically a "lab-paced" semester. The students, working in pairs, are required to use 1970 census data in replicating, as far as possible, studies in the area of education and earnings, migration, and regional income differences. The lecture, along with the traditional development of microeconomic theory, develops the theoretical framework for the empirical studies. Each research assignment is divided into two parts. For instance, the migration study is divided into two parts: a descriptive and an analytic component. The guide for the descriptive component is the article by A. Taeuber and K. Taeuber, "The Changing Character of Negro Migration," *American Journal of Sociology* (January 1965), which is a description of black migration patterns. The guide to the analytic aspect of the study is the article by D. Kaun, "Negro Migration and Unemployment," *Journal of Human Resources* (Spring 1970), which develops and tests an economic theory of migration. In addition, each student must complete a fourth study, on a topic of his choice, from the range of possible topics coming from the lectures or found in the text.[5]

What do we mean by replication? The students have available the fourth count of the 1970 census of housing and population for states and Standard Metropolitan Statistical Areas (SMSA). In the first week of the second semester, they are taught how to access these materials using prewritten programs. The lab manual then discusses two studies in each of the noted areas

Time	Lecture		Laboratory	
Period	Topic	Purpose	Topic	Purpose
1	Philosophy of	Understanding of	Computer	To show the student
2	Science	the scientific pro-	programming	how to handle data
3	"	cess and the mean-	"	on the computer
4	"	ing of inquiry in	"	and
5	Macroeconomic	the social sciences	"	how to test hypothe-
6	Topics		"	ses using appropriate
7	"	Understanding of	"	statistical tests
8	"	the content area	"	
9	"	of macroeconomics	"	
10	"		Hypothesis testing	To show the student
11	"		of macroeconomic	how to set up hypothe-
12	"		hypotheses	ses from theory and
13	"		"	how to empirically
14	"		"	test them.

Figure 9.1. Economics 101, Macroeconomics: First Semester. Lecture-Lab Relationship

of education and earnings, migration, and regional income differentials. The first study discussed, in some detail, for each area is the descriptive analysis. The second study considered in each instance is the analytic study. The analytic studies were chosen because each developed a hypothesis or hypotheses and tested each hypothesis using some variation of census data and regression analysis.

It is in this second semester that the analogy to the natural sciences is most correct, for here the type of learning that occurs is most closely allied to the laboratory approach of the natural sciences. The students gain (1) an understanding of the process of inquiry which science adheres to (2) experience with the actual steps of scientific research and (3) an understanding of the type of "knowledge" that can be attained by this effort.

Since the first semester of the course covers macroeconomics, concentration in what follows will be on that semester.

The third course, Economics 121, which is included in the following discussion, is used as a type of control course. It is a one-semester freshman course, meeting three times each week on a lecture or lecture-discussion basis with the assigned teacher meeting the course for each of the three weekly sessions. Normally about seventy-five students self-select into the course. The major concentration of the course is on current policy issues, One-third of the course was spent on wage-and-price controls during the fall period, 1973, at the time the course was evaluated for this study. In keeping with this general trend, three paperbacks were used which emphasized this macroeconomic policy approach. This course did not have a computer element either as computer-assisted-instruction or as a laboratory to the lecture sequence.

The above discussion highlights some of the differences between the alternative approaches but does not explain why these differences exist. The structure for Economics 223 results from its being the first of a two-course sequence required of all College of Business students. As such, it places a heavy emphasis on conventional macroeconomic content. The 121 course exists because it allows students of all colleges to use economics to satisfy a social science requirement. It utilizes a current macroeconomic problems approach in order to stimulate student interest in economics. The 101-102 sequence was created because we felt it was a "better way" to teach economics and at the same time better serve the educational objectives of the freshman year.

The question now is what are the expectations about the outcomes of the different approaches, or, more precisely, "if the Economics Department were to teach all introductory courses in the form of 101, what cognitive and affective tradeoffs would be involved?"[6] Given our specification of the courses' educational objectives, our expectations are that in comparison with the 223 approach, there would be a loss in the pure content area as measured by TUCE. However, we would expect TUCE performance to be comparable to the national norm and to exceed that of 121. Turning to the affective domain, the impact of 101 should be less than that of the more topical course 121. However, we would expect that both 101 and 121 would be superior to 223 in this domain. The following sections will indicate that our expectations are generally correct, and that we are able to specify the types of tradeoffs that would occur if 101 became the norm for introductory courses.

Before turning to the results of the analysis of the tradeoffs among the courses, it will be useful to indicate the characteristics of the students in each of the courses, since no attempt was made to assign students randomly.[7]

In examining the data presented in Table 9.1, it would appear that the students in the three courses do differ in some major respects. The 223 students have higher MSAT and VSAT scores as well as a higher projected university GPA. The 101 students follow, with the 121 students having the lowest MSAT, VSAT, and projected university GPA. In terms of the other two characteristics–percentage male and percentage white–the three classes seem quite similar. The students do not differ significantly (at the 5-percent level) on the TUCE precourse test. Finally,as stated previously, all the 101 and 121 students are freshmen–indeed first-semester freshmen. The 223 students on the other hand are exclusively nonfreshmen, with 80 percent of them being sophomores.

C. Cognitive Outcomes

As stated, we expected that a course such as 101 would yield less cognitive attainment as ordinarily measured by researchers on economic education than a course like 223. The basis for this expectation is straightforward; the time spent on economic content in lecture is less, and the lab period develops skills which do not translate directly into content knowledge. Thus the question to be answered in this section is: What is the extent of the tradeoff?

Before attempting to answer this question, it is important to state explicitly why we are willing to accept less cognitive attainment in 101, as measured by TUCE. There are two reasons. First, other knowledge and skills are developed as a substitute–philosophy of science, computer programming, use of statistics, and hypothesis testing–and we feel that these are valuable in the context of modern economics.[8] Second, we feel that the reduction in cognitive attainment will not occur evenly; that is, 101 emphasizes the "process of economic analysis" and, thus, these students will do relatively better on problems that require analysis and thought.

In measuring the cognitive dimension of the courses, we utilized the TUCE Part I (macroeconomics), Form A, as both a precourse test and a

TABLE 9.1

Selected Characteristics of Students
(Standard Deviations in Parenthesis)

CHARACTERISTIC	101	121	223
Verbal Scholastic Aptitude Test Score (VSAT)	539.44 (76.34)	526.35 (86.08)	567.51 (86.54)
Mathematical Scholastic Aptitude Test Score (MSAT)	602.78 (69.27)	590.00 (68.98)	620.09 (78.04)
Projected University Grade Point Average*	2.81 (0.668)	2.66 (0.668)	2.855 (0.567)
Percent Male	78%	85%	82%
Percent White	97%	96%	95%
Precourse TUCE Score	12.39 (3.57)	12.37 (3.39)	13.04 (3.86)
Number of Students**	36	74	205

*The Projected university grade point average is calculated using a formula which includes VSAT, MSAT, and rank in high school class. Weights are assigned to each variable with rank in high school class receiving the highest weight. The conceptual range here is from 0.00 to 4.00.

**Although there are more than 300 students in 223, we have selected only those students who have had no previous college economics. This was done so that the comparison is in effect between students who are experiencing their first college economics course. Note that we are specifically using students from Section 62 of Economics 223 as taught during the 1973–74 academic year. This was done because the lecturer in this course was also the lecturer in the 101 course. In addition the 223 students included both controls and experimentals as these terms were used in the previous chapters.

postcourse test. Several different types of information are available from the TUCE and are presented below in Table 9.2.

The first of these is student performance on the entire thirty-three-question exam. These results correspond to our expectations. The 223 course is more effective in teaching content as measured by TUCE. The 101 course, although yielding significantly less cognitive attainment than 223, does produce significantly better results than either the national norm or 121. Given that maximization of TUCE-type performance is not the sole goal of 101, we find that the tradeoff between broader types of knowledge attained in 101 and TUCE is not severe, and the students actually perform quite well. Yet this loss of

TABLE 9.2

*Test of Difference of Means (t-test) on TUCE Postcourse Test**

Mean of Economics 101 20.89 (15.78)**

Comparison Course	Mean	t-value	Significant at .05***
National Norm	19.22	1.70	yes
Economics 121	18.31 (14.35)**	2.27	yes
Economics 223	23.35 (17.91)**	-2.27	yes

*There was no significant difference in performance on the precourse test across the courses.

**The values in parenthesis are the means on twenty-five questions which the instructors felt were covered in all three courses, although the coverage was not the same in breadth or depth. The results of the comparison of means is the same for this common core as for the overall TUCE. Thus the discussion will concentrate on the whole TUCE.

***In this chapter we have used a one-tailed "t" test.

content knowledge must be taken into account in choosing the particular approach to the introductory course.

Another type of insight into cognitive attainment is available from a disaggregation of the TUCE postcourse test scores into "objective categories." These include recognition and understanding, simple application, and complex application. This categorization was suggested by the authors of TUCE and results in three eleven-question divisions. As noted above we would expect the 101 students to do relatively better on questions that require more complex thought and reasoning patterns, that is, on complex application as opposed to recognition questions. Table 9.3 presents the results of this disaggregation of TUCE performance.

In examining these results, we find some confirmation of our hypothesis that the loss in TUCE performance for the 101 students would decline as we moved to more complex skills. Although the 101 students attained a significantly lower total TUCE score than the students in 223, there was no significant difference on the complex application questions—a result in accordance with our expectations. Nonetheless, the major difference between the 101 and 223 students is on the simple application questions, which is not the expected result. The comparison of 101 and 121 shows exactly the pattern expected, 101 providing a lower (insignificant) score on recognition and understanding questions and in the other two categories yielding higher and significant results. The same pattern seems to be indicated when 101 is compared to the

TABLE 9.3

Test of Difference of Means on Objective Categories
TUCE Postcourse Test

	Mean	t-value	Significant at .05
Recognition and Understanding			
Econ 101 = 7.39			
Comparison Course			
National Norm**	7.41	-	
121	7.64	-0.34	No
223	8.16	-1.12	No
Simple Application			
Econ 101 = 6.97			
Comparison Course			
National Norm**	6.17	+	
121	5.49	+2.06	Yes
223	8.21	-1.89	Yes
Complex Application			
Econ 101 = 6.53			
Comparison Course			
National Norm**	5.03	+	
121	5.17	+2.11	Yes
223	6.98	-0.62	No

*There was no significant difference in performance on the precourse test across the courses in any of the objective categories. The means on the objective categories were as follows: recognition and understanding 5.00 (101), 5.11 (121), 5.14 (223); simple application 4.16 (101), 3.99 (121), 4.27 (223), and complex application 3.22 (101), 3.27 (121), 3.63 (223).

**Note: No standard deviations are available for the national norming data and thus tests cannot be performed.

national norm. There, 101 is very slightly below the national norm on recognition and understanding and then rises to 12 percent and then to 30 percent superiority as we move to simple and complex application questions. These results, when added to the overall results have the effect of reducing the negative impact of the TUCE tradeoff: the loss in TUCE performance occurs in "skill areas" that are not stressed within the 101 course.

The final information on cognitive attainment as measured by the TUCE involves a disaggregation by "content categories." The TUCE developers have established seven content categories. An analysis of the courses on this basis is important, for the courses differ in topical coverage and the emphasis given to covered topics. It is also important because the objective categories of the TUCE vary with content.

Given the large number of categories and the difference in the number of items per category, it will be easier to deal with these results in terms of the percentage of questions in each content category answered correctly on the postcourse test. Our expectations were that the 223 students would do better in most or all categories and that 101, while not performing as well as 223, should perform better than the 121 in most or all categories. The one possible exception was the content category labeled "determinants of economic growth." Here 121 might be superior because this is the only course which spends any time on growth per se.

These results (Table 9.4) in general also confirm our expectations. The 223 students perform best in six of the seven content categories and are second best in the remaining category. The 101 students are second in five of the seven categories while 121 students return the highest percentage in the growth category, second in another, and on the other five categories are in third place. Again, 101 performs in an acceptable manner yielding its poorest performance in the growth area—an area not specifically covered in the course. It was also lowest in the determination of GNP, a result that was not expected but whose negative impact is reduced because of the absence of complex application questions.

As expected, the results of the cognitive measures indicate that 101 does not maximize TUCE performance. But the loss in performance, whether measured in terms of total loss, loss by objective category, or by content category, is more than compensated for by gains in areas that are not captured by the TUCE exam. It should also be noted that these losses are only relative to a course like 223, which has as its objective the maximization of TUCE-like performance.[9] Comparison with national norms or current events type courses are favorable to 101. Perhaps even more important is the fact that there is little loss in simple or complex application areas.

D. Attitudinal Outcomes.

Our expectations are that there will be a tradeoff in the affective dimension among the three courses. In particular we would expect the 121 course to have more of an impact in the affective area than either 101 or 223. This is because of the nature of the course, which takes a much more topical approach to macroeconomics and relates the material directly to current economic questions. The 223 course should yield the worst results because it is a large lecture class and is taken as a required course by a majority of students.

One commonly used measure in the affective domain is the course evalu-

TABLE 9.4

Content Category Results of the TUCE Postcourse Test
*Percent Correct**

Category	101	121	223
A. Scarcity, functioning of economic systems, base elements of supply and demand	70.8	65.7	76.2
B. Macroeconomic Accounting	86.0	69.8	87.0
C. Determination of GNP (income-expenditure theory)	46.5	49.3	59.5
D. Money, banking, and monetary policy	64.8	50.3	70.9
E. Government fiscal policies	60.0	47.0	68.1
F. Determinants of economic growth	45.8	70.9	63.4
G. Policies for stabilization and growth	56.4	52.2	61.6

*On the precourse test there were only two differences which were significant: on Category D 223 was significantly above 101 ($t = 2.77$) and Category E 101 was significantly above 121 ($t = 1.91$). In terms of the above postcourse test, 223 is significantly better than 121 on categories A through E and significantly better than 101 on topics C and F. In turn 121 is significantly better than 101 on category F with no other significant differences appearing.

ation form. On the particular form used at Notre Dame students are asked to rate the instructor and the course on a variety of items using a scale from 1 to 4, with 4 being the highest possible rating. Within the Economics Department the scores on the items seldom fall below 2.5, with a typical range between 3.0 and 3.5. The evaluation is taken toward the end of the semester, normally within the last two weeks.

The course evaluations for the three alternative approaches are reproduced in Table 9.5. In summarizing these results, we can begin by making three observations: (1) in general, 101 receives the highest rating, even though it engendered the heaviest work load; (2) 121 was rated close to 101, with major differences appearing on three items—teacher's ability to encourage independent thinking, quality of text, and work load; and (3) 223 receives the lowest overall rating, and, even though this course yields superior TUCE results, it was rated lowest in terms of work load.

Examination of the patterns on specific items or the overall average indicates partial confirmation of our expectations in the affective domain. As

TABLE 9.5

University Course Evaluation
(4.0 Point Scale)

Category	101	121	223
1. Knowledge of subject matter.	3.93	3.91	3.94
2. Enthusiasm for subject.	3.96	3.94	3.86
3. Effectiveness of class teaching or direction.	3.64	3.56	3.44
4. Ability to stimulate student interest in the subject.	3.58	3.43	3.14
5. Interest in students–e.g., availability, helpfulness, etc.	3.61	3.41	2.89
6. Fairness in dealing with students.	3.67	3.58	3.31
7. Respect for student's viewpoint.	3.70	3.55	3.23
8. Organization and management of course.	3.58	3.65	3.59
9. What overall rating would you give this teacher as compared with other teachers you have at Notre Dame?	3.83	3.78	3.57
10. Teacher's ability to lecture in a clear, interesting manner.	3.80	3.70	3.71
11. Teacher's ability to encourage independent thinking.	3.60	3.25	3.05
12. Teacher's carefulness of preparation for class.	3.75	3.67	3.74
13. Teacher's promptness in returning student's work.	3.73	3.70	3.88
14. Intellectual level of the lecture.	3.67	3.63	3.43
15. Quality of text.	3.48	3.18	3.22
16. Personal value of the course to you.	3.60	3.52	3.29
17. Standards for students performance required for this course.	3.46	3.31	3.27
18. Compared with other courses you have taken or are taking at Notre Dame, the work load for this course was:	3.45	3.13	2.79
Average	3.67	3.55	3.41

expected, both 101 and 121 yield ratings that are superior to the 223 course. Contrary to expectation, the 101 course is more successful than 121; with the exception of one item, 101 receives higher ratings.

A second measure within the affective domain is student attitudes regarding economics as a discipline. Specifically, students were given five descriptors of economics and were asked to rank their attitudes on a scale from 1 to 5. For example, one descriptor was "hard" with a 1 implying that economics was not very hard, while a 5 means that it was very hard. The data were collected on a precourse and postcourse basis. Table 9.6 presents these results for the three courses. Here the 101 and 223 results are quite similar, on all five descriptors the postcourse survey yielded higher values than the precourse survey. Thus these students found economics harder, more abstract, more useful, more theoretical, and more relevant than they had originally thought. The 121 students moved up the scale on these descriptors, but they found economics less abstract and less theoretical than they had anticipated.

In interpreting these results we felt that economics courses, particularly intorductory courses, should be perceived by students as useful and relevant. Indeed the 121 course is designed to stimulate interest in economics and, thus, presumably should yield the highest postcourse values on the useful and relevant descriptors. Relative to the 223 course, this result was obtained, but contrary to our expectations the 101 course matches 121 on the useful descriptor (a difference of only .01) and surpasses 121 on the relevant descriptor (a difference of .15). Thus the tradeoff expected between 101 and 121 in this aspect of the affective domain is not realized; indeed, this measure as well as the previous measure imply that 101 is the most successful of the three courses.

The third and final measure in the affective domain is student opinion regarding certain economic institutions, problems, and policies. Again surveys were administered on a precourse and postcourse basis. On these surveys an issue—for example, inflation—is presented and under it are listed a series of semantic differentials such as "bad-good," "inevitable-controllable," "demand pull-cost push," and so forth. Each semantic differential represents a continuum ranging from 1 to 5 with a 3 representing a middle-of-the-road position or no opinion. Eight macroeconomic issues were given with a total of forty-one semantic differentials.

TABLE 9.6

Attitudes Toward Economics as a Discipline
(Scale of 1 to 5)

DESCRIPTOR	101		121		223	
	PRE	POST	PRE	POST	PRE	POST
Hard	2.99	3.61	3.16	3.86	3.19	3.58
Abstract	2.69	2.80	2.71	2.63	2.81	3.00
Useful	4.38	4.54	4.48	4.55	4.15	4.34
Theoretical	3.72	4.06	3.64	3.55	3.57	3.62
Relevant	4.36	4.70	4.45	4.55	4.20	4.42

Table 9.7 presents these results. To summarize these data we can establish ranges of opinion change: (1) no effect–average opinion change of less than .100, (2) intermediate effect–average opinion change of between .100 and .500, and (3) significant effect–average opinion change greater than .500. Using these ranges, 223 generates the largest number of significant changes–eight–followed by 101 and 121 each with five significant changes. In only two instances did the significant changes occur for the same semantic differential in all three courses. For the intermediate range there were sixteen such changes for 101 and fourteen for both 121 and 223. Eight of these occurred simultaneously across all three courses, and four are concentrated within the issue of poverty.

On this basis, then, it appears that 101 and 223 students have a slightly higher propensity to change opinions than 121 students, and in the case of 223 the changes appear to be somewhat stronger.[10] With the exception of the poverty issue, these changes do not occur consistently–each course seems to have its own impact. These results are contrary to our expectations and indicate that if there is a tradeoff, it is not between 101 and 121 (101 performs better) but between 101 and 223.

Another possible measure is to examine the "no opinion" students, that is those who were noncommittal or "3" initially and remained as such on the postcourse survey. This case is viewed as the extreme of "no impact": a course did not provide any information–as perceived by the student–upon which to form an opinion.[11] To summarize the data, we can compare the number of semantic differentials (out of a total of forty-one for each course for which less than 50 percent of the initial 3's remained 3's. We find that this is the case for twenty semantic differentials in 101, twenty-three in 121, and thirty-one in 223. Thus, 223 is most successful. This analysis is, for the most part, inconsistent with our expectations: inconsistent in that 223 is more successful than 101 and 121, but consistent in that 121 is more successful than 101 in changing student opinions on economic issues.

While there is no agreed upon method of assessing the impact of a course in the affective domain, the combined evidence indicates that the tradeoff expected between 101 and 121 did not occur. To express it more positively, 101 performed much better than expected relative to 121.

E. Regression Analysis of Cognitive Achievement

Previously it was argued that the expected tradeoff of less cognitive achievement as measured by the total TUCE for 101 relative to 223 was realized. That conclusion, however, is suspect, for as Table 9.1 indicates, the 101 students had lower MSAT and VSAT scores than their 223 counterparts.

TABLE 9.7

Opinions of Economic Institutions, Problems, and Policies (Scale 1 to 5)

	101		121		223	
Issue	Ending Position	Change**	Ending Position	Change	Ending Position	Change
Decision-making for National Economics Policy						
Simple–Complex	4.581	+.275	4.452	+.074	4.585	+.119
Random–Rational	4.032	-.032	3.932	+.040	4.126	+.329
Political–Apolitical	2.400	-.145	1.986	-.109	2.189	+.134
Important to me–Irrelevant to me	2.097	-.264	.905	+.243	1.881	-.041
Important to society–Irrelevant to society	1.355	-.589	1.432	+.094	1.333	-.217
Government Spending Deficit						
Undesirable–Desirable	3.097	+.375	2.527	-.068	3.433	+.802
Democratic–Republican	3.065	+.176	2.986	+.027	2.936	-.034
Promotes Prosperity–Promotes Depression	2.414	-.142	2.342	-.239	2.234	-.484
Increases Aggregate Demand–Decreases Aggregate Demand	2.290	-.571	2.055	-.769	2.241	-.505
Government Controls such as Wage-Price Freezes						
Undesirable–Desirable	2.871	-.407	3.027	-.041	2.975	-.080
Democratic–Republican	3.433	+.044	3.351	-.128	3.509	+.154
Free Enterprise–Socialism	3.677	+.306	3.730	+.525	3.509	+.099
Effective–Ineffective	3.914	+1.081	3.027	-.189	3.224	-.022
Facilitate Market Operations–Distort Market Operations	3.677	+.177	3.658	+.266	3.696	+.226
Poverty						
Laziness–Lack of Opportunity	3.355	+.469	3.644	+.320	3.873	+.323
Serious–Unimportant	1.163	-.054	1.419	-.054	1.503	+.003
Market Determined–Discrimination	2.677	-.209	2.890	+.196	2.615	-.103
No Jobs–No Skills	3.194	-.149	3.423	+.342	2.949	-.239
Inevitable–Can be Eliminated	3.000	+.056	2.905	-.234	3.283	+.159
Individual Responsibility–Social Responsibility	3.571	+.257	3.676	+.224	3.870	+.357

TABLE 9.7

(Continued)

Issue	101 Ending Position*	101 Change**	121 Ending Position	121 Change	223 Ending Position	223 Change
Inflation						
Bad–Good	2.633	+.462	1.932	-.257	2.704	+.508
Recession–Prosperity	3.500	+.250	2.973	-.203	3.660	+.635
Inevitable–Controllable	3.452	-.005	3.365	+.014	3.403	-.178
Democratic–Republican	2.900	-.267	3.203	+.054	3.019	-.031
Demand Pull–Cost Push	3.267	-.019	3.563	+.320	3.342	+.179
High Unemployment						
Democratic–Republican	3.233	+.073	3.315	+.099	3.208	-.018
Recession–Prosperity	2.194	+.033	2.324	+.256	2.120	-.042
Inflation–Deflation	3.167	+.024	3.189	+.459	3.465	+.449
Controllable–Fact of Life	2.467	+.238	2.541	+.365	2.132	-.098
Bad–Good	1.935	+.324	1.589	+.008	1.767	+.159
Federal Income Tax						
Progressive–Regressive	2.097	-.292	2.486	+.222	1.742	-.833
Good–Bad	2.097	-.292	2.351	+.036	2.006	-.556
Democratic–Republican	2.839	-.078	3.027	+.137	2.881	-.045
Free Enterprise–Socialism	2.710	+.127	2.662	+.216	2.648	-.017
Too High–Too Low	2.806	+.112	2.541	+.089	2.722	+.356
Fair–Unfair	2.710	-.290	3.014	-.081	2.673	-.644
Increasing the Money Supply						
Helps People–Hurts People	2.484	-.766	2.669	-.861	2.296	-.838
Inflation–Recession	2.033	-.189	2.028	+.731	2.184	+.106
More Gold–More Paper	3.677	+.594	3.919	+.824	3.829	+.464
Democratic–Republican	3.033	+.144	2.959	-.069	3.006	+.031
Free Enterprise–Socialism	2.710	-.033	2.608	-.172	2.491	-.297

*Ending position is defined as $\frac{\sum_{i=1}^{N} O_i}{N}$ where O_i represents the opinions of the ith student and N the number of students. Change is defined as the difference between ending and beginning positions.

**A plus sign indicates that ending position represented a higher score than initial position.

The counterargument, then, is that the tradeoff occurred not because of a difference between courses but because of differences between *students* in the courses. In order to control for this possibility and other differences, we can employ multiple-regression analysis of TUCE performance.

While the general construction developed previously is applied in the present case, data limitations forced certain changes in the equations actually estimated. In addition, the comparison in this case is among three alternatives, necessitating two dummy variables. Economics 101 is the standard of comparison, that is, the dummies both have a value of zero for it, and thus coefficient estimates indicate differences from the 101 intercept.

The following are the variables that enter the regressions. In terms of human capital variables three are employed in all regressions. They are MSAT, VSAT, and rank in high school class (RHSC). The latter was included on the presumption that human capital may not be fully captured by MSAT and VSAT. Of course the three variables are not perfect measures of the stock of human capital at the time the students began the respective courses. In the case of the 223 students, mainly sophomores, these variables measure human capital as it existed some two years previously.

Proxies for utilization rates were the most troublesome to quantify. Our measure of utilization rates was taken from the university course evaluation. Specifically, we employed the last item presented in Table 9.5 on "work load" (CE 20). This variable is particularly troublesome because the question which generates it is stated in a relative sense. Thus, a student who spends little time in all courses including economics would give a middle ranking, as would a student who spends much time on all courses including economics.

For the efficiency variables we have a number to choose from. Again using the course evaluation, we selected items 9 (CE9), 15 (CE15), and 16 (CE16), capturing the students' evaluations of the teacher in an overall sense, of the texts, and of the entire course.[12] In addition we have included the change in student opinion regarding economic policy—the first issue presented in Table 9.7 (OPI). This variable is the absolute sum of the change on each of the five semantic differentials listed under this item.[13] This variable is included as an efficiency variable because it measures, presumably, the extent to which a student has internalized the content presented in the course.

Finally, the major purpose of the regression analysis is to determine whether the differential cognitive results reported earlier could be attributed to the courses themselves. Thus we have included two dummy variables. The first is DV223, which was coded as a 1 for all 223 students and 0 for all others. The other is DV121, which was coded as a 1 for all 121 students and 0 for all others. In this way we can compare the 101 students to each of the other groups by examining the sign and significance of the two dummy variables.

The regression version of the model thus appears as

$$CA = a_1 + b_1\ (MSAT) + b_2\ (VSAT) + b_3\ (RHSC) + b_4\ (CE20) + b_5\ (CE9) + b_6\ (CE15) + b_7\ (CE16) + b_8\ (OPI) + b_9\ (DV223) + b_{10}\ (DV121) + u$$

All of the variables–excluding DV223 and DV121–are expected to operate positively on cognitive achievement. The elimination of pre-TUCE scores as an independent variable was justified on the basis of using the gap-closing specification of the dependent variable.[14] Regressions were run on the total TUCE as well as the three objective categories. The results are presented in Table 9.8.

These results offer insights in many areas, but the two of concern here are the explanatory ability of the model and the impact of the courses themselves. With respect to the former we can begin by examining the R^2 values. We find that the model works fairly well in explaining total TUCE performance ($R^2 = 0.395$) but then unevenly among the objective categories. Here the model performed best in the simple-application category ($R^2 = 0.425$) and worst in the recognition-and-understanding category ($R^2 = 0.101$).

Another aspect of the model's efficacy is the sign and significance of the coefficients. Of the three human-capital variables, we find that MSAT is the most consistent–significant and positive in three of the four regressions. VSAT has one incorrect sign but is insignificant here, and in the one instance that it is significant, it has the proper sign.

CE20 represented the single utilization rate variable. Its performance is disappointing–insignificant in all four regressions, with one incorrect sign. As stated previously, the wording of the question on the course evaluation form may explain the poor performance of this variable.

With the four efficiency variables, the results are also disappointing. The sign of the teacher evaluation is consistently negative and in two instances it is significant. The text evaluation has two unexpected signs but in all four regressions is insignificant. The course evaluation is consistently positive but insignificant. OPI operates positively in all four regressions and is significant in the complex-application regression.

Turning to the question of the effects of the courses, the sign and significance of the dummy variables support our earlier assertions. In the total TUCE regression we find that DV223 is positive while DV121 is negative with both variables significant. The 223 students, after controlling for the other independent variables, obtain higher total TUCE scores than the 101 students; but the 101 students are significantly better than the 121 students. On recognition and understanding questions, 223 is again significantly better than 101, but there is no difference between 101 and 121. With simple applications, 223 is significantly better and 121 significantly worse than 101.

TABLE 9.8

Regression Results
Total TUCE and the Three Objective Categories

Dependent Variable		Constant	MSAT	VSAT	RHSC	CE20	CE9
	b value	-0.07497	0.00967	0.00010	0.00070	0.01474	-0.06314
Total TUCE	beta weights		0.22995	0.04109	0.03757	0.04858	-0.15704
	t-ratio		3.762*	0.677	0.646	0.843	2.568*
Recognition	b value	-0.12403	0.00075	-0.00040	0.00233	0.02562	-0.06576
and	beta weights		0.18879	-0.11844	0.09241	0.06200	-0.12006
Understanding	5-ratio		2.533*	1.602	1.303	0.883	1.610
	b value	-0.17902	0.00079	0.00060	-0.00153	-0.00313	-0.04617
Simple	beta weights		0.18091	0.16223	-0.05493	-0.00688	-0.07663
Application	t-ratio		3.036*	2.744*	0.969	0.122	1.285
	b value	-0.06328	0.00046	0.00011	0.00177	0.04120	-0.08625
Complex	beta weights		0.11317	0.03089	0.06855	0.09745	-0.15393
Application	t-ratio		1.603	0.441	1.021	1.465	2.180*

*Indicates significance at the .05 level

We had expected that the 223–101 comparison would not be significant in this category. On the complex application we do obtain our expected results—no significant difference between 223 and 101, and 101 is significantly better than 121. Simply, the results of the regression analysis do confirm the earlier reported results, again rejecting only one of our a priori expectations.

F. Conclusions

In the teaching of any course, the instructor must identify his objectives, develop a strategy for obtaining these objectives, and determine the extent to which the objectives have been obtained. The same is true of a department that offers alternative introductory courses. Objectives identified in this chapter include both cognitive and affective outcomes for three different courses. By comparing the results of the courses in these areas, we were able to indicate likely tradeoffs from adopting one or the other of these approaches. In general, the results indicated that our objectives in each course were being attained; courses indeed can be designed to achieve different outcomes. Also the performance of a course that integrates the computer as a laboratory seems quite good—the loss coming in an area of cognitive achievement which was not stressed.

TABLE 9.8
(continued)

CE15	CE16	OPI	DV223	DV121	R^2	N	F Statistic
0.00290	0.03313	0.01058	0.13190	-0.10449	0.39538	226	14.12506
0.01119	0.11655	0.08949	0.30552	-0.22477			
.178	1.722	1.637	3.496*	2.642*			
0.00651	0.05645	0.00225	0.13795	0.02775	0.10131	226	2.43511
0.01840	0.14592	0.01397	0.23456	0.04382			
0.240	1.767	0.209	2.202*	0.421			
-0.00022	0.01805	0.00703	0.20277	-0.17036	0.42528	226	15.98347
-0.00057	0.04241	0.03967	0.31343	-0.24455			
0.000	0.642	0.744	3.679*	2.948*			
-0.00001	0.03372	0.02398	0.06927	-0.14165	0.19388	226	5.19506
-0.00003	0.08520	0.14556	0.11513	-0.21864			
0.000	1.089	2.306*	1.141	2.225*			

This chapter should provide a starting point for other comparisons of alternative approaches. In these activities, as indicated by our own difficulties, special attention should be given the TUCE and to data collection. In particular the dual disaggregation of the TUCE provides extensive analytical capabilities. If one is teaching an analytical course, particular attention should be paid to the objective category results, but care should be taken that the content coverage of the course parallels that of the TUCE. Finally, it appears that individuals must be careful in specifying what they believe to be the educational process taking place in their courses before proceeding to empirical analysis. It should also be realized that if a computer is used in relation to a course, there are a number of ways it may be incorporated. Using it as a laboratory is one very promising approach. Indeed it appears that the use of the computer in 101 generated results more closely in line with our expectations then did the CAI system used in 223 and evaluated in preceding chapters.

10

SUMMARY & CONCLUSIONS

In the preceding chapters we have attempted to both explain and evaluate our efforts in intergrating the computer into the teaching of introductory economics. It should be clear that these efforts have involved two very different approaches. One approach may be labeled *Computer Assisted Instruction* (CAI) and is represented by our efforts in conjunction with the Economics 223-224 sequence. We feel that the term "assisted" is appropriate because the computer materials (review, demonstration, and game-simulation routines) as well as the use of the computer itself do not involve a restructuring of educational objectives but an alternative method for achieving given objectives. The other approach may be labeled *Computer-Based Instruction* (CBI) and is represented by the Economics 101-102 sequence. Here the term "based" is appropriate because new educational objectives are specified and, effectively, there is no alternative to using the computer.

With respect to evaluation we have concentrated on CAI. Specifically for the 1973-74 academic year we ask the question: Relative to discussion classes what are the effects of CAI on the cognitive achievement and attitudes of students and on educational costs? Although the empirical analyses used to answer these questions are not all we would like them to be—indeed we have attempted to improve the state of the art at least as it is practiced in economic education—we believe the following conclusion is in order: Relative to discussion classes CAI is an effective substitute; that is, it yields approximately equivalent levels of cognitive achievement, it does not exert an independent influence on student attitudes, and it compares favorably in terms of costs. Note, however, that these conclusions are relative to discussion classes; further evaluations should be made comparing CAI to still other instructional alternatives. In addition further research should be undertaken to establish whether the rate in which economic knowledge deteriorates is affected by CAI. This suggests that we should undertake a follow-up study to determine whether CAI operates differentially on this deterioration rate.

During the 1974-75 academic year CAI was used in conjunction with discussion classes. The evidence from the 223 course indicates that CAI can handle the more traditional tasks of the discussion classes and, therefore, the discussion class can be used to broaden the content of an introductory course without a loss in cognitive achievement. The results for the 224 course suggest that only CAI or the discussion class should be used if the discussion class has no unique objectives. Overall the empirical evidence indicates that CAI will be used by those students who think it is useful.

We should also add that CAI, at least the version we employed, could be improved. Specifically the review routines should be constructed so as to provide better clues to the student as to what he knows and what he does not know. The demonstration and game-simulation routines would then be keyed in such a way that once a weakness is revealed the student can turn to an appropriate routine to obtain further instruction. In short we believe CAI's effectiveness could be increased if it were redesigned along the lines of the TIPS system developed by Allan Kelley. We would, however, retain the prompts for both correct and incorrect answers for the review routine questions.

In addition the CAI system could be improved in a number of technical ways: by allowing students to begin and/or end a routine at any point, by speeding up the printing process, by allowing exploration of other responses to a question before the end of a routine, and so on. We believe that our system could be improved by making both basic and technical modifications.

With regard to CBI, we have not compiled as much evidence here relative to CAI. Nonetheless, the evidence on CBI, according to our own criterion, is superior to conventional approaches to introductory economics. But this is because we are willing to sacrifice some cognitive achievement as measured by the TUCE to obtain other objectives that we consider more important both in the context of introductory economics and in terms of a university education. Others may be unwilling to accept such a tradeoff.

Aside from the evidence on CAI and CBI the methodology employed in answering the basic questions we have raised is important. With respect to the learning model of cognitive achievement what we attempted to do is specify the variables in the regression equations through a deductive process. that is, one must begin with a conceptual view before collecting data. The difficulty with the data stems in part from an inability to articulate fully both model and its implications before beginning the data-collection process. We shall have to be engaged in further activity here as well. Even given these problems we think we have underscored a point that to a large extent has been ignored in evaluation of educational innovations in the teaching of economics; that is, the absence of any consideration of utilization rates.

On the attitudinal side our primary efforts were to isolate determinants of attitudinal change on economic issues. To say that further work in this area is needed is to say the obvious. Here we would hope that our results would be interpreted as an initial endeavor, stimulating others to undertake further investigations.

The cost area is becoming increasingly important as colleges and universities respond to both decreasing revenues or at least a slowing down of revenue growth and increasing costs. In determining the cost impact of an educational innovation, one must grapple with differences between fixed and variable costs as identified by a budgeting process and as seen by the economist. The resolution of these differences is not easy but is critical when attempting to ascertain cost impacts. We hope that we have highlighted these difficulties and their importance.

Indeed simply addressing all of the questions we have posed for CAI and CBI has forced us to make a systematic inquiry into all aspects of the educational endeavor. As such we recommend that all teachers undertake such an inquiry, for the inquiry itself is a learning process for the teacher, which perhaps will lead to better instruction for our students.

Finally, we suspect that our evidence, like all evidence is not conclusive. After all, we are evaluating only a particular CAI system and a particular CBI sequence. We do think that the evidence we have presented is encouraging: CAI can be an effective substitute for certain instructional elements, and CBI can provide a whole new approach to introductory economics.

APPENDIXES

APPENDIX A

Questionnaires on Instructional Elements

PART I

University Course Evaluation Form
(administered within two weeks of the end of the semester)

Please circle the grade you would give your teacher on each of the following (circle NA if the item does not apply).

	(very high)			(very low)	
Knowledge of subject matter	A	B	C	D	NA
Enthusiasm for subject	A	B	C	D	NA
Effectiveness of class teaching or direction	A	B	C	D	NA
Ability to stimulate student interest in the subject	A	B	C	D	NA
Interest in students–for example, availability, helpfulness, etc.	A	B	C	D	NA
Fairness in dealing with students	A	B	C	D	NA
Respect for student's viewpoint	A	B	C	D	NA
Organization and management of course	A	B	C	D	NA
What overall rating would you give this teacher as compared with other teachers you have at Notre Dame?	A	B	C	D	NA
Teacher's ability to lecture in a clear, interesting manner	A	B	C	D	NA
Teacher's ability to encourage independent thinking	A	B	C	D	NA
Teacher's carefulness of preparation for class	A	B	C	D	NA
Teacher's promptness in returning student's work	A	B	C	D	NA
Intellectual level of lectures	A	B	C	D	NA
Quality of text	A	B	C	D	NA
Personal value of the course to you	A	B	C	D	NA
Standards for students performance required for this course	A	B	C	D	NA

Compared with other courses you have taken or are taking at Notre Dame, the work load for this course was:

A (heavier)
B (heavy)
C (somewhat lighter)
D (much lighter)
NA

PART II

Attitudes on General Instructional Elements
(administered both at the beginning and the end of the semester)

In the following items, please circle the number which corresponds with your feeling on the item. If you have no opinion, please circle number 3.

	strongly disagree	disagree	undecided	agree	strongly agree
1. LARGE LECTURES ARE:					
A good teaching method	1	2	3	4	5
A good way to present information	1	2	3	4	5
Useful for presenting policy questions	1	2	3	4	5
Useful for presenting theory	1	2	3	4	5
A good way to relate to the text	1	2	3	4	5
Boring	1	2	3	4	5
Stifling to creative thought	1	2	3	4	5
2. OBJECTIVE TESTS ARE:					
Fair measures of knowledge	1	2	3	4	5
Good if limited to specific kinds of knowledge	1	2	3	4	5
Superior to subjective (essay) tests	1	2	3	4	5
Requires memorization and penalizes true understanding	1	2	3	4	5
Useful for testing knowledge of theory	1	2	3	4	5
Useful for testing knowledge of policy questions	1	2	3	4	5
3. TEXTBOOKS ARE:					
A good teaching device	1	2	3	4	5
Useful for presenting policy questions	1	2	3	4	5
Useful for presenting theory	1	2	3	4	5
Always dull	1	2	3	4	5
Not relevant to class goals	1	2	3	4	5
Not suitable for tutorial discussions	1	2	3	4	5
Not integrated into lectures	1	2	3	4	5

PART III

Attitudes on Specific Instructional Elements
(administered within two weeks of the end of the semester)

1. In preparing for your examinations, how much did you rely on each of the following? Check the appropriate response. Leave blank any items which do not pertain to your particular situation

	None	Very Little	Some	A Lot
The Samuelson text	____	____	____	____
Lectures	____	____	____	____
Class handouts	____	____	____	____
Computer simulations	____	____	____	____
Computer reviews (multiple choice)	____	____	____	____
Computer demonstrations	____	____	____	____
Individual meetings with tutorial instructor	____	____	____	____
Discussion in tutorial classes	____	____	____	____
Review sheets from tutorial class	____	____	____	____
Working with others outside class	____	____	____	____
Memorization	____	____	____	____
Thinking about ideas and concepts	____	____	____	____
Individual meetings with professor	____	____	____	____

2. How much have each of the following contributed to your understanding of the topics covered thus far in the course?

The Samuelson text	____	____	____	____
Lectures	____	____	____	____
Class handouts	____	____	____	____
Computer simulations	____	____	____	____
Computer reviews (multiple choice)	____	____	____	____
Computer demonstrations	____	____	____	____
Individual meetings with tutorial instructor	____	____	____	____
Discussion in tutorial class	____	____	____	____
Review sheets from tutorial class	____	____	____	____
Working with others outside class	____	____	____	____
Memorization	____	____	____	____
Thinking about ideas and concepts	____	____	____	____
Individual meetings with professor	____	____	____	____

PART III
(continued)

3. Which of the following have you found difficult in the course? Check all that apply.

_____ Understanding how economic principles are applied
_____ Understanding lecture material
_____ Incorporating information from the course into *your point* of economic life
_____ Doing the computer exercises
_____ Finding the computer available
_____ Understanding the text
_____ Getting interested in the course
_____ Having questions answered by the lecturer
_____ Having questions answered by the tutorial instructor
_____ Understanding the vocabulary used in the text or lectures
_____ Integrating computer exercises into course
_____ Integrating tutorial discussion into course
_____ Other: Please specify ________________________________

PART IV

Attitudes on CAI
(administered within two weeks of the end of the semester)

TO BE ANSWERED ONLY IF YOU ARE ASSIGNED TO A TUTORIAL CLASS USING THE COMPUTER

1. Which of the following points on the continuum describes the effect of using the computer on your understanding of Economics?

	strongly disagree	disagree	undecided	agree	strongly agree	
Helpful	1	2	3	4	5	Harmful
Relevant	1	2	3	4	5	Irrelevant
Clarifying	1	2	3	4	5	Confusing
Redundant	1	2	3	4	5	Necessary

2. Which of the following describes your *first* reaction to computer usage?

Interesting	1	2	3	4	5	Boring
Stifling	1	2	3	4	5	Stimulating
Additional work	1	2	3	4	5	Helpful Technique
Fun	1	2	3	4	5	Bothersome
Intriguing	1	2	3	4	5	Redundant

3. My feeling toward computers *now* is:

Interesting	1	2	3	4	5	Boring
Stifling	1	2	3	4	5	Stimulating
Additional work	1	2	3	4	5	Helpful Technique
Fun	1	2	3	4	5	Bothersome
Intriguing	1	2	3	4	5	Redundant

PART IV

(continued)

4. Overall, what has been your reaction to your experience with use of the computer in this course?

	strongly disagree	disagree	undecided	agree	strongly agree
A. The computer has complemented the course well.	1	2	3	4	5
B. The computer is available at convenient times	1	2	3	4	5
C. The computer is an effective way to review material	1	2	3	4	5
D. The computer has increased the value of the course	1	2	3	4	5
E. The computer has depersonalized the course too much	1	2	3	4	5

5. Are you satisfied with your experience with the computer?

____ Very unsatisfied

____ Unsatisfied

____ Slightly satisfied

____ Very satisfied

6. Why or why not?____

____

____

7. How often did you use the computer?

____ Every week (ran all programs regularly as assigned)

____ Fairly regularly (every other week)

____ Only a few times

____ Never

PART IV

(continued)

8. Of the 23 review programs with multiple choice questions, how many did you use?

____ all 23

____ 18–22

____ 13–17

____ 8–12

____ 3–7

____ 0–2

9. Of the five demonstrations, how many did you use?

____ all 5

____ 2–4

____ less than 2

10. Did you run the simulation?

____ Yes ____ No

11. Which type of program did you feel helped you the most in learning economics?

____ Review (multiple choice) (23)

____ Demonstrations (5)

____ Simulation (1)

12. Which type of program did you feel helped you the most in preparing for for the tests?

____ Reviews (multiple choice) (23)

____ Demonstrations (5)

____ Simulation (1)

PART V

Attitudes on Discussion Classes
(administered within two weeks of the end of the semester)

1. Which of the following points on the continuum describes the effect of your tutorial class on your understanding of Economics?

	Strongly Disagree	Disagree	Undecided	Agree	Strongly Agree	
Helpful	1	2	3	4	5	Harmful
Relevant	1	2	3	4	5	Irrelevant
Clarifying	1	2	3	4	5	Confusing
Redundant	1	2	3	4	5	Necessary

2. Which of the following points describes your *first* reaction to tutorial classes?

Interesting	1	2	3	4	5	Boring
Stifling	1	2	3	4	5	Stimulating
Additional Work	1	2	3	4	5	Helpful Technique
Fun	1	2	3	4	5	Bothersome
Intriguing	1	2	3	4	5	Redundant

3. My feeling toward tutorial classes *now* is:

Interesting	1	2	3	4	5	Boring
Stifling	1	2	3	4	5	Stimulating
Additional Work	1	2	3	4	5	Helpful Technique
Fun	1	2	3	4	5	Bothersome
Intriguing	1	2	3	4	5	Redundant

4. Overall, what has been your reaction to your experience with the tutorial classes in this course?

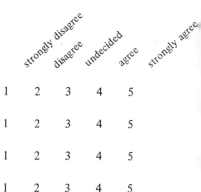

	strongly disagree	disagree	undecided	agree	strongly agree
A. The tutorial class has complemented the course well	1	2	3	4	5
B. The tutorial class is an effective way to review material	1	2	3	4	5
C. The tutorial class has increased the value of the course	1	2	3	4	5
D. The personal element of the tutorial instructor is important to learning	1	2	3	4	5

PART V
(continued)

5. Are you satisfied with you experience in the discussion group?

____ Very satisfied
____ Slightly satisfied
____ Unsatisfied
____ Very unsatisfied

6. Why or why not? ____

____

____

7. How often did you attend your discussion group?

____ Every week
____ Fairly regularly
____ Only a few times
____ Never

8. Did you have access to computer terminal use even though you were in a tutorial? ____Yes ____No

9. Did you have frequent access to computer printouts (not questions) even though you were in a tutorial? ____Yes ____No

APPENDIX B

Attitudes toward Economics as a Discipline (administered both at the beginning and end of each semester)

1. In the following item please circle the number which corresponds with your feeling (Strongly Agree, 5; Agree, 4; Undecided, 3; Disagree, 2; and Strongly Disagree, 1) on the item. If you have no opinion, please circle number 3.

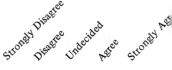

ECONOMICS AS A COURSE IS:	Strongly Disagree	Disagree	Undecided	Agree	Strongly Agree
Hard	1	2	3	4	5
Abstract	1	2	3	4	5
Useful	1	2	3	4	5
Theoretical	1	2	3	4	5
Relevant	1	2	3	4	5

2. Your instructor has certain goals in mind for this course. Which *one* of the following do you feel is most important or significant for you?

_____ An understanding of tools of economic analysis

_____ An understanding of types of economic institutions and economic problems in our economy

_____ An understanding of how to manipulate the tools in analyzing and seeking solutions to problems

3. Here is a list of topics explored in this course. Please check the *three* that most interest you.

_____ 1. Inflation

_____ 2. Federal Reserve System

_____ 3. Law of Diminishing returns

_____ 4. Causes of poverty

_____ 5. Law of Demand

_____ 6. Taxation

_____ 7. Law of Increasing Resource Cost

_____ 8. Monetary policy

_____ 9. Current anti-poverty programs
_____ 10. Unemployment
_____ 11. Fiscal policy
_____ 12. Economic growth
_____ 13. Meaning and size of gross national product
_____ 14. Fluctuation in the price of a commodity
_____ 15. Money
_____ 16. Negative income tax
_____ 17. Government spending
_____ 18. Production and distribution of goods and services
_____ 19. Adding to the capital stock
_____ 20. Consumer spending

4. Would you expect this course to help you understand discussions of economic issues as presented in the news media such as the New York *Times, Newsweek,* the Wall Street *Journal*?

_____ Yes
_____ No

APPENDIX C

Attitudes toward Economic Institutions, Problems, and Policies (administered both at the beginning and end of the semester)

The following are questions dealing with your attitudes toward certain economic terms. Please circle the number on the continuum which most closely reflects your attitudes. If you do not understand the term or are otherwise undecided, circle number 3.

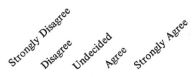

	Strongly Disagree	Disagree	Undecided	Agree	Strongly Agree	
1. DECISION-MAKING FOR NATIONAL ECONOMIC POLICY						
Simple	1	2	3	4	5	Complex
Random	1	2	3	4	5	Rational
Political	1	2	3	4	5	Apolitical
Important to me	1	2	3	4	5	Irrelevant to me
Important to society	1	2	3	4	5	Irrelevant to society
2. GOVERNMENT SPENDING DEFICIT						
Undesirable	1	2	3	4	5	Desirable
Democratic	1	2	3	4	5	Republican
Promotes inflation	1	2	3	4	5	Promotes depression
Increases aggregate demand	1	2	3	4	5	Decreases aggregate demand
3. GOVERNMENT CONTROLS SUCH AS WAGE AND PRICE FREEZES						
Undesirable	1	2	3	4	5	Desirable
Democratic	1	2	3	4	5	Republican
Free enterprise	1	2	3	4	5	Socialism
Effective	1	2	3	4	5	Ineffective
Facilitate market operations	1	2	3	4	5	Distort market operations
4. POVERTY						
Laziness	1	2	3	4	5	Lack of opportunity
Serious	1	2	3	4	5	Unimportant

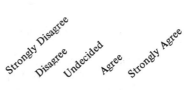

	Strongly Disagree	Disagree	Undecided	Agree	Strongly Agree	
4. POVERTY (continued)						
Market determined	1	2	3	4	5	Overt discrimination
No jobs	1	2	3	4	5	No skills
Inevitable	1	2	3	4	5	Can be eliminated
Individual responsibility	1	2	3	4	5	Social responsibility
5. INFLATION						
Bad	1	2	3	4	5	Good
Recession	1	2	3	4	5	Prosperity
Inevitable	1	2	3	4	5	Controllable
Democratic	1	2	3	4	5	Republican
Demand pull	1	2	3	4	5	Cost push
6. HIGH UNEMPLOYMENT						
Democratic	1	2	3	4	5	Republican
Recession	1	2	3	4	5	Prosperity
Inflation	1	2	3	4	5	Deflation
Controllable	1	2	3	4	5	Fact of life
Bad	1	2	3	4	5	Good
7. FEDERAL INCOME TAX						
Progressive	1	2	3	4	5	Regressive
Good	1	2	3	4	5	Bad
Democratic	1	2	3	4	5	Republican
Free enterprise	1	2	3	4	5	Socialism
Too high	1	2	3	4	5	Too low
Fair	1	2	3	4	5	Unfair
8. INCREASING THE MONEY SUPPLY						
Helps people	1	2	3	4	5	Hurts people
Inflation	1	2	3	4	5	Recession
More gold	1	2	3	4	5	More paper
Democratic	1	2	3	4	5	Republican
Free enterprise	1	2	3	4	5	Socialism

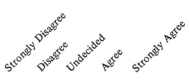

	Strongly Disagree	Disagree	Undecided	Agree	Strongly Agree	
9. FOREIGN TRADE						
Desirable	1	2	3	4	5	Undesirable
Should be encouraged	1	2	3	4	5	Should be discouraged
Unimportant	1	2	3	4	5	Important
Should be political	1	2	3	4	5	Should be apolitical
Should be free	1	2	3	4	5	Should be controlled
10. LABOR UNIONS						
Good	1	2	3	4	5	Bad
Effective	1	2	3	4	5	Ineffective
Important	1	2	3	4	5	Unimportant
Fair	1	2	3	4	5	Unfair
Responsible	1	2	3	4	5	Irresponsible
Capitalistic	1	2	3	4	5	Socialistic
Greedy	1	2	3	4	5	Selfless
Necessary	1	2	3	4	5	Unnecessary
11. BIG BUSINESS						
Good	1	2	3	4	5	Bad
Growing in importance	1	2	3	4	5	Declining importance
Should be controlled	1	2	3	4	5	Should be free
Pays its share	1	2	3	4	5	Has a free ride
Socially responsible	1	2	3	4	5	Socially irresponsible
Monopolistic	1	2	3	4	5	Competitive
Politically involved	1	2	3	4	5	Politically uninvolved
12. CAPITALISM						
A reality	1	2	3	4	5	A non-reality
Desirable	1	2	3	4	5	Undesirable
Declining	1	2	3	4	5	Growing
Superior to socialism	1	2	3	4	5	Inferior to socialism
Should be controlled	1	2	3	4	5	Should be free
Efficient	1	2	3	4	5	Inefficient
Equitable	1	2	3	4	5	Inequitable

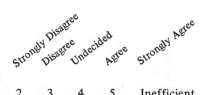

13. MARKET MECHANISMS

	Strongly Disagree	Disagree	Undecided	Agree	Strongly Agree	
Efficient	1	2	3	4	5	Inefficient
Theoretical	1	2	3	4	5	Practical
Workable	1	2	3	4	5	Unworkable
Desirable	1	2	3	4	5	Undesirable
Abstract	1	2	3	4	5	Concrete
High prices	1	2	3	4	5	Low prices
Allocates	1	2	3	4	5	Do not allocate

APPENDIX D

Regression Results on Student Attitudes
*Section 61, Economics 223**

ISSUE	AGE 1		HIGH SCHOOL 2		VSAT 3		MSAT 4		SEX 5		EXPCODE 6	
1. Decision-Making for National Economic Policy:												
Simple-Complex	-.020	.319	-.059	.744	.0006	1.164	.0005	.905	.460	2.159	.018	.228
Random-Rational	-.006	.105	.070	.935	.0003	.581	.0004	.922	.279	1.407	-.061	.782
Apolitical-Political	-.081	.912	-.167	1.486	.0007	1.022	-.0003	.458	-.037	.126	-.072	.625
Important to me-Irrelevant to me	-.109	1.517	-.021	.243	.0005	.895	-.0002	.430	-.390	1.643	.016	.182
Important to society-Irrelevant to society	-.071	1.119	.00004	0	-.0002	.465	-.0001	.173	-.165	.791	.068	.823
2. Government Spending Deficit												
Desirable-Undesirable	.047	.489	.154	1.294	-.001	1.500	-.0004	.532	-.072	.237	-.039	.320
Democratic-Republican	-.045	.677	.082	1.058	-.0001	.197	-.0004	.879	.168	.827	-.023	.322
Promotes inflation-Promotes depression	.063	.864	.175	1.951	-.0007	1.225	-.0006	.974	.232	.988	-.113	1.229
Decreases demand-Increases demand	.021	.335	.053	.703	-.0001	.262	.0006	1.173	-.156	.789	-.028	.371
3. Government Controls such as Wage-Price Freezes:												
Undesirable-Desirable	.094	1.155	-.126	1.227	-.001	2.303	.001	1.582	.370	1.356	.061	.576
Democratic-Republican	-.022	.402	.132	1.861	.0008	1.693	-.0006	1.350	-.126	2.16	-.031	.437
Socialism-Free enterprise	.064	.825	-.024	.249	-.0008	1.214	.0001	.151	.238	.931	.045	.446
Ineffective-Effective	-.111	1.490	-.011	.126	.0001	.210	.0001	.184	-.181	-.727	.067	.698
Distort market operations-Facilitate market operations	-.182	2.254	.052	.512	.0008	1.113	-.0005	.708	-.013	.055	-.018	.176

*First entry in a column is the regression coefficient and the second entry is the "t" statistic.

APPENDIX D
(continued)

ISSUE	RELIGION 7		TUCE IMP 8		SWAT 9		ATT 10		R^2 11	F 12	CONSTANT 13	OTHER VARIABLES** 14
1. Decision-Making for National Economic Policy:												
Simple-Complex	.228	1.346	-.003	.435	1.076	8.609	.584	8.752	.38	12.1	.877	5
Random-Rational	.096	.609	-.008	1.132	1.097	10.544	.624	11.502	.45	16.1	1.068	
Apolitical-Political	-.536	2.307	.009	.827	1.471	9.187	.451	6.573	.32	9.2	3.060	7
Important to me-Irrelevant to me	.0004	0	.005	.559	1.334	12.954	.598	12.004	.55	24.1	2.77	5
Important to society-Irrelevant to society	.363	2.205	.018	2.316	1.378	14.060	.191	4.583	.54	22.8	2.35	7, 8
2. Government Spending Deficit:												
Desirable-Undesirable	-.094	.385	.0007	.054	1.676	9.386	.308	5.244	.36	10.8	1.357	
Democratic-Republican	-.102	.636	.011	1.453	1.116	9.111	.414	8.336	.35	10.1	2.37	
Promotes inflation-Promotes depression	-.137	.733	.005	.603	1.205	9.970	.270	5.127	.38	11.5	.586	2
Decreases demand-Increases demand	.251	1.606	-.0001	0	1.343	15.753	.599	10.005	.59	27.6	.524	7
3. Government Controls such as Wage-Price Freezes:												
Undesirable-Desirable	-.087	.411	.007	.681	1.518	11.036	.650	12.320	.52	20.7	-1.38	3
Democratic-Republican	.036	.249	.013	1.754	1.345	13.682	.455	10.436	.53	21.5	1.88	2, 3, 5, 8
Socialism-Free enterprise	.125	.620	.007	.782	1.388	10.89	.322	6.880	.41	13.7	- .018	
Ineffective-Effective	.026	.130	-.005	.591	1.671	14.869	.745	14.433	.61	30.5	2.449	
Distorts market operations-Facilitates market operations	.289	1.377	-.003	.375	1.554	12.10	.593	10.286	.48	18.2	3.847	1

**Column number identifying those variables other than ATT and SWAT which were significant in a particular regression.

APPENDIX D
(continued)

Regression Results on Student Attitudes
Section 61, Economics 223

ISSUE	AGE 1		HIGH SCHOOL 2		VSAT 3		MSAT 4		SEX 5		EXPCODE 6	
4. Poverty:												
Laziness-Lack of opportunity	.011	.148	.050	.541	.0002	.350	.0009	1.413	.230	.882	.001	0
Unimportant-Serious	-.072	1.043	-.159	1.824	-.0007	1.228	.0005	.933	.143	.628	-.015	.173
Market determined-Overt discrimination	-.020	.279	.014	.158	.001	2.781	-.001	2.594	.019	.070	-.158	1.648
No skills-No job	-.054	.702	.019	.202	-.0005	.729	.0008	1.190	.179	.653	-.072	.713
Inevitable-Can be eliminated	-.193	2.044	.028	.243	.001	1.763	-.001	1.465	.257	.822	.136	1.112
Individual responsibility-Social responsibility	-.058	.657	.146	1.313	-.0003	.453	-.0009	1.253	-.158	.505	-.129	1.112
5. Inflation:												
Bad-Good	-.042	.640	.068	.807	-.001	2.252	.0004	.723	.387	1.732	.086	.989
Recession-Prosperity	.012	.138	.051	.444	-.0006	.866	-.0003	.400	.093	.306	.187	1.566
Inevitable-Controllable	-.103	1.190	.160	1.480	.0004	.575	.0002	.379	.053	.187	.080	.711
Democratic-Republican	-.020	.348	.007	.105	-.0003	.626	.0003	.644	.275	1.432	-.097	1.288
Cost push-Demand pull	-.138	1.661	-.026	.249	-.006	.890	-.0001	.226	-.243	.892	.069	.631
6. High Unemployment:												
Democratic-Republican	-.042	.664	.017	.219	.001	2.371	-.0005	1.001	.154	.738	.124	1.507
Recession-Prosperity	-.065	.838	.065	.667	.0002	.421	.001	1.469	-.02	.084	-.054	.541
Inflation-Deflation	-.065	.718	-.067	.592	.0007	.997	.001	1.290	-.278	.926	.052	.445
Fact of life-Controllable	-.062	.900	-.120	1.374	-.0002	.032	.0001	.170	-.049	.212	.071	.792
Bad-Good	-.019	.345	.045	.635	0	0	-.00003	.734	.018	.095	.035	.489

APPENDIX D
(continued)

ISSUE	RELIGION 7		TUCE IMP 8		SWAT 9		ATT 10		R^2 11	F 12	CONSTANT 13	OTHER VARIABLES 14
4. Poverty:												
Laziness-Lack of opportunity	-.013	.071	-.001	.138	1.47	13.883	.785	17.092	.66	36.4	- .697	
Unimportant-Serious	.087	.480	-.003	.345	1.264	7.197	.682	9.659	.37	11.3	2.494	2
Market determined-Overt discrimination	-.058	.290	-.0007	.077	1.443	12.734	.415	6.997	.48	18.1	1.715	3, 4, 6
No skills-No job	-.027	.137	-.007	.777	1.439	12.985	.691	13.264	.58	26.3	1.169	
Inevitable-Can be eliminated	-.077	.316	.021	1.787	1.853	12.557	.658	11.739	.53	21.4	3.650	1, 3, 8
Individual responsibility-Social responsibility	.095	.418	.004	.401	1.673	12.042	.789	13.308	.54	22.0	2.298	
5. Inflation:												
Bad-Good	-.030	.176	.001	.126	1.661	18.027	.766	16.425	.69	42.9	1.032	3, 5
Recession-Prosperity	.223	.930	-.011	.936	1.631	10.827	.588	8.982	.41	13.1	1.192	
Inevitable-Controllable	.205	.907	.018	1.689	1.623	11.160	.639	10.327	.46	16.6	1.921	8
Democratic-Republican	.152	.965	.001	.247	.943	7.905	.400	8.347	.34	9.9	1.725	
Cost push-Demand pull	-.514	2.304	-.011	1.060	1.533	12.153	.518	8.247	.49	17.8	4.314	1, 7
6. High Unemployment:												
Democratic-Republican	.066	.384	-.005	.635	1.142	8.509	.431	8.312	.37	11.2	1.859	3
Recession-Prosperity	.075	.370	-.0007	.071	1.347	10.934	.441	7.204	.40	12.9	1.33	
Inflation-Deflation	-.130	.546	.032	2.742	1.816	13.347	.682	11.901	.54	22.9	.641	8
Fact of life-Controllable	-.215	1.166	.007	.848	1.235	10.085	.509	8.772	.37	11.6	2.736	
Bad-Good	.075	.848	.003	.420	1.243	15.146	.653	13.304	.60	29.0	.934	

APPENDIX D
(continued)

Regression Results on Student Attitudes
Section 61, Economics 223

ISSUE	AGE		HIGH SCHOOL		VSAT		MSAT		SEX		EXPCODE	
	1		2		3		4		5		6	
7. Federal Income Tax:												
Progressive-Regressive	-.018	.235	.021	.210	.0009	.141	.0003	.512	.167	.640	-.088	.860
Bad-Good	.003	.055	-.179	2.249	.0006	1.158	.0002	.359	-.330	1.556	.142	1.743
Democratic-Republican	-.005	.095	.059	.833	-.00001	.032	-.00006	.130	.134	.729	-.046	.639
Socialism-Free enterprise	.056	.658	.098	.893	-.0007	1.036	-.00007	.089	-.009	.031	-.189	1.704
Too high-Too low	-.046	.774	-.076	1.010	.0005	1.077	.0002	.544	.160	.806	-.168	2.160
Unfair-Fair	.046	.573	-.217	2.112	-.001	1.421	.0002	.310	.149	.547	-.056	.533
8. Increasing the Money Supply:												
Hurts people-Helps people	-.045	.740	.070	.901	.0001	.298	-.0001	.270	-.056	.276	.057	.716
Inflation-Recession	-.077	1.277	-.036	.477	.00005	.105	-.0006	1.247	.322	1.602	-.093	1.203
More paper-More gold	.098	1.318	.170	1.819	-.0001	.221	.0004	.729	.050	.202	-.172	1.787
Democratic-Republican	-.066	1.191	-.092	1.302	.0002	.556	.0009	.182	-.236	1.296	.018	.253
Free enterprise-Socialism	-.138	1.822	-.149	1.586	.001	1.563	.0002	.300	-.200	.809	-.003	.032
9. Foreign Trade:												
Desirable-Undesirable	-.008	.145	.036	.493	-.0003	.760	.0008	1.571	-.192	.982	.044	.565
Should be encouraged-Should be discouraged	-.046	.783	.033	.453	.0001	.245	.0006	1.185	.153	.791	.049	.658
Important-Unimportant	-.083	1.488	-.013	.190	-.0001	.373	.0006	1.255	-.086	.467	-.024	.344
Should be apolitical-Should be political	-.194	2.332	.013	.130	.001	1.668	.0001	.176	.096	.351	-.017	.161
Should be free-Should be controlled	.030	.308	-.014	1.177	-.0001	.214	-.0005	.679	-.050	.155	.029	.235

APPENDIX D
(continued)

ISSUE	RELIGION		TUCE IMP		SWAT		ATT		R^2	F	CONSTANT	OTHER VARIABLES
	7		8		9		10		11	12	13	14
7. Federal Income Tax:												
Progressive-Regressive	-.436	2.015	.007	.667	1.74	10.536	.436	8.706	.46	16.4	.904	7
Bad-Good	-.129	.744	-.004	.503	1.341	11.287	.704	12.791	.49	18.5	.781	2, 6
Democratic-Republican	-.006	.045	-.00009	0	.943	8.252	.337	5.621	.27	7.09	1.866	
Socialism-Free enterprise	-.015	.063	.037	3.308	1.837	12.094	.178	2.717	.51	20.2	.742	6, 8
Too high-Too low	-.420	2.556	.011	1.438	1.141	11.974	.626	11.207	.51	19.8	1.02	6, 7
Unfair-Fair	.284	1.277	.010	.971	1.708	13.849	.736	13.968	.57	25.8	.029	2
8. Increasing the Money Supply:												
Hurts people-Helps people	.291	1.725	.013	1.699	1.326	14.422	.564	10.922	.53	22.0	1.968	7, 8
Inflation-Recession	-.320	1.934	.012	1.541	1.067	11.256	.312	6.730	.44	14.9	2.62	5, 7
More paper-More gold	.183	.894	.002	.286	1.029	7.778	.285	6.618	.30	8.2	- .99	2, 6
Democratic-Republican	.091	.602	.002	.292	1.103	9.792	.353	6.285	.38	11.4	3.12	
Free enterprise-Socialism	.077	.381	.010	1.093	1.410	11.167	.446	7.740	.45	15.5	3.153	1
9 Foreign Trade:												
Desirable-Undesirable	-.176	1.092	.011	1.500	1.08	13.088	.556	11.473	.54	23.1	.481	
Should be encouraged-Should be discouraged	-.028	.179	.004	.528	1.05	12.486	.517	11.832	.53	21.6	1.164	
Important-Unimportant	.032	.214	.018	2.581	1.048	12.724	.444	9.584	.49	19.0	2.006	8
Should be apolitical-Should be political	.291	1.288	-.001	.130	1.537	12.880	.571	11.188	.51	20.6	3.48	1, 3
Should be free-Should be controlled	.004	0	-.003	.274	1.906	11.136	.744	13.012	.52	20.8	.415	

APPENDIX D
(continued)

Regression Results on Student Attitudes
Section 61, Economics 223

ISSUE	AGE 1		HIGH SCHOOL 2		VSAT 3		MSAT 4		SEX 5		EXPCODE 6	
10. Labor Unions:												
Bad-Good	.056	.760	-.047	.506	-.0005	.933	-.0001	.249	-.025	.105	-.001	0
Ineffective-Effective	.007	.114	-.128	1.513	-.001	1.987	-.0003	.566	-.022	.100	.070	.816
Important-Unimportant	-.040	.723	.019	.281	.0007	1.599	-.0001	.370	.081	.439	-.05	.687
Unfair-Fair	-.075	1.148	.024	.297	.0006	1.121	-.0003	.595	-.051	.232	.050	.599
Irresponsible-Responsible	-.002	.032	-.052	.608	-.0007	1.250	.0002	.352	.105	.464	-.006	.071
Socialistic-Capitalistic	-.018	.217	-.074	.691	.0001	.138	.0003	.464	-.060	.214	.023	.217
Greedy-Selfless	.011	.182	.023	.286	.0001	.302	-.0003	.541	.303	1.323	-.009	.114
Unnecessary-Necessary	-.081	1.141	-.104	1.161	-.0008	1.332	.0002	.465	.041	.176	.032	.349
11. Big Business:												
Good-Bad	.028	.400	.098	1.089	-.0001	.235	.0003	.559	.007	.032	-.035	.385
Declining-Growing	.067	1.170	-.060	.832	.0004	.946	.0005	1.01	.153	.812	.004	.055
Should be free-Should be controlled	.011	.134	-.067	.632	-.00002	.032	-.0008	1.093	.083	.295	.213	1.948
Pays share-Has a free ride	.019	.192	-.109	.849	0	0	.0005	.553	.059	.176	.089	.680
Socially responsible-Socially irresponsible	.089	1.014	-.071	.642	.0005	.756	-.0002	.338	.436	1.511	.011	.105
Competitive-Monopolistic	.052	.607	-.127	1.179	-.0002	.363	.00008	.100	-.037	.134	-.029	.274
12. Capitalism:												
A reality-A non-reality	-.068	.954	.151	1.692	.00002	.444	.0007	1.184	-.096	.416	-.110	1.208
Desirable-Undesirable	-.001	0	-.016	.232	.0004	.974	-.0005	1.086	-.071	.391	.152	2.119
Declining-Growing	.032	.437	.100	1.068	.0003	.574	.0003	.541	-.086	.351	.486	.508

APPENDIX D
(continued)

ISSUES	RELIGION 7		TUCE IMP 8		SWAT 9		ATT 10		R^2 11	F 12	CONSTANT 13	OTHER VARIABLES 14
10. Labor Unions:												
Bad-Good	-.059	.217	.0007	.077	1.42	11.130	.795	17.477	.62	31.3	- .179	
Ineffective-Effective	-.017	.095	.019	2.182	1.223	9.636	.559	11.118	.46	16.8	2.026	3, 8
Important-Unimportant	-.143	.938	.005	.700	1.124	12.184	.642	15.103	.60	28.8	.868	
Unfair-Fair	-.211	1.180	.002	.318	1.334	13.008	.689	16.157	.63	33.2	1.774	
Irresponsible-Responsible	-.228	1.223	.0003	.363	1.346	12.357	.728	16.089	.64	35.0	.719	
Socialistic-Capitalistic	.375	1.549	.004	.438	1.581	11.305	.705	13.293	.52	20.6	.607	
Greedy-Selfless	-.231	1.316	.005	.691	1.217	11.934	.656	12.627	.54	22.9	.085	
Unnecessary-Necessary	-.048	.247	-.0009	.100	1.295	10.063	.720	15.377	.58	27.1	2.51	
11. Big Business:												
Good-Bad	.121	.661	.002	.251	1.224	10.742	.571	12.116	.51	20.1	- .080	
Declining-Growing	.125	.840	-.005	.754	1.103	9.746	.644	12.624	.48	17.8	.732	
Should be free-Should be controlled	.059	.268	-.010	.964	1.407	9.028	.640	10.668	.42	14.0	1.192	6
Pays share-Has a free ride	-.137	.513	-.016	1.238	1.765	9.995	.534	8.786	.40	12.6	.189	
Socially responsible-Socially irresponsible	-.469	2.044	-.005	.456	1.829	11.844	.642	12.277	.56	24.2	-1.732	7
Competitive-Monopolistic	.010	.045	-.012	1.096	1.279	8.60	.539	8.696	.35	10.2	.693	
12. Capitalism:												
A reality-A non-reality	-.242	1.318	.002	.307	1.328	12.656	.623	12.389	.56	24.5	1.44	2
Desirable-Undesirable	-.095	.650	.008	1.198	1.292	15.55	.757	18.054	.69	43.4	.238	6
Declining-Growing	-.314	1.600	.004	.439	1.601	14.199	.662	13.255	.60	28.2	- .509	7

APPENDIX D
(continued)

Regression Results on Student Attitudes
Section 61, Economics 223

ISSUE	AGE 1		HIGH SCHOOL 2		VSAT 3		MSAT 4		SEX 5		EXPCODE 6	
12. Capitalism (continued):												
Superior to socialism-Inferior to socialism	-.051	.701	-.118	1.270	.0007	1.166	.0002	.300	.423	1.745	.073	.769
Socially irresponsible-Socially responsible	-.050	.606	-.018	.176	.0006	.959	.00001	0	-.422	1.574	.152	1.421
Monopolistic-Competitive	-.002	.045	.038	.497	-.0002	.422	-.0002	.513	-.401	1.916	-.078	.979
Politically involved-Politically uninvolved	-.021	.288	-.096	1.067	.0006	.993	-.0004	.643	.292	1.234	.044	.479
13. Market Mechanisms:												
Efficient-Inefficient	-.081	1.406	-.115	1.574	.0006	1.339	.0009	1.921	.069	.366	-.064	.876
Practical-Theoretical	.005	.071	.018	.184	-.0009	1.470	-.0001	.224	.461	1.797	.100	1.012
Workable-Unworkable	-.028	.522	-.018	.279	-.0001	.290	.0007	1.552	-.001	0	.018	.274
Desirable-Undesirable	-.060	1.108	.013	.190	.0002	.558	.0003	.620	-.185	1.029	.034	.486
Abstract-Concrete	-.018	.281	-.034	.417	-.0001	.214	.001	2.154	-.329	1.533	-.165	1.939
High prices-Low prices	.047	.819	.117	1.619	-.0009	1.939	.001	2.247	.28	1.466	-.063	.851
Allocates-Does not allocate	.049	.775	.123	1.523	-.001	2.161	.001	3.142	.135	.600	-.151	1.852

APPENDIX D
(continued)

ISSUE	RELIGION 7		TUCE IMP 8		SWAT 9		ATT 10		R^2 11	F 12	CONSTANT 13	OTHER VARIABLES 14
12. Capitalism (continued):												
Superior to socialism-Inferior to socialism	.128	.668	-.006	.716	1.28	10.794	.576	11.694	.50	18.9	.789	5
Socially irresponsible-Socially responsible	-.032	.155	.006	.587	1.52	11.224	.702	12.498	.49	18.6	1.48	
Monopolistic-Competitive	-.020	.126	.010	1.308	1.338	15.013	.733	14.839	.64	34.1	1.04	5
Politically involved-Politically uninvolved	.058	.315	-.007	.801	1.47	13.960	.600	10.756	.54	22.2	.87	
13. Market Mechanisms:												
Efficient-Inefficient	-.163	1.084	.004	.594	1.364	14.05	.430	9.306	.54	22.3	1.56	4
Practical-Theoretical	.114	.571	-.003	.355	1.636	13.67	.568	10.025	.57	25.7	.784	5
Workable-Unworkable	-.257	1.857	.001	.148	1.276	13.51	.37	8.240	.53	21.5	1.29	7
Desirable-Undesirable	-.052	.366	-.010	1.439	1.24	13.20	.437	8.295	.49	18.3	2.03	
Abstract-Concrete	-.416	2.456	-.001	.161	1.36	13.89	.586	10.972	.57	25.1	1.12	4, 6, 7
High prices-Low prices	.089	.592	.006	.865	1.196	11.98	.668	11.645	.50	19.2	- .728	2, 3, 4
Allocates-Does not allocate	-.386	2.319	.008	.991	1.241	9.92	.529	7.804	.44	15.2	- .563	3, 4, 6, 7

APPENDIX E

Regression Results on Student Attitudes
Section 62, Economics 223

ISSUE	AGE 1		HIGH SCHOOL 2		VSAT 3		MSAT 4		SEX 5		EXPCODE 6	
1. Decision Making:												
Simple-Complex	.04	.915	.10	1.200	.0009	1.528	.00004	.054	-.3924	2.238	-.130	1.590
Random-Rational	.015	.346	.039	.497	.0007	1.301	.0004	.744	.261	1.652	.06	.784
Apolitical-Political	.010	.144	.217	1.843	-.0004	.498	.007	.854	.374	1.566	-.123	1.098
Important to me-Irrelevant to me	-.040	.837	-.016	.187	-.0009	1.558	.0003	.566		1.459	.117	1.445
Important to society-Irrelevant to society	-.04	1.344	.003	.063	-.0002	.622	.0002	.469	-.317	1.154	.030	.558
2. Government Spending Deficit:												
Desirable-Undesirable	.1398	2.190	-.044	.384	-.0014	1.753	.001	1.316	.0995	.427	.038	.352
Democratic-Republican	.024	.492	-.024	.279	.00004	.063	.0001	.238	-.223	1.247	-.113	1.396
Promotes inflation-Promotes depression	-.022	.435	-.132	1.452	-.0007	1.117	-.0007	1.076	.229	1.199	-.014	.158
Decreases demand-Increases demand	.065	1.378	.1295	1.544	.00016	.272	.0006	1.008	.257	1.145	.147	1.830
3. Government Controls such as Wage-Price Freezes:												
Undesirable-Desirable	-.069	1.006	.072	.600	.0007	.793	.0003	.393	-.0295	.118	-.018	.151
Democratic-Republican	-.143	3.079	.002	.31	.0002	.330	-.0002	.426	.1097	.664	.066	.839
Socialism-Free enterprise	.0187	.343	-.025	.256	-.0006	.965	-.0002	.282	-.085	.431	-.171	1.842
Ineffective-Effective	-.040	.679	.015	.141	-.0005	.692	.0007	1.012	-.235	1.104	-.055	.543
Distort market operations-Facilitate market operations	-.083	1.387	.144	1.367	-.00096	1.323	.0002	.225	.159	.736	.036	.354

*First entry in a column is the regression coefficient and the second entry is the "t" statistic.

APPENDIX E
(continued)

ISSUE	RELIGION 7		TUCEIMP 8		SWAT 9		ATT 10		R^2 11	F 12	CONSTANT 13	OTHER VARIABLES** 14
1. Decision Making:												
Simple-Complex	.137	.447	.003	.266	1.1097	7.896	.600	7.744	.34	9.75	.617	5
Random-Rational	.116	.626	-.009	.999	1.15	11.175	.595	11.157	.49	17.9	.236	5
Apolitical-Political	.038	.134	-.011	.796	1.240	6.682	.542	6.877	.27	7.0	1.38	2
Important to me-Irrelevant to me	-.216	1.068	-.0055	.548	1.364	14.487	.488	10.940	.59	26.7	1.342	
Important to society-Irrelevant to society	-.2396	1.794	.003	.393	1.234	15.482	.175	6.503	.58	26.3	1.794	7
2. Government Spending Deficit:												
Desirable-Undesirable	-.295	1.073	-.016	1.205	1.535	8.729	.320	6.172	.35	10.1	-1.2099	1, 3
Democratic-Republican	-.5796	2.884	-.006	.596	1.385	11.104	.568	9.235	.43	15.3	.81468	7
Promotes inflation-Promotes depression	.2596	1.212	.0002	0	1.367	10.881	.485	8.848	.46	15.6	1.74166	
Decreases demand-Increases demand	.075	.375	.005	.534	1.39	14.508	.753	11.229	.595	27.0	-1.06233	6
3. Government Controls such as Wage-Price Freezes;												
Undesirable-Desirable	.2698	.942	.0075	.535	1.7117	11.108	.782	14.138	.55	23.3	.75866	
Democratic-Republican	.121	.627	-.0096	1.028	1.350	14.932	.501	9.579	.59	27.0	4.16204	1
Socialism-Free enterprise	-.099	.428	-.015	1.288	1.479	12.385	.515	10.784	.54	21.7	1.30996	6
Ineffective-Effective	.083	.333	-.006	.476	1.596	13.088	.733	15.241	.62	29.9	1.16740	
Distort market operations-Facilitate market operations	.351	1.312	-.0095	.764	1.729	13.292	.563	10.387	.54	21.5	2.24064	

**Column number identifying those variables other than ATT and SWAT which were significant in a particular regression.

APPENDIX E
(continued)

Regression Results on Student Attitudes
Section 62, Economics 223

ISSUE	AGE 1		HIGH SCHOOL 2		VSAT 3		MSAT 4		SEX 5		EXPCODE 6	
4. Poverty:												
Lazy-Lack of opportunity	.046	1.171	-.022	.313	-.0007	1.392	-.0001	.194	.059	.419	-.065	.967
Unimportant-Serious	.020	.450	.0995	1.257	-.0005	.994	-.0002	.400	.0467	.288	-.158	2.098
Market determined-Overt discrimination	-.060	1.198	-.002	0	.0008	1.357	.0001	.197	-.327	1.818	.057	.679
No skills-No jobs	-.085	1.603	-.039	.412	-.0004	.568	.0007	1.063	.108	.524	-.055	.606
Inevitable-Can be eliminated	-.009	.134	.014	.118	.0007	.843	.0001	.167	.263	1.072	.050	.453
Individual responsibility-Social responsibility	-.0498	.875	-.058	.572	.0003	.496	-.0006	.841	-.313	1.413	-.132	1.362
5. Inflation:												
Bad-Good	.0496	.896	.0696	.702	-.0008	1.226	.005	.718	.368	1.833	-.151	1.618
Recession-Prosperity	-.049	.780	-.168	1.590	.0015	2.019	-.00006	.077	-.016	.070	.167	1.573
Inevitable-Controllable	-.009	.134	.062	.541	.001	1.701	-.0004	.544	-.004	0	-.044	.400
Democrat-Republican	-.0009	0	-.110	1.455	-.0009	1.716	.0009	1.679	.301	1.944	-.061	.834
Cost push-Demand pull	-.016	.256	-.085	.793	-.0007	.996	.0008	1.053	.114	.503	.066	.639
6. High Unemployment:												
Democrat-Republican	.0112	.279	.0897	1.289	-.0007	1.523	.0009	1.786	-.284	2.008	-.037	.554
Recession-Prosperity	-.018	.346	-.076	.824	-.001	2.048	.0006	1.003	.40036	2.056	.024	.272
Inflation-Deflation	.018	.236	.183	1.384	-.00008	.089	.0009	.999	-.2095	.751	.156	1.238
Fact of life-Controllable	-.015	.286	-.048	.522	.0004	.651	.001	1.906	.048	.254	.048	.548
Bad-Good	-.041	1.013	.024	.331	-.001	2.207	.0007	1.437	-.108	.744	.059	.861

APPENDIX E
(continued)

ISSUE	RELIGION 7		TUCEIMP 8		SWAT 9		ATT 10		R^2 11	F 12	CONSTANT 13	OTHER VARIABLES 14
4. Poverty:												
Lazy-Lack of opportunity	.223	1.354	.006	.761	1.334	14.785	.750	17.885	.66	36.0	.23246	
Unimportant-Serious	-.107	.561	.0098	1.047	1.065	8.300	.494	6.920	.34	9.2	1.94433	6
Market determined-Overt discrimination	-.084	.401	-.0138	1.344	1.299	11.653	.420	7.602	.45	15.0	2.21500	5
No skills-No jobs	-.028	.130	-.0005	.044	1.554	13.960	.625	12.525	.58	25.1	1.99551	1
Inevitable-Can be eliminated	.079	.288	-.001	.070	1.794	12.660	.689	12.331	.53	21.2	- .13543	
Individual responsibility-Social responsibility	.007	.031	.0009	.077	1.4988	11.580	.619	11.528	.49	17.4	2.70035	
5. Inflation:												
Bad-Good	.034	.148	.002	.202	1.771	16.238	.711	12.965	.62	31.2	- .77549	5, 6
Recession-Prosperity	-.0339	1.277	.006	.478	1.367	9.199	.458	7.389	.35	10.3	1.71190	3
Inevitable-Controllable	.385	1.413	.001	.109	1.5396	9.964	.637	9.782	.43	14.2	.47868	3
Democrat-Republican	.157	.866	.0002	0	1.179	10.568	.564	9.279	.45	15.6	.85520	3, 4, 5
Cost push-Demand pull	.126	.491	.0006	.044	1.684	12.202	.4298	7.489	.47	16.5	1.10639	
6. High Unemployment:												
Democrat-Republican	-.032	.192	-.011	1.402	1.309	12.489	.531	11.278	.53	21.2	1.35518	4, 5
Recession-Prosperity	.052	.234	-.002	.212	1.317	11.836	.296	5.630	.46	15.8	1.35002	3, 5
Inflation-Deflation	.1296	.415	-.029	1.901	1.869	11.920	.624	9.354	.45	15.7	.09837	8
Fact of life-Controllable	.265	1.209	.007	.612	1.255	9.492	.454	7.409	.35	10.1	.97102	4
Bad-Good	.241	1.415	-.007	.840	1.302	16.053	.605	11.063	.61	29.98	1.43705	3

APPENDIX E
(continued)

Regression Results on Student Attitudes
Section 62, Economics 223

ISSUE	AGE 1		HIGH SCHOOL 2		VSAT 3		MSAT 4		SEX 5		EXPCODE 6	
7. Federal Income Tax:												
Progressive-Regressive	.048	.884	.052	.543	-.0001	.221	-.001	1.648	-.2699	1.387	.095	1.032
Bad-Good	.024	.472	.022	.242	-.0001	.173	.0009	1.460	.191	1.011	.104	1.220
Democrat-Republican	-.029	.732	-.025	.359	-.00037	.785	.0002	.494	-.043	.303	-.002	.031
Socialism-Free enterprise	-.0177	.279	.023	.202	.002	2.254	-.0001	.181	-.271	1.134	-.040	.372
Too high-Too low	.0285	.823	-.063	1.025	-.0008	1.933	.0007	1.624	.1326	1.061	.076	1.291
Unfair-Fair	.037	.631	-.045	.431	-.001	1.688	.0017	2.386	.425	2.002	.243	2.454
8. Increasing the Money Supply:												
Hurts people-Helps people	.02605	.598	.05626	.736	-.00065	1.273	.00038	.712	.08926	.572	.14452	1.982
Inflation-Recession	.08500	1.757	-.15689	1.830	.00053	.922	-.00015	.248	-.08013	.450	-.04105	.502
More paper-More gold	.06884	1.347	-.21904	2.402	.00028	.452	.00019	.306	-.23756	1.286	-.08354	.965
Democratic-Republican	-.01954	.536	.02877	.459	.00037	.879	.00021	.480	-.01387	.109	.03686	.613
Free enterprise-Socialism	.02257	.430	-.22869	2.428	.00052	.835	-.00040	.624	-.12724	.667	-.01258	.141
9. Foreign Trade:												
Desirable-Undesirable	.00071	.000	.01522	.234	-.00082	1.878	.00113	2.464	-.00416	.031	.03269	.525
Should be encouraged-Should be discouraged	.03374	.848	.01125	.158	-.00102	2.134	.00137	2.779	.25721	1.784	.08763	1.294
Important-Unimportant	.05114	1.311	.01623	.234	-.00162	3.524	.00150	3.132	.07921	.541	.08984	1.366
Should be apolitical-Should be political	.01105	.173	-.14560	1.297	-.00010	.134	.00001	0	-.01854	.083	.14734	1.387
Should be free-Should be controlled	-.05043	.709	.18292	1.438	-.00184	2.169	.00064	.721	.42456	1.594	-.15265	1.275

APPENDIX E
(continued)

ISSUE	RELIGION 7		TUCEIMP 8		SWAT 9		ATT 10		R^2 11	F 12	CONSTANT 13	OTHER VARIABLES 14
7. Federal Income Tax:												
Progressive-Regressive	.093	.412	-.016	1.427	1.407	8.757	.228	4.868	.36	10.7	1.24167	4
Bad-Good	.0199	.094	.0006	.054	1.154	10.348	.570	10.639	.455	15.7	.27892	
Democrat-Republican	-.244	1.487	-.0014	.167	.866	7.596	.371	5.779	.2699	6.95	2.37671	
Socialism-Free enterprise	.392	1.460	-.0035	.260	1.674	10.578	.128	1.856	.45	15.3	1.63702	3
Too high-Too low	.1238	.854	-.0016	.232	1.160	15.934	.752	17.798	.687	41.4	- .15438	3, 4
Unfair-Fair	.076	.308	.001	.083	1.615	14.384	.715	14.074	.61	29.96	-1.21161	3, 4, 5, 6
8. Increasing the Money Supply:												
Hurts people-Helps people	-.09988	.545	.01362	1.530	1.13938	11.811	.57536	11.789	.51	19.5	.66333	6
Inflation-Recession	-.22797	1.119	.00067	.063	1.21925	12.181	.53335	9.617	.49	17.8	- .91732	1, 2
More paper-More gold	-.16015	.746	-.01780	1.649	.95453	8.123	.39272	9.340	.385	11.7	- .00899	2, 8
Democratic-Republican	-.08527	.575	.00289	.397	.99137	9.421	.52954	9.544	.397	12.4	1.25841	
Free enterprise-Socialism	-.40674	1.842	-.01639	1.503	1.36534	10.908	.40208	7.280	.42	13.8	1.11618	2, 7
9. Foreign Trade:												
Desirable-Undesirable	.18078	1.171	-.01115	1.453	1.11116	15.175	.59116	13.475	.63	32.4	.28996	3, 4
Should be encouraged Should be discouraged	.12636	.756	-.00479	.573	1.19978	15.234	.60689	13.322	.64	33.1	- .78939	3, 4, 5
Important-Unimportant	.07574	.462	-.00782	.940	1.20790	15.782	.63698	11.811	.64	34.0	- .64171	3, 4
Should be apolitical-Should be political	.26754	.955	.02294	1.756	1.66825	13.791	.51932	9.808	.56	23.97	.21093	8
Should be free-Should be controlled	.24136	.812	.00004	0	1.74959	11.049	.74586	13.053	.52	20.4	1.46310	3

APPENDIX E
(continued)

Regression Results on Student Attitudes
Section 62, Economics 223

ISSUE	AGE 1		HIGH SCHOOL 2		VSAT 3		MSAT 4		SEX 5		EXPCODE 6	
10. Labor Unions:												
Bad-Good	-.055	.932	.026	.246	.0003	.537	-.0007	1.067	.211	.947	-.169	1.685
Ineffective-Effective	.046	.868	-.162	1.717	-.0004	.658	.001	1.870	.132	.661	-.056	.622
Important-Unimportant	.030	.772	.026	.376	-.0003	.633	.0001	.328	-.050	.349	-.100	1.489
Unfair-Fair	.006	.137	-.02	.230	.001	1.705	-.0004	.759	.131	.700	-.039	.474
Irresponsible-Responsible	.015	.298	-.064	.709	.0004	.770	-.0008	1.329	.087	.452	-.089	1.042
Socialistic-Capitalistic	.047	.810	-.093	.892	.0002	.383	-.00006	.077	-.011	.054	-.037	.374
Greedy-Selfless	.0146	.275	-.017	.181	.007	1.122	.001	1.507	.208	1.075	-.045	.500
Unnecessary-Necessary	.02236	.392	-.02821	.279	-.00026	.388	.00046	.639	.33100	1.599	.07014	.723
11. Big Business:												
Good-Bad	-.06035	1.179	-.08133	.909	-.00028	.471	-.00064	1.013	-.04209	.223	-.06529	.766
Declining-Growing	-.02125	.491	.09632	1.265	.00083	1.627	-.00045	.855	.06369	.407	.04477	.620
Should be free-Should be controlled	.01204	.212	.02049	.204	-.00099	1.486	.00072	1.032	.10081	.498	-.17842	1.860
Pays share-Has a free ride	-.00430	.054	.20774	1.598	-.00059	.678	.00179	1.962	.16476	.622	.02590	.209
Socially responsible-Socially irrespoinsible	.04180	.609	-.04550	.376	-.00152	1.873	.00138	1.632	-.07017	.284	-.03588	.314
Competitive-Monopolistic	-.06965	1.201	-.01586	.154	-.00084	1.235	.00120	1.684	.13535	.655	.04297	.444
12. Capitalism:												
A reality-A non-reality	-.043	.850	.0007	0	-.00002	.044	.0001	.270	-.109	.597	-.015	.176
Desirable-Undesirable	.021	.431	-.032	.378	-.0001	.313	-.0003	.610	-.073	.415	-.060	.738
Declining-Growing	.041	.732	-.040	.410	.0008	1.220	-.001	2.019	-.003	0	-.030	.322

APPENDIX E
(continued)

ISSUE	RELIGION 7		TUCEIMP 8		SWAT 9		ATT 10		R^2 11	F 12	CONSTANT 13	OTHER VARIABLES 14
10. Labor Unions:												
Bad-Good	-.236	.957	.330	2.749	1.45	10.536	.78	16.752	.63	32.2	1.212	6, 8
Ineffective-Effective	-.231	1.029	.006	.601	1.40	9.622	.796	13.382	.51	19.4	-1.06	2, 4
Important-Unimportant	.304	1.835	-.002	.331	1.17	13.257	.698	15.596	.63	33.3	.0007	7
Unfair-Fair	.148	.719	.016	1.587	1.39	12.503	.781	17.774	.65	35.5	- .43	3
Irresponsible-Respoinsible	-.188	.884	.006	.590	1.306	11.485	.787	13.507	.64	33.3	.187	
Socialistic-Capitalistic	-.029	.118	.007	.597	1.568	12.716	.682	13.438	.56	24.7	- .235	
Greedy-Selfless	.34426	1.545	.01746	1.580	1.23915	10.261	.56059	9.887	.446	15.26	- .96020	
Unnecessary-Necessary	.06595	.273	.01617	1.369	1.53571	11.099	.80790	14.632	.566	24.74	- .78384	
11. Big Business:												
Good-Bad	.07359	.347	.00238	.228	1.43522	14.219	.68886	14.710	.62	31.3	2.20500	
Declining-Growing	.18035	.997	.00653	.729	1.28381	11.636	.61516	12.103	.49	18.3	1.27538	3
Should be free-Should be controlled	.05791	.240	-.00761	.652	1.36916	9.853	.72163	11.907	.465	16.3	.67729	6
Pays share-Has a free ride	.27748	.908	-.02626	1.722	1.71635	9.944	.67301	11.471	.48	17.6	- .29187	4, 8
Socially responsible Socially irresponsible	.26298	.925	-.00964	.672	1.64188	10.526	.70759	12.641	.51	19.6	- .19929	3, 4
Competitive-Monopolistic	.44741	1.866	-.02172	1.815	1.32166	8.994	.51944	8.757	.36	10.5	2.58516	4, 7, 8
12. Capitalism:												
A reality-A non-reality	-.041	.197	-.020	1.951	1.320	13.318	.549	11.836	.56	24.8	1.657	8
Desirable-Undesirable	-.118	.580	-.015	1.576	1.109	10.440	.437	8.192	.42	13.6	1.12	
Declining-Growing	.335	1.410	-.011	.929	1.62	14.081	.758	14.710	.61	30.5	.046	4

APPENDIX E
(continued)

Regression Results on Student Attitudes
Section 62, Economics 223

ISSUE	AGE 1		HIGH SCHOOL 2		VSAT 3		MSAT 4		SEX 5		EXPCODE 6	
12. Capitalism (continued):												
Superior to socialism-Inferior to socialism	.011	.236	.011	.134	-.001	3.281	.0005	.843	-.047	.275	.171	2.118
Socially irresponsible-Socially responsible	-.053	.863	.044	.412	-.001	1.396	.0002	.354	.120	.544	-.031	.304
Monopolistic-Competitive	-.030	.657	-.045	.564	-.0005	1.025	.0008	1.465	-.005	.031	.008	.114
Politically involved-Politically uninvolved	-.080	1.679	-.036	.434	-.0002	.450	.0001	.298	.086	.494	-.165	2.101
13. Market Mechanism:												
Efficient-Inefficient	.045	.883	-.0001	0	.0001	.246	.0004	.642	.304	1.685	-.013	.158
Practical-Theoretical	-.044	.712	.159	1.466	-.001	1.503	.002	3.277	-.09	.411	.21	2.039
Workable-Unworkable	.077	1.886	.085	1.177	-.0001	.200	.0009	1.796	-.067	.464	-.042	.618
Desirable-Undesirable	.078	1.685	.026	.320	.0001	.322	-.0006	1.041	-.045	.275	-.013	.170
Abstract-Concrete	.023	.386	-.093	.888	.002	2.951	-.001	1.618	-.088	.411	.101	1.004
High prices-Low prices	-.051	1.126	-.179	2.256	-.0002	.448	.00006	.118	.055	.334	-.094	1.264
Allocates-Does not allocate	.046	.861	.119	1.272	-.0003	.044	.0009	1.392	.092	.484	-.009	.109

APPENDIX E
(continued)

ISSUE	RELIGION 7		TUCEIMP 8		SWAT 9		ATT 10		R^2 11	F 12	CONSTANT 13	OTHER VARIABLES 14
12. Capitalism (continued):												
Superior to socialism-Inferior to socialism	-.138	.693	-.016	1.660	1.346	12.880	.703	15.514	.64	33.2	1.040	3, 6, 8
Socially irresponsible-Socially responsible	.360	1.386	-.008	.667	1.507	10.592	.719	12.320	.49	18.3	1.794	
Monopolistic-Competitive	.125	.654	-.017	1.876	1.169	11.419	.484	9.934	.47	17.0	1.512	8
Politically involved-Politically uninvolved	.111	.563	-.012	1.255	1.42	14.425	.634	12.750	.60	28.9	2.324	1, 6
13. Market Mechanism:												
Efficient-Inefficient	-.013	.063	-.001	.158	1.300	10.109	.348	6.395	.38	11.9	- .421	5
Pracitcal-Theoretical	.214	.823	-.007	.673	1.72	13.660	.584	9.262	.56	24.5	.594	4, 6
Workable-Unworkable	.125	.735	-.007	.832	1.223	11.979	.328	6.625	.47	16.8	- .71	1, 4
Desirable-Undesirable	-.093	.486	-.008	.903	1.251	10.601	.449	8.012	.42	13.6	- .287	1
Abstract-Concrete	-.100	.404	-.002	.161	1.56	12.645	.664	9.506	.51	19.9	- .274	3, 4
High prices-Low prices	-.067	.361	-.026	2.880	1.214	11.108	.537	7.687	.42	13.7	2.34	2, 8
Allocates-Does not allocate	.204	.924	-.013	1.258	1.54	12.448	.665	9.243	.48	17.7	-1.046	

APPENDIX F

Regression Results on Student Attitudes
Section 63, Economics 224

ISSUE	AGE 1		HIGH SCHOOL 2		VSAT 3		MSAT 4		SEX 5		EXPCODE 6	
1. Decision Making:												
Simple-Complex	-.032	.620	-.040	.502	-.0001	.363	-.0006	1.205	.246	1.515	.028	.389
Random-Rational	-.031	.462	-.139	1.379	.0002	.316	-.0006	.867	-.332	1.616	-.011	.118
Apolitical-Political	-.019	.152	.040	.207	-.0009	.832	.002	1.840	.289	.742	-.195	1.103
Important to me-Irrelevant to me	.097	1.228	-.139	1.168	-.0003	.540	-.0005	.648	.133	.552	-.206	1.829
Important to society-Irrelevant to society	.008	.100	.050	.379	.0002	.243	-.001	1.202	-.092	.341	-.024	.202
2. Government Spending Deficit:												
Desirable-Undesirable	.194	2.459	.056	.505	.0005	.813	-.001	1.647	.002	0	.061	.556
Democratic-Republican	-.181	2.121	-.033	.274	.0007	1.014	.0004	.479	-.165	.619	-.114	.974
Promotes inflation-Promotes depression	-.016	.238	-.045	.447	.0004	.760	.0003	.485	.268	1.295	.038	.406
Decreases demand-Increases demand	-.102	1.368	-.022	.192	.00003	.045	.0006	.793	.059	.253	.006	.063
3. Government Controls such as Wage-Price Freeze												
Undesirable-Desirable	-.075	.608	-.174	.951	-.001	1.555	.0004	.369	.638	1.766	.210	1.262
Democratic-Republican	-.151	1.672	-.046	.121	.001	1.734	.0003	.389	.391	1.441	.017	.020
Socialism-Free enterprise	-.168	2.242	-.013	.118	.0003	.464	.0004	.527	.321	1.400	-.201	1.905
Ineffective-Effective	.007	.063	-.241	1.332	-.001	1.066	.0007	.573	.315	.877	-.078	.477
Distort market operations-Facilitate market operations	-.128	1.296	-.099	.672	-.005	.554	-.0007	.669	.220	.718	-.240	1.701

APPENDIX F
(continued)

ISSUE	RELIGION 7		TUCEIMP 8		SWAT 9		ATT 10		BG1359 11		FAGE 12	
1. Decision Making:												
Simple-Complex	.061	.241	-.010	.976	1.039	7.860	.861	8.63	-.020	.828	-.015	1.319
Random-Rational	-.007	0	.006	.460	1.195	8.425	.639	8.34	-.005	.187	.005	.382
Apolitical-Political	.693	1.133	-.019	.753	1.257	4.62	.568	4.483	.073	1.239	.009	.318
Important to me-Irrelevant to me	-.149	.395	.014	.941	1.553	11.674	.755	9.448	-.008	.221	-.017	.984
Important to society-Irrelevant to society	.129	.308	.002	.152	1.466	9.411	.589	4.617	.009	.214	-.009	.467
2. Government Spending Deficit:												
Desirable-Undesirable	.304	.797	.024	1.554	1.272	8.854	.582	9.195	-.116	3.133	.008	.480
Democratic-Republican	-.163	.412	.024	1.492	1.065	5.908	.390	3.634	.012	.313	.011	.593
Promotes inflation-Promotes depression	.213	.638	-.007	.564	1.289	10.748	.842	10.180	.025	.801	-.016	1.072
Decreases demand-Increases demand	-.258	.723	-.018	1.258	1.251	8.104	.644	8.121	-.007	.212	-.001	.071
3. Government Controls such as Wage-Price Freeze												
Undesirable-Desirable	.798	1.391	.004	.187	1.968	7.696	.685	7.580	-.011	.040	-.084	3.125
Democratic-Republican	-.575	1.354	-.016	.826	1.362	6.984	.454	5.165	.004	.105	.014	.738
Socialism-Free enterprise	-.119	.332	.005	.132	1.423	10.489	.721	9.705	.013	.389	.011	.663
Ineffective-Effective	.057	.106	.025	1.053	1.535	6.897	.617	6.863	-.086	1.543	-.014	.549
Distort market operations-Facilitate market operations	.312	.670	.044	2.276	1.433	7.772	.428	6.141	.001	.032	-.015	.683

APPENDIX F
(continued)

Regression Results on Student Attitudes
Section 63, Economics 224

ISSUE	MAGE 13		FED 14		MED 15		CONSTANT 16	R^2 17	F 18	OTHER VARIABLES 19
1. Decision Making:										
Simple-Complex	.019	1.532	.005	.429	.009	.554	1.254	.57	7.002	
Random-Rational	.014	.910	-.007	.414	.040	1.845	2.462	.58	7.29	5, 15
Apolitical-Political	.025	.837	-.096	2.938	.030	.713	- .470	.41	3.69	4, 14
Important to me-Irrelevant to me	.007	.402	.015	.727	-.019	.724	- .621	.72	13.41	6
Important to society-Irrelevant to society	.010	.486	.036	1.612	-.031	1.074	.735	.62	8.49	14
2. Government Spending Deficit:										
Desirable-Undesirable	-.0008	.045	.024	1.198	-.018	.478	-2.673	.65	9.72	1, 4, 11
Democratic-Republican	-.022	1.092	.029	1.332	.0005	0	4.33	.41	3.64	1
Promotes inflation-Promotes depression	.009	.612	-.003	.221	-.001	.077	.614	.70	12.13	
Decreases demand-Increases demand	.016	.950	-.040	2.066	-.014	.563	2.859	.60	7.805	14
3. Government Controls such as Wage-Price Freeze										
Undesirable-Desirable	.065	2.321	-.017	.538	.021	.518	2.808	.59	7.366	5, 12, 13
Democratic-Republican	-.010	.508	-.016	.731	.018	.643	3.04	.52	5.589	1, 3
Socialism-Free enterprise	-.003	.176	.013	.705	-.026	1.038	2.55	.71	12.78	1, 6
Ineffective-Effective	-.005	.184	-.004	.161	.019	.481	1.381	.54	6.06	
Distort market operations-Facilitate market operations	-.002	.095	.015	.609	.004	.134	4.103	.58	7.139	6, 8

APPENDIX F
(continued)

ISSUE	AGE 1		HIGH SCHOOL 2		VSAT 3		MSAT 4		SEX 5		EXPCODE 6	
4. Poverty:												
Lazy-Lack of opportunity	-.065	.770	.140	1.099	-.0006	.851	-.001	1.547	.005	0	-.122	1.027
Unimportant-Serious	-.0007	0	-.026	.081	-.00001	0	-.0007	1.112	.192	1.019	.057	.675
Market determined-Overt discrimination	-.076	.949	-.019	.161	-.005	.729	-.0005	.605	.140	.556	-.093	.678
No skills-No jobs	.164	1.708	-.271	1.908	.0005	.432	.001	1.750	-.052	.182	-.051	.373
Inevitable-Can be eliminated	-.161	1.559	.047	.297	.001	1.308	-.0005	.430	.330	1.040	-.125	.832
Individual responsibility-Social responsibility	-.242	2.353	.050	.311	-.0001	.192	0	0	-.088	.265	-.251	1.724
5. Inflation:												
Bad-Good	.105	1.134	-.032	.224	-.001	1.237	.0007	.703	.046	.164	-.049	.370
Recession-Prosperity	-.130	.943	.133	.613	-.0004	.365	.002	1.887	-.116	.274	.075	.382
Inevitable-Controllable	.0006	0	-.018	.114	.002	2.364	-.002	1.743	.133	.409	-.083	.542
Democrat-Republican	-.209	3.258	-.057	.602	.001	2.347	-.0006	.881	-.032	.173	-.171	1.886
Cost push-Demand pull	.125	1.040	.124	.689	-.001	1.228	.0001	.105	.665	1.832	-.053	.305
6. High Unemployment:												
Democrat-Republican	.054	.693	-.076	.616	.0007	.965	-.0008	1.013	-.0007	.032	-.101	.905
Recession-Prosperity	-.052	.486	.108	.650	-.0008	.863	.0003	.261	-.092	.286	.103	.683
Inflation-Deflation	.170	1.259	.141	.684	.0008	.633	-.00008	.055	-.194	.467	.005	.032
Fact of life-Controllable	-.103	1.121	.190	1.327	.0007	.823	-.0002	.237	.131	.463	-.152	1.167
Bad-Good	.111	1.324	-.041	.316	.00008	.105	-.0003	.339	-.164	.639	.178	1.502

APPENDIX F
(continued)

Regression Results on Student Attitudes
Section 63, Economics 224

ISSUE	RELIGION 7		TUCEIMP 8		SWAT 9		ATT 10		BG1359 11		FAGE 12	
4. Poverty:												
Lazy-Lack of opportunity	.341	.835	.019	1.125	1.400	10.299	.915	11.459	-.029	.744	-.011	.344
Unimportant-Serious	.168	.322	-.002	.567	1.074	9.211	.821	9.575	.002	.095	-.007	.512
Market determined-Overt discrimination	.129	.333	.038	2.422	1.378	10.412	.683	8.088	-.025	.675	.013	.731
No skills-No jobs	.030	.063	.009	.513	1.573	7.487	.673	7.861	-.019	.442	-.031	1.477
Inevitable-Can be eliminated	-.412	.650	.012	.578	1.427	7.060	.740	9.195	.044	.930	.024	1.032
Individual responsibility Social responsibility	.015	.032	-.022	1.096	1.709	8.887	.899	8.703	.118	2.488	-.007	.332
5. Inflation:												
Bad-Good	.122	.276	.024	1.264	1.605	7.546	.735	11.066	-.029	.691	.002	.118
Recession-Prosperity	-.534	.804	-.008	.303	1.750	5.703	.510	4.270	.008	.130	.031	.952
Inevitable-Controllable	-.462	.896	.016	.746	1.308	5.764	.577	5.559	.148	2.952	.002	.095
Democrat-Republican	-.102	.352	-.035	2.904	1.263	8.078	.537	7.249	-.002	.100	.004	.326
Cost push-Demand pull	-.109	.190	-.004	.176	1.543	5.648	.413	3.437	-.078	1.443	-.005	.221
6. High Unemployment:												
Democrat-Republican	-.260	.670	.006	.428	1.315	6.669	.625	6.129	-.059	1.519	-.004	.239
Recession-Prosperity	.125	.247	-.020	.975	1.511	7.675	.536	5.337	-.005	.110	-.027	1.141
Inflation-Deflation	.743	1.149	.021	.760	1.988	7.579	.662	7.280	-.011	.182	.056	1.794
Fact of life-Controllable	-.140	.319	-.008	.486	1.169	5.977	.543	4.788	.064	1.509	.041	1.941
Bad-Good	.023	.055	.005	.316	1.603	10.237	.695	6.443	.054	1.349	-.004	.239

APPENDIX F
(continued)

ISSUE	MAGE 13		FED 14		MED 15		CONSTANT 16	R^2 17	F 18	OTHER VARIABLES 19
4. Poverty:										
Lazy-Lack of opportunity	.021	1.064	.003	.148	.022	.816	1.659	.72	13.26	
Unimportant-Serious	.017	1.181	-.0009	.063	.009	.439	.339	.65	9.80	
Market determined-Overt discrimination	-.017	.927	.021	1.002	-.026	1.014	2.677	.70	12.34	8
No skills-No jobs	.032	1.436	-.002	.114	.024	.799	-4.277	.57	7.02	1, 2, 4
Inevitable-Can be eliminated	-.014	.572	-.019	.680	.066	1.939	3.347	.65	9.54	15
Individual responsibility-Social responsibility	.031	1.310	.038	1.370	-.066	1.978	3.758	.63	8.32	1, 6, 11, 15
5. Inflation:										
Bad-Good	.015	.686	-.021	.792	-.014	.467	-2.063	.72	12.93	
Recession-Prosperity	-.040	1.179	-.027	.731	.055	.110	2.795	.42	3.60	4
Inevitable-Controllable	-.019	.750	-.011	.387	-.066	1.820	2.702	.56	6.45	3, 4, 11, 15
Democrat-Republican	-.018	1.251	-.017	1.053	-.008	.418	6.36	.68	10.88	1, 3, 6, 8
Cost push-Demand pull	-.005	.210	-.004	.152	-.005	.145	.356	.39	3.275	5
6. High Unemployment:										
Democrat-Republican	.0001	0	-.025	1.119	.011	.423	.904	.59	7.277	
Recession-Prosperity	.021	.849	.002	.089	.038	1.062	1.889	.525	5.471	
Inflation-Deflation	-.065	2.004	.026	.720	-.059	1.316	-2.605	.570	6.654	12, 13
Fact of life-Controllable	-.032	1.464	-.020	.829	-.049	1.593	3.352	.460	4.268	12
Bad-Good	-.0009	.045	-.028	1.263	.014	.476	-1.364	.657	9.460	

APPENDIX F
(continued)

Regression Results on Student Attitudes
Section 63, Economics 224

ISSUE	AGE 1		HIGH SCHOOL 2		VSAT 3		MSAT 4		SEX 5		EXPCODE 6	
7. Federal Income Tax:												
Progressive-Regressive	.161	1.455	-.042	.255	-.0005	.557	-.0001	.141	.253	.760	.086	.557
Bad-Good	.015	.148	.190	1.210	-.0006	.632	.002	1.890	-.145	.456	.230	1.550
Democrat-Republican	-.145	2.804	-.00005	0	.0002	.524	-.0007	.122	-.043	.268	-.095	1.270
Socialism-Free enterprise	.027	.239	.122	.713	.0005	.463	-.0008	.696	.133	.385	.326	2.043
Too high-Too low	-.049	.592	-.152	1.217	.0001	.232	.001	1.163	-.041	.167	.110	.952
Unfair-Fair	.036	.295	.041	.217	-.0001	.118	-.001	1.486	.051	.134	-.021	.118
8. Increasing Money Supply:												
Hurts people-Helps people	.117	1.207	-.057	.390	.0003	.405	-.0005	.476	.039	.134	-.065	.473
Inflation-Recession	.035	.493	.010	.100	.0006	.908	-.001	1.967	-.299	1.387	.027	.268
More paper-More gold	.035	.531	.133	1.276	.001	3.133	-.0006	.686	-.151	.764	-.044	.470
Democratic-Republican	-.062	.961	.063	.641	-.00009	.152	.003	.427	-.135	.679	-.069	.758
Free enterprise-Socialism	.025	.326	-.114	.974	.0004	.578	-.0004	.517	.209	.880	.018	.167
9. Foreign Trade:												
Desirable-Undesirable	.069	1.155	.184	1.996	.0003	.691	-.001	1.702	-.0003	0	-.094	1.110
Should be encouraged-Should be discouraged	.068	1.088	.208	2.191	.0002	.356	.0001	.256	-.011	.054	-.106	1.236
Important-Unimportant	.108	1.565	.069	.673	.0005	.788	.0001	.151	-.215	1.007	-.007	.077
Should be apolitical-Should be political	.207	1.826	.193	1.157	.0001	.100	.0004	.375	-.568	1.687	.309	1.948
Should be free-Should be controlled	.073	.462	.126	.510	-.001	1.103	-.001	.730	-.038	.077	.434	1.926

APPENDIX F
(continued)

ISSUE	RELIGION 7		TUCEIMP 8		SWAT 9		ATT 10		BG1359 11		FAGE 12	
7. Federal Income Tax:												
Progressive-Regressive	-.408	.784	-.030	1.406	1.723	9.587	.577	5.998	-.021	.420	-.010	.407
Bad-Good	.184	.374	-.045	2.209	1.513	7.173	.771	7.502	.094	1.970	.025	1.105
Democrat-Republican	-.069	.274	-.024	2.311	.879	6.080	.355	5.144	.028	1.141	-.006	.554
Socialism-Free enterprise	.587	1.091	.011	.510	1.370	6.647	.649	7.139	-.043	.825	.026	1.034
Too high-Too low	-.119	.302	-.008	.532	1.415	8.532	.848	9.251	.020	.540	.005	.286
Unfair-Fair	.423	.707	-.008	.336	1.799	7.429	.608	6.766	.060	1.052	.028	1.009
8. Increasing Money Supply:												
Hurts people-Helps people	.136	.297	.005	.302	1.202	5.054	.608	5.742	-.103	2.304	.003	.138
Inflation-Recession	-.132	.387	-.011	.766	.990	6.438	.463	6.058	-.032	.995	-.008	.509
More paper-More gold	.768	2.369	-.026	1.932	1.215	8.790	.411	5.479	.008	.255	.034	2.263
Democratic-Republican	-.055	.176	.011	.872	.952	5.806	.369	2.984	-.003	.105	-.002	.190
Free enterprise-Socialism	-.337	.906	.005	.358	1.126	7.801	.448	5.236	.041	1.167	.019	1.104
9. Foreign Trade:												
Desirable-Undesirable	.284	.980	.001	.152	.850	3.996	.352	5.207	.007	.235	.012	.927
Should be encouraged-Should be discouraged	.305	1.038	.008	.709	.938	4.684	.380	5.814	-.051	1.772	-.016	1.162
Important-Unimportant	.206	.632	.004	.303	.971	5.141	.253	3.967	-.030	.937	.001	.083
Should be apolitical-Should be political	-.482	.911	-.017	.777	1.509	7.817	.669	8.218	-.027	.534	-.031	1.235
Should be free-Should be controlled	.360	.472	-.058	1.811	2.048	5.719	.561	5.145	-.038	.494	-.060	1.679

APPENDIX F
(continued)

Regression Results on Student Attitudes
Section 63, Economics 224

ISSUE	MAGE 13		FED 14		MED 15		CONSTANT 16	R^2 17	F 18	OTHER VARIABLES 19
7. Federal Income Tax:										
Progressive-Regressive	.002	.084	-.055	1.885	.008	.217	- .936	.648	9.204	14
Bad-Good	-.031	1.279	.006	.228	-.005	.145	- .915	.581	6.958	4, 8, 11
Democrat-Republican	.007	.568	-.006	.436	.010	.566	4.564	.502	5.044	1, 8
Socialism-Free enterprise	-.024	.910	.004	.161	-.086	2.299	1.201	.534	5.743	6, 15
Too high-Too low	-.026	1.366	.029	1.318	-.006	.064	.997	.639	8.855	
Unfair-Fair	-.037	1.253	-.011	.333	.040	.946	.787	.559	6.353	
8. Increasing Money Supply:										
Hurts people-Helps people	-.015	.670	-.007	.303	-.001	.045	- .056	.416	3.565	11
Inflation-Recession	-.006	.379	.037	1.999	-.005	.217	1.553	.507	5.159	4, 14
More paper-More gold	-.035	2.176	-.008	.451	-.016	.713	.120	.653	9.301	3, 7, 8, 12, 13
Democratic-Republican	-.018	1.186	.155	1.418	-.014	.674	3.702	.406	3.422	
Free enterprise-Socialism	-.023	1.279	.037	1.749	.006	.232	- .212	.598	7.459	14
9. Foreign Trade:										
Desirable-Undesirable	-.020	1.419	.007	.465	-.002	.118	.007	.430	3.881	2, 4
Should be encouraged Should be discouraged	.003	.242	-.005	.371	-.002	.137	- .043	.477	4.634	2, 11
Important-Unimportant	-.168	.104	-.017	.959	-.002	.094	- .945	.395	3.364	
Should be apolitical-Should be political	.020	.760	-.019	.678	.022	.628	-2.287	.634	8.784	1, 5, 6
Should be free-Should be controlled	.048	1.270	-.005	.141	.028	.536	1.764	.438	4.010	6, 8, 12

APPENDIX F
(continued)

Regression Results on Student Attitudes
Section 63, Economics 224

ISSUE	AGE 1		HIGH SCHOOL 2		VSAT 3		MSAT 4		SEX 5		EXPCODE 6	
10. Labor Unions:												
Bad-Good	-.060	.547	-.017	.104	-.002	2.016	.001	1.571	.472	1.373	.069	.451
Ineffective-Effective	.091	.840	-.121	.730	.00008	.083	.00009	.077	-.007	.031	-.016	.109
Important-Unimportant	.064	.829	-.030	.264	-.00004	.054	.0001	.219	.021	.089	-.004	.044
Unfair-Fair	-.006	.089	.088	.721	-.001	2.010	.0007	.941	.271	1.116	.011	.100
Irresponsible-Responsible	.005	.063	.072	.508	-.0008	.934	.0007	.796	.315	1.121	.111	.836
Socialistic-Capitalistic	-.186	1.790	.053	.337	.004	.510	.0004	.400	-.040	.126	-.062	.421
Greedy-Selfless	-.013	.170	.028	.234	.0002	.164	.0002	.333	.094	.386	-.076	.660
Unnecessary-Necessary	-.091	.934	-.037	.248	-.0009	1.053	.001	.981	.359	1.202	-.076	.551
11. Big Business:												
Good-Bad	.104	1.272	.011	.094	-.0008	1.059	.0003	.419	.124	.493	-.063	.557
Declining-Growing	-.045	.516	.072	.547	.001	2.203	0	0	-.643	2.421	-.066	.543
Should be free-Should be controlled	-.044	.772	.047	.523	-.0001	.207	-.0008	.122	.090	.498	-.047	.585
Pays share-Has a free ride	.052	.463	.281	1.644	-.001	1.057	.001	1.477	.422	1.223	.250	1.568
Socially responsible-Socially irresponsible	.097	.938	-.112	.717	-.0005	.600	-.0002	.178	.448	1.417	.259	1.787
Competitive-Monopolistic	-.035	.403	.151	1.145	-.001	1.770	.002	2.637	.221	.807	-.050	.407
12. Capitalism:												
Reality-Non-reality	-.068	.900	.192	1.684	-.0005	.762	.0003	.466	.312	1.325	.039	.368
Desirable-Undesirable	.103	1.318	-.002	0	.00003	.031	.001	1.366	-.054	.236	.151	1.413
Declining-Growing	.095	.973	-.012	.089	-.0002	.298	.0008	.822	.014	.044	.068	.497

APPENDIX F
(continued)

Regression Results on Student Attitudes
Section 63, Economics 224

ISSUE	RELIGION 7		TUCEIMP 8		SWAT 9		ATT 10		BG1359 11		FAGE 12	
10. Labor Unions:												
Bad-Good	.228	.432	.015	.728	1.379	7.085	.830	9.356	.018	.359	.015	.618
Ineffective-Effective	.023	.044	-.012	.594	1.361	6.599	.653	6.334	-.069	1.384	.022	.886
Important-Unimportant	-.084	.228	.0004	.031	1.337	9.851	.588	6.531	.023	.655	-.021	1.236
Unfair-Fair	-.223	.602	-.008	.546	1.327	9.930	.862	13.205	.039	1.085	-.013	.766
Irresponsible-Responsible	.328	.756	.004	.234	1.383	8.956	.772	10.445	-.054	1.287	-.007	.378
Socialistic-Capitalistic	.494	.985	.028	1.338	1.397	7.505	.698	7.898	-.057	1.170	-.002	.094
Greedy-Selfless	.383	.967	-.006	.398	1.231	8.994	.686	7.868	-.026	.688	-.017	.969
Unnecessary-Necessary	.069	.148	-.018	.978	1.479	7.168	.666	8.173	.056	1.196	.032	1.479
11. Big Business:												
Good-Bad	-.340	.863	-.011	.670	1.379	9.617	.730	11.010	.035	.919	.001	.077
Declining-Growing	-.972	2.328	-.022	1.280	1.214	7.999	.636	5.541	.012	.298	.018	.898
Should be free-Should be controlled	-.077	.275	-.006	.560	1.157	11.650	.759	14.007	-.006	.248	-.011	.834
Pays share-Has a free ride	.573	1.052	-.016	.726	1.827	9.188	.748	9.356	-.074	1.428	.004	.167
Socially responsible-Socially irresponsible	.196	.391	-.005	.242	1.743	10.283	.772	9.779	-.067	1.407	.004	.161
Competitive-Monopolistic	.487	1.144	-.018	1.072	1.298	6.921	.899	10.415	.008	.197	.036	1.829
12. Capitalism:												
Reality-Non-reality	-.049	.134	.041	2.734	1.427	11.145	.656	10.171	.005	.151	-.010	.618
Desirable-Undesirable	-.148	.407	-.010	.689	1.349	8.582	.621	8.061	.030	.844	-.005	.333
Declining-Growing	-.350	.740	.012	.616	1.625	9.346	.790	10.535	-.007	.173	-.011	.532

APPENDIX F
(continued)

ISSUE	MAGE 13		FED 14		MED 15		CONSTANT 16	R^2 17	F 18	OTHER VARIABLES 19
10. Labor Unions:										
Bad-Good	-.011	.442	.028	.967	-.007	.216	.083	.653	9.693	3
Ineffective-Effective	-.003	.141	.073	1.331	.004	.118	-2.056	.524	5.577	
Important-Unimportant	.008	.473	-.032	1.618	.002	.089	.318	.651	9.583	14
Unfair-Fair	.010	.568	.051	2.552	.012	.472	- .766	.772	17.383	3, 14
Irresponsible-Responsible	.021	.973	.026	1.146	.007	.260	-1.183	.726	13.668	
Socialistic-Capitalistic	.002	.100	-.057	2.142	.020	.563	4.206	.622	8.462	1, 14
Greedy-Selfless	.030	1.611	-.011	.535	.024	.935	.174	.650	9.574	
Unnecessary-Necessary	-.018	.788	.017	.674	-.012	.376	1.181	.609	8.004	
11. Big Business:										
Good-Bad	-.003	.040	-.034	1.638	-.018	.676	- .679	.725	13.589	14
Declining-Growing	-.009	.480	.003	.176	.011	.158	1.143	.566	6.702	3, 5, 7
Should be free-Should be controlled	.009	.658	-.004	.282	-.005	.311	1.932	.788	19.098	
Pays share-Has a free ride	-.007	.273	-.027	.919	-.010	.289	- .870	.641	9.195	2
Socially responsible-Socially irresponsible	-.005	.216	-.022	.824	-.009	.272	- .870	.690	11.473	6
Competitive-Monopolistic	.009	.449	-.004	.200	-.018	.652	1.454	.666	10.252	3, 4, 12
12. Capitalism:										
Reality-Non-reality	.011	.646	.003	.202	-.017	.692	1.072	.740	14.667	2, 8
Desirable-Undesirable	.032	1.787	-.008	.415	.019	.783	-3.657	.650	9.561	13
Declining-Growing	.021	.938	-.017	.700	.030	.961	-2.683	.673	10.447	

APPENDIX F
(continued)

Regression Results on Student Attitudes
Section 63, Economics 224

ISSUE	AGE 1		HIGH SCHOOL 2		VSAT 3		MSAT 4		SEX 5		EXPCODE 6	
12. Capitalism (continued):												
Superior to socialism-Inferior to socialism	-.004	.044	-.041	.275	.0002	.242	.0008	.792	-.398	1.269	.091	.649
Socially irresponsible-Socially responsible	.020	.207	.112	.752	.001	1.234	.0002	.242	-.303	.993	.003	.031
Monopolistic-Competitive	.067	.760	-.044	.339	.001	1.485	.0001	.109	-.051	.192	.133	1.104
Politically involved-Politically uninvolved	.002	.031	.098	.702	-.00009	1.059	.0006	.598	-.229	.798	.089	.678
13. Market Mechanism:												
Efficient-Inefficient	-.018	.977	.079	.646	.0009	1.191	-.0002	.260	-.198	.789	.013	.114
Practical-Theoretical	-.037	.298	.098	.535	-.0007	.689	.001	.839	.015	.044	.114	.672
Workable-Unworkable	.054	.711	-.099	.859	-.00001	0	-.0003	.402	.018	.083	-.006	.063
Desirable-Undesirable	.080	1.264	-.089	.932	-.0009	1.617	.00006	.077	.287	1.504	-.086	.976
Abstract-Concrete	.076	.781	-.295	2.007	-.001	1.989	.001	1.355	.269	.897	-.142	1.038
High prices-Low prices	.073	1.045	-.225	2.174	.0003	.462	-.0007	1.001	-.014	.070	.031	.339
Allocates-Does not allocate	-.007	.083	.151	1.138	-.0001	.114	-.0008	.083	.115	.430	.033	.270

APPENDIX F
(continued)

ISSUE	RELIGION 7		TUCEIMP 8		SWAT 9		ATT 10		BG1359 11		FAGE 12	
12. Capitalism (continued):												
Superior to socialism-Inferior to socialism	.493	1.057	-.016	.820	1.373	6.410	.724	8.845	.013	.289	.014	.429
Socially irresponsible-Socially responsible	.048	.104	-.009	.514	2.029	9.987	1.032	11.223	.097	2.168	.036	1.615
Monopolistic-Competitive	-.118	.286	.005	.324	1.412	8.006	.587	7.176	.034	.834	-.013	.684
Politically involved-Politically uninvolved	-.094	.214	-.004	.236	1.608	10.120	.789	9.721	-.004	.104	.028	1.339
13. Market Mechanism:												
Efficient-Inefficient	-.379	.957	-.023	1.452	1.408	7.590	.326	4.030	.096	2.508	.007	.396
Practical-Theoretical	-.531	.909	.025	1.044	1.886	8.924	.426	4.281	-.068	1.175	.0005	0
Workable-Unworkable	.042	.118	-.011	.741	1.337	7.879	.328	3.821	-.027	.776	-.007	.205
Desirable-Undesirable	-.320	1.054	-.003	.252	1.130	8.482	.413	5.482	.029	1.014	-.035	2.505
Abstract-Concrete	-.274	.573	-.016	.836	1.300	7.314	.439	4.485	.025	.548	.038	1.734
High prices-Low prices	-.091	.270	-.014	1.060	.969	6.765	.462	4.685	-.004	.137	-.043	2.818
Allocates-Does not allocate	-.220	.519	-.017	.984	1.592	9.280	.473	5.611	.043	1.053	.006	.296

APPENDIX F
(continued)

Regression Results on Student Attitudes
Section 63, Economics 224

ISSUE	MAGE 13		FED 14		MED 15		CONSTANT 16	R^2 17	F 18	OTHER VARIABLES 19
12. Capitalism (continued):										
Superior to socialism-Inferior to socialism	-.025	1.050	.008	.317	.041	1.293	- .078	.578	7.048	
Socially irresponsible-Socially responsible	-.012	1.008	-.047	1.902	.014	.472	-2.00	.678	10.818	11, 12, 14
Monopolistic-Competitive	.025	1.221	.00002	0	-.001	.054	- .736	.597	7.631	
Politically involved-Politically uninvolved	-.024	1.134	.020	.857	.013	.446	- .295	.666	10.273	
13. Market Mechanism:										
Efficient-Inefficient	-.011	.598	-.017	.821	-.031	1.163	3.258	.503	5.206	11
Practical-Theoretical	-.025	.884	.034	1.104	.021	.524	1.792	.557	6.456	
Workable-Unworkable	.006	.382	.0002	0	-.007	.314	.844	.523	5.635	
Desirable-Undesirable	.023	1.622	-.036	2.200	-.028	1.404	.451	.597	7.624	3, 12, 13, 14
Abstract-Concrete	.036	1.569	-.053	.200	.006	.200	1.007	.496	5.056	2, 3, 12
High prices-Low prices	.050	3.084	-.010	.618	.023	1.063	.267	.560	6.558	2, 12, 13
Allocates-Does not allocate	-.030	1.423	-.036	1.580	-.028	.941	2.954	.628	8.701	

APPENDIX G

Regression Results on Student Attitudes
Section 64, Economics 224

ISSUE	AGE 1		HIGH SCHOOL 2		VSAT 3		MSAT 4		SEX 5		EXPCODE 6	
1. Decision Making:												
Simple-Complex	-.04344	.583	-.03881	.472	-.00135	2.373	.00069	1.153	.36285	1.604	-.01325	.164
Random-Rational	-.05281	.595	.11750	1.195	-.00056	.821	.00050	.707	.17240	.649	.16791	1.766
Apolitical-Political	-.08036	.789	-.09766	.870	.00018	.236	-.00060	.737	.20064	.667	.02232	.202
Important to me-Irrelevant to me	.11124	1.243	.20842	2.104	-.00169	2.484	.00041	.566	.27951	1.040	-.02649	.277
Important to society-Irrelevant to society	.10770	1.398	.28383	3.376	-.00053	.923	-.00031	.511	-.19682	.867	.03588	.439
2. Government Spending Deficit:												
Desirable-Undesirable	-.08498	.945	-.13136	1.317	.00071	1.031	-.00137	1.919	-.02790	.104	.01141	.118
Democratic-Republican	-.06758	.864	.14613	1.708	-.00082	1.366	.00060	.972	.20596	.894	.03053	.363
Promotes inflation-Promotes depression	.01486	.189	-.07241	.836	-.00047	.783	.00025	.402	-.27864	1.178	.03959	.467
Decreases demand-Increases demand	.06242	.859	-.15454	1.942	.00064	1.152	.00072	1.256	-.15331	.707	.04910	1.215
3. Government controls such as Wage-Price Freezes:												
Undesirable-Desirable	.08662	.748	.05604	.443	-.00071	.736	.00035	.372	.22943	.664	.07170	.569
Democratic-Republican	-.16161	2.377	.05691	.767	-.00026	.489	.00015	.286	.28310	1.417	-.07165	.992
Socialism-Free enterprise	-.03285	.354	.13371	1.304	-.00179	2.465	-.00009	.122	-.08453	.304	.21044	2.110
Ineffective-Effective	-.03894	.319	.16650	1.242	-.00064	.656	.00015	.151	-.22549	.625	.07687	.585
Distorts market operations-Facilitates market operations	-.02071	.200	.07375	.641	-.00074	.883	.00108	1.272	-.65288	2.095	.00207	0

APPENDIX G
(continued)

Regression Results on Student Attitudes
Section 64, Economics 224

ISSUE	RELIGION 7		TUCEIMP 8		SWAT 9		ATT 10		BG1359 11		FAGE 12	
1. Decision Making:												
Simple-Complex	.29151	1.628	-.03080	1.628	1.06982	9.655	.75428	10.847	.02091	.801	.00433	.447
Random-Rational	-.24247	1.162	-.01168	.914	1.36700	12.121	.76701	10.907	.03447	1.124	.01275	1.116
Apolitical-Political	.09202	.384	.02157	1.454	1.42230	9.802	.64922	8.400	.01749	.496	-.01386	1.062
Important to me-Irrelevant to me	-.23476	1.116	.02564	1.989	1.54857	13.457	.50711	9.768	-.03871	1.253	-.00421	.367
Important to society Irrelevant to society	-.24557	1.341	.00688	.616	1.27934	12.722	.24449	4.780	-.04839	1.836	-.01231	1.259
2. Government Spending Deficit:												
Desirable-Undesirable	.36159	1.707	.02380	1.816	1.32662	11.011	.47034	8.670	-.01445	.463	.02948	2.517
Democratic-Republican	-.24477	1.336	-.01126	1.003	1.10957	8.115	.59406	7.351	-.05373	2.003	.01928	1.910
Promotes inflation-Promotes depression	.08779	.477	.01218	1.083	1.15971	10.370	.45194	7.860	-.00614	.225	.02115	2.098
Decreases demand-Increases demand	-.12591	.740	.00180	.173	1.28533	12.085	.72826	12.406	-.03566	1.408	-.00800	.844
3. Government controls such as Wage-Price Freezes												
Undesirable-Desirable	-.14954	.550	.00203	.122	1.73693	11.469	.58618	8.857	-.04356	1.096	-.01086	.725
Democratic-Republican	-.00537	.031	.00065	.070	1.16671	12.234	.68249	12.891	-.01387	.589	-.00110	.126
Socialism-Free enterprise	-.39837	1.808	-.00929	.692	1.27652	9.482	.56616	9.373	-.00605	.187	.00140	.118
Ineffective-Effective	-.06488	.225	.00387	.219	1.62432	9.447	.70896	10.264	-.00329	.077	-.01820	1.162
Distorts market operations-Facilitates market operations	-.41122	1.669	-.00246	.164	1.60277	11.003	.65538	10.696	.00628	.173	-.01530	1.143

APPENDIX G
(continued)

ISSUE	MAGE 13		FED 14		MED 15		CONSTANT 16	R^2 17	F 18	OTHER VARIABLES 19
1. Decision Making:										
Simple-Complex	-.01047	1.004	.00681	.473	-.02072	1.201	2.37894	.56	11.50106	3, 5, 7, 8
Random-Rational	.01399	1.133	-.00865	.526	.02427	1.188	- .26531	.637	15.73921	6
Apolitical-Political	-.00267	.187	.00404	.212	-.01380	.592	3.32020	.48	8.19700	
Important to me-Irrelevant to me	.00788	.631	-.00390	.232	.05164	2.500	-2.04943	.685	19.46477	2, 3, 8, 15
Important to society-Irrelevant to society	.00587	.552	-.02425	1.702	.05022	2.857	- .51354	.612	14.14535	2, 11, 14, 15
2. Government Spending Deficit:										
Desirable-Undesirable	-.01701	1.300	.00667	.397	-.01587	.762	2.32046	.607	13.83047	4, 7, 8, 12
Democratic-Republican	-.02553	2.349	-.00476	.328	.03103	1.741	2.27387	.437	6.90124	2, 11, 12, 13, 15
Promotes inflation-Promotes depression	-.02109	1.955	.00626	.430	-.02351	1.307	1.19155	.50	9.16815	12, 13
Decreases demand-Increases demand	.00968	.944	.00425	.314	-.00515	.306	- .86256	.63	15.34557	2
3. Government Controls such as Wage-Price Freezes										
Undesirable-Desirable	.02201	1.376	-.00035	0	-.01396	.527	-1.31445	.63	15.63791	
Democratic-Republican	-.00591	.626	.01732	1.384	-.01112	.703	3.95165	.675	18,30411	1
Socialism-Free enterprise	-.00266	.204	-.03167	1.822	.02889	1.350	2.53388	.617	14.45011	3, 6, 7, 14
Ineffective-Effective	.03308	1.930	-.04461	1.967	.01220	.437	1.29404	.585	12.53767	13, 14
Distorts market operations-Facilitates market operations	.01710	1.178	-.04199	2.155	.01141	.476	1.55805	.63	15.29943	5, 7, 14

APPENDIX G
(continued)

Regression Results on Student Attitudes
Section 64, Economics 224

ISSUE	AGE 1		HIGH SCHOOL 2		VSAT 3		MSAT 4		SEX 5		EXPCODE 6	
4. Poverty:												
Lazy-Lack of Opportunity	-.21075	2.264	.01751	.170	.00015	.202	-.00089	1.212	-.03422	.126	.02531	.252
Unimportant-Serious	.02539	.402	-.00103	0	-.00023	.477	.00014	.281	.15194	.814	.13938	2.067
Market determined-Overt discrimination	.22696	2.330	.03490	.322	-.00160	2.157	.00103	1.299	.09877	.337	-.08807	.839
No skills-No jobs	.04394	.407	.01424	.122	.00062	.759	.00134	1.583	-.18473	.538	-.04847	.423
Inevitable-Can be eliminated	-.05646	.558	.19682	1.750	.00030	.388	-.00035	.427	-.35127	1.160	.19774	1.806
Individual responsibility-Social responsibility	-.11020	1.049	-.06174	.541	.00099	1.218	-.00023	.279	-.02595	.083	.00397	.031
5. Inflation:												
Bad-Good	-.03931	.383	.01194	.104	-.00109	1.381	.00098	1.184	.12749	.414	-.31517	2.811
Recession-Prosperity	-.04695	. .389	-.07281	.532	.00121	1.305	.0015	.158	-.01916	.054	.03913	.294
Inevitable-Controllable	-.11211	1.066	.04184	.363	.0058	.725	-.00187	2.259	-.13917	.447	-.02902	.254
Democrat-Republican	-.05336	.777	.01591	.212	-.00064	1.210	.00113	2.068	.21792	1.087	.03664	.504
Cost Push-Demand Pull	.01532	.134	-.13420	1.044	.00148	1.672	-.00021	.223	-.64683	1.903	-.04583	.366
6. High Unemployment:												
Democrat-Republican	-.04018	.621	-.11701	1.639	.00070	1.384	.00017	.340	-.06746	.352	-.06127	.880
Recession-Prosperity	.02840	.337	-.10820	1.164	.00014	.209	.00016	.242	.16118	.644	-.03703	.408
Inflation-Deflation	-.30296	2.382	-.03977	.281	.00106	1.074	-.00131	1.281	.10524	.275	-.16099	1.160
Fact of life-Controllable	-.09446	.974	.06059	.559	.00026	.363	-.00087	1.144	-.28474	1.000	.09307	.875
Bad-Good	.02290	.268	-.00085	0	-.00006	.094	-.00010	.148	.31130	1.216	-.07953	.857

APPENDIX G
(continued)

ISSUE	RELIGION 7		TUCEIMP 8		SWAT 9		ATT 10		BG1359 11		FAGE 12	
4. Poverty:												
Lazy-Lack of Opportunity	.00900	.044	.02049	1.522	1.58173	12.979	.72143	13.625	.00930	.289	-.03097	2.617
Unimportant-Serious	.01073	.070	-.01401	1.544	1.09166	12.127	.71016	14.591	.00604	.277	-.01003	1.246
Market determined-Overt discrimination	.12121	.523	.02743	1.934	1.45808	11.904	.56862	8.233	-.00826	.244	.01764	1.392
No skills-No jobs	.03852	.151	.02644	1.716	1.49695	11.191	.64764	10.207	.08038	2.159	-.01032	.750
Inevitable-Can be eliminated	.09203	.380	-.00925	.622	1.52516	11.605	.85907	16.989	.01798	.507	-.02042	1.552
Individual responsibility-Social responsibility	-.11959	.486	.00748	.500	1.60928	10.933	.83824	14.858	.02012	.554	-.02587	1.932
5. Inflation:												
Bad-Good	.10165	.419	.01153	.778	1.67902	11.879	.68701	11.751	.08166	2.277	-.00880	.660
Recession-Prosperity	.11869	.414	.02612	1.453	1.68971	9.478	.73265	9.268	.00082	0	-.03306	2.108
Inevitable-Controllable	.14871	.590	-.02509	1.660	1.36559	8.245	.72722	11.064	.06521	1.790	-.01436	1.072
Democrat-Republican	-.16348	1.031	.02670	2.729	1.18077	9.825	.70168	9.876	-.00615	.258	.00677	.776
Cost push-Demand pull	-.42318	1.522	-.00409	.244	1.53910	8.080	.36222	4.090	-.03812	.948	.02087	1.431
6. High Unemployment:												
Democrat-Republican	-.07933	.524	.01859	1.998	1.22275	13.228	.65034	12.625	-.02099	.934	.00319	.387
Recession-Prosperity	-.01477	.070	-.00596	.491	1.53062	12.827	.31815	5.184	.02981	1.031	.00555	.515
Inflation-Deflation	-.06374	.209	-.03133	1.650	1.79006	9.882	.64697	9.285	.07722	1.739	.00151	.089
Not controllable-Controllable	.10469	.463	.00526	.376	1.15352	7.922	.53193	5.850	.00055	0	-.00853	.687
Bad-Good	.13955	.686	-.00532	.430	1.30959	9.629	.40887	6.696	.03773	1.272	-.00031	.031

APPENDIX G
(continued)

Regression Results on Student Attitudes
Section 64, Economics 224

ISSUE	MAGE 13		FED 14		MED 15		CONSTANT 16	R^2 17	F 18	OTHER VARIABLES 19
4. Poverty:										
Lazy-Lack of opportunity	.01870	1.444	-.00439	.254	.00513	.234	5.68609	.685	19.16835	1, 12
Unimportant-Serious	.01182	1.351	-.00641	.547	-.01514	1.043	.79386	.667	17.90011	6
Market determined-Overt discrimination	-.01145	.839	-.00068	.031	.00387	.170	-3.89714	.57	12.07727	1, 3, 8
No skills-No jobs	.00886	.599	-.03165	1.588	.04523	1.808	-1.84794	.60	13.46160	8, 11, 15
Inevitable-Can be eliminated	.02211	1.557	-.01621	.847	-.00212	.089	1.58968	.72	23.25329	2, 6
Individual responsibility-Social responsibility	.01884	1.303	-.02778	1.401	.02778	1.165	2.28999	.66	17.16272	12
5. Inflation:										
Bad-Good	.00964	.653	-.02957	1.536	.04029	1.692	.47368	.655	16.88113	6, 11, 15
Recession-Prosperity	.03053	1.790	-.00021	0	.01403	.500	.48522	.498	8.67569	12, 13
Inevitable-Controllable	.02416	1.657	-.00652	.333	.00029	0	3.32974	.538	10.43056	4, 8, 11, 13
Democrat-Republican	-.01354	1.418	-.01021	.812	.01928	1.207	1.15134	.538	10.20308	4, 8
Cost push-Demand pull	-.01539	.957	-.03154	1.460	.00464	.170	1.20757	.39	5.55850	3, 5
6. High Unemployment:										
Democrat-Republican	.00955	1.046	-.01603	1.343	.01000	.665	.84609	.695	19.95406	2, 8
Recession-Prosperity	-.02082	1.781	.00602	.383	-.00865	.448	.94639	.60	13.40823	13
Inflation-Deflation	.01303	.728	-.01163	.485	.01280	.435	5.83407	.53	10.12333	1, 8, 11
Not controllable-Controllable	.00275	.204	-.00122	.070	.01188	.536	4.10096	.36	5.08727	
Bad-Good	-.00095	.077	.00358	.221	-.01140	.577	.16345	.477	8.10812	

APPENDIX G
(continued)

ISSUE	AGE 1		HIGH SCHOOL 2		VSAT 3		MSAT 4		SEX 5		EXPCODE 6	
7. Federal Income Tax:												
Progressive-Regressive	.03814	.419	.00470	.044	.00107	1.526	.00100	1.378	-.33366	1.225	0.6533	.664
Bad-Good	-.18174	1.736	-.11316	.968	.00066	.822	-.00141	1.683	-.05742	.181	-.32830	2.906
Democrat-Republican	-.07289	.910	.07051	.791	-.00009	.137	-.0032	.507	.28066	1.194	-.00785	.089
Socialism-Free enterprise	-.15040	1.234	.25304	1.870	-.00055	.594	.00024	.250	-.02233	.063	-.12197	.923
Too high-Too low	.02728	.304	-.14167	1.431	.00064	.948	-.00037	.514	.16112	.607	-.00848	.089
Unfair-Fair	-.17286	1.432	.01525	.114	-.00118	1.270	-.00030	.309	.44768	1.233	-.10561	.807
8. Increasing Money Supply:												
Hurts people-Helps people	.10232	.954	.01959	.170	-.00074	.931	.00139	1.696	.10624	.343	-.02885	.258
Inflation-Recession	.05284	.732	-.08162	1.018	-.00024	.428	.00023	.403	.23841	.1097	.03365	.431
More paper-More gold	.23248	2.847	.03206	.349	.00098	1.561	-.00030	.443	.25081	1.032	.24300	2.760
Democratic-Republican	.04720	.565	-.05528	.604	-.00136	2.128	.00022	.339	.25704	1.057	.08234	.929
Free enterprise-Socialism	.11035	1.131	-.13282	1.222	.00054	.731	.00130	1.784	.20361	.699	-.14808	1.389
9. Foreign Trade:												
Desirable-Undesirable	.80817	1.044	-.09069	1.077	.00005	.089	.00040	.648	.14208	.624	-.06644	.801
Should be encouraged-Should be discouraged	.02576	.349	-.11415	1.407	-.00041	.734	.00100	1.697	-.04264	.194	-.04342	.547
Important-Unimportant	.07305	1.000	-.05528	.685	.00027	.475	.00076	1.276	-.05930	.272	.05261	.661
Should be apolitical-Should be political	.16488	1.416	-.07424	.570	-.00093	1.040	.00011	.114	.34763	.988	-.06326	.501
Should be free-Should be controlled	.13110	.878	-.19959	1.205	-.00060	.530	-.00030	.252	.29518	.665	-.07583	.471

APPENDIX G
(continued)

Regression Results on Student Attitudes
Section 64, Economics 224

ISSUE	RELIGION 7		TUCEIMP 8		SWAT 9		ATT 10		BG1359 11		FAGE 12	
7. Federal Income Tax:												
Progressive-Regressive	-.28364	1.309	.00109	.083	1.55184	13.045	.50764	8.156	-.00102	.031	.00344	.289
Bad-Good	.06366	.256	.02813	1.838	1.34887	8.572	.62700	7.301	-.01390	.382	.00266	.194
Democrat-Republican	.16751	.900	.01331	1.164	.99929	6.105	.43862	5.195	.02777	1.008	.00103	.100
Socialism-Free enterprise	.18691	.649	.02904	1.655	1.56945	9.306	.71573	10.093	-.05133	1.291	.01154	.730
Too high-Too low	.23164	1.096	.02198	1.707	1.37502	8.881	.86442	11.507	.02532	.817	-.01195	1.039
Unfiar-Fair	.09498	.330	.3909	2.225	1.63064	9.023	.78784	10.726	-.03514	.835	-.02586	1.649
8. Increasing Money Supply:												
Hurts people-Helps people	.33188	1.363	-.00565	.379	1.18946	6.678	.53190	6.427	.01360	.379	.00839	.618
Inflation-Recession	-.04792	.279	.00137	.130	1.22053	12.578	.46065	7.511	.00552	.221	.01282	1.337
More paper-More gold	-.25701	1.334	.00398	.334	1.32135	12.051	.54658	8.835	.00109	.031	.00317	.294
Democratic-Republican	-.06250	.324	-.01982	1.665	.73683	4.973	.17351	1.908	.00962	.336	-.01718	1.592
Free enterprise-Socialism	.01210	.054	.00172	.122	1.38263	10.160	.53273	7.810	-.04188	1.238	.04558	3.611
9. Foreign Trade:												
Desirable-Undesirable	.25831	1.430	-.00272	.246	1.02382	6.303	.52574	9.454	-.01356	.514	-.00347	.354
Should be encouraged-Should be discouraged	.15260	.879	-.00058	.054	1.13053	7.719	.40833	7.635	-.00120	.044	.01324	1.397
Important-Unimportant	.18688	1.077	.00399	.375	1.12984	6.698	.42039	6.529	.05236	2.067	.00307	.322
Should be apolitical-Should be political	-.52107	1.858	-.00299	.176	1.73991	10.295	.74916	10.461	.04160	1.067	-.00394	.262
Should be free-Should be controlled	.32811	.927	.01006	.467	1.92490	8.873	.72741	9.241	.08240	1.518	-.00851	.438

APPENDIX G
(continued)

ISSUE	MAGE 13		FED 14		MED 15		CONSTANT 16	R^2 17	F 18	OTHER VARIABLES 19
7. Federal Income Tax:										
Progressive-Regressive	-.00280	.216	.00613	.359	.01536	.730	-1.36586	.609	13.95571	
Bad-Good	.00631	.418	.01176	.599	.01208	.493	4.35584	.465	7.73543	1, 4, 6, 8
Democrat-Republican	-.00840	.742	-.01512	1.027	.00145	.077	3.08503	.306	3.85096	
Socialism-Free enterprise	-.00677	.393	-.00656	.288	-.01270	.452	3.34787	.50	10.44393	2, 8
Too high-Too low	.00192	.151	-.00592	.352	.01483	.707	- .61690	.565	11.43917	8
Unfair-Fair	.01572	.914	.00989	.434	.02810	.997	3.56962	.53	10.05018	8
8. Increasing Money Supply:										
Hurts people-Helps people	-.00141	.094	.00388	.200	-.00798	.334	-1.50097	.375	5.32696	4
Inflation-Recession	-.01041	1.023	.02478	1.826	-.01753	1.041	- .65040	.58	12.28286	14
More paper-More gold	-.00311	.266	-.01032	.670	-.02067	1.095	-4.10142	.61	13.98106	1, 6
Democratic-Republican	.01134	.969	.01433	.938	-.01366	.709	2.14494	.286	3.47371	3, 8
Free enterprise-Socialism	-.02613	1.900	.01926	1.057	.02277	1.010	-4.00435	.528	9.95013	4, 12, 13
9. Foreign Trade:										
Desirable-Undesirable	.00745	.703	-.00293	.204	-.04314	2.450	-0.77700	.493	8.77800	15
Should be encouraged-Should be discouraged	-.00728	.707	-.01140	.825	-.01969	1.162	0.15972	.467	7.85499	4
Important-Unimportant	-.00694	.680	-.02794	2.041	-.01333	.792	-0.58417	.419	6.45544	11, 14
Should be apolitical-Should be political	-.00030	.000	.00044	.000	-.02120	.784	-2.45800	.548	10.83377	7
Should be free-Should be controlled	-.01402	.668	-.00144	.054	-.02341	.681	4.14894	.499	8.91981	

APPENDIX G
(continued)

Regression Results on Student Attitudes
Section 64, Economics 224

ISSUE	AGE 1		HIGH SCHOOL 2		VSAT 3		MSAT 4		SEX 5		EXPCODE 6	
10. Labor Unions:												
Bad-Good	-.04567	.475	-.04238	.400	-.00009	.118	-.00034	.442	.13998	.489	-.00016	.000
Ineffective-Effective	-.01577	.192	.02740	.304	-.00001	.000	.00013	.197	.13238	.542	.00168	.000
Important-Unimportant	-.12100	1.668	.00077	.000	-.00061	1.105	.00036	.633	.09379	.434	.04273	.552
Unfair-Fair	.15914	1.766	-.01907	.189	-.00057	.825	-.00060	.843	-.11538	.430	.06100	.628
Irresponsible-Responsible	-.03142	.334	.03281	.316	-.00079	1.074	.00011	.151	.10057	.357	.04830	.477
Socialistic-Capitalistic	.02134	.194	-.10367	.861	.00069	.828	.00044	.497	-.36117	1.115	.04508	.374
Greedy-Selfless	-.04885	.599	-.06816	.746	.00040	.651	-.00046	.705	.18399	.752	-.20470	2.323
Unnecessary-Necessary	.02411	.289	-.01599	.170	-.00042	.660	.00036	.543	.09656	.391	.12388	1.389
11. Big Business:												
Good-Bad	-.06702	.734	-.17101	1.736	.00030	.451	-.00022	.309	-.06113	.234	-.19288	1.994
Declining-Growing	.10791	1.293	-.03297	.370	.00054	.880	-.00015	.238	-.22011	.933	.05733	.657
Should be free-Should be controlled	-.18810	2.028	-.03729	.382	-.00054	.797	.00031	.427	-.05303	.202	-.00528	.054
Pays share-Has a free ride	-.17982	1.508	.04269	.337	.00004	.044	-.00129	1.430	-.35029	1.042	-.23983	1.960
Socially responsible-Socially irresponsible	-.01955	.173	-.00951	.077	.00040	.473	.00028	.325	.32643	1.010	-.07067	.604
Competitive-Monopolistic	-.01937	.164	-.09359	.743	.00013	.154	-.00104	1.146	.05253	.158	.04983	.408
12. Capitalism:												
Reality-Non-reality	.12738	1.437	.06178	.647	-.00019	.296	.00087	1.289	.04181	.167	.02752	.301
Desirable-Undesirable	-.00752	.063	.21187	1.722	-.00114	1.347	.00060	.685	.02888	.089	-.18479	1.549
Declining-Growing	.02098	.212	-.04650	.428	-.00059	.801	.00007	.094	-.15883	.563	.01150	.109

APPENDIX G
(continued)

ISSUE	RELIGION 7		TUCEIMP 8		SWAT 9		ATT 10		BG1359 11		FAGE 12	
10. Labor Unions:												
Bad-Good	.08948	.393	-.00160	.114	1.37029	10.222	.73484	12.440	-.01800	.542	-.00408	.324
Ineffective-Effective	.37521	1.940	-.00128	.109	1.06776	7.505	.50677	6.649	-.00744	.260	-.00353	.334
Important-Unimportant	-.12053	.707	.01418	1.339	1.02684	7.409	.36455	6.344	-.10989	.788	.00419	.450
Unfair-Fair	.00248	.000	.01324	1.004	1.35012	11.599	.78142	12.999	-.01878	.600	.00151	.130
Irresponsible-Responsible	.13434	.604	.01434	1.050	1.46667	11.367	.75675	12.204	-.00045	.000	-.01781	1.442
Socialistic-Capitalistic	.03481	.134	.01785	1.129	1.67712	11.352	.76220	12.065	-.01911	.507	.00971	.691
Greedy-Selfless	-.00528	.031	.01769	1.492	1.22865	10.702	.63802	11.350	-.00132	.044	-.01774	1.667
Unnecessary-Necessary	.34868	1.778	-.01327	1.107	1.30235	10.025	.81875	14.198	-.01801	.621	.02333	2.136
11. Big Business:												
Good-Bad	.04694	.228	-.00663	.527	1.39824	13.022	.58143	10.244	.01124	.367	.00828	.730
Declining-Growing	-.23163	1.231	-.00218	.189	1.20473	10.331	.67936	10.102	-.01252	.444	-.00332	.322
Should be free-Should be controlled	.11386	.551	-.01027	.806	1.24408	10.383	.72219	11.895	-.01847	.598	-.01075	.930
Pays share-Has a free ride	-.02624	.100	-.01327	.816	1.63991	12.135	.69005	11.820	.01907	.478	.00202	.134
Socially responsible-Socially irresponsible	-.03123	.122	-.01501	.969	1.60918	12.189	.73915	12.671	.00503	.130	.01529	1.087
Competitive-Monopolistic	.11765	.444	-.00389	.238	1.65925	10.324	.62449	7.664	.00022	.000	-.01831	1.250
12. Capitalism:												
Reality-Non-reality	.04171	.207	-.00727	.604	1.43827	13.204	.78028	13.212	.04085	1.373	.01300	1.191
Desirable-Undesirable	-.19745	.758	.00919	.564	1.68898	13.390	.45313	5.060	-.00159	.044	-.01058	.742
Declining-Growing	-.06774	.300	.02242	1.624	1.62677	13.272	.76832	14.100	-.03800	1.148	-.00270	.219

APPENDIX G
(continued)

Regression Results on Student Attitudes
Section 64, Economics 224

ISSUE	MAGE 13		FED 14		MED 15		CONSTANT 16	R^2 17	F 18	OTHER VARIABLES 19
10. Labor Unions:										
Bad-Good	-.00051	.031	.00326	.181	.01356	.611	1.81957	.59	12.95640	
Ineffective-Effective	-.01125	.980	0.00578	.375	-.02873	1.516	3.01000	.39	5.74450	7
Important-Unimportant	-.00110	.109	-.00709	.525	.00726	.437	3.18833	.43	6.77284	1
Unfair-Fair	-.00231	.184	-.00135	.077	.01542	.741	-2.06819	.65	16.63553	1
Irresponsible-Responsible	-.00412	.309	-.01495	.841	.02648	1.197	2.14932	.64	16.02950	
Socialistic-Capitalistic	-.01048	.692	-.03066	1.507	-.02232	.884	0.51313	.60	13.50872	
Greedy-Selfless	.01007	.879	-.00092	.063	.00671	.356	1.71822	.627	15.02390	6, 12
Unnecessary-Necessary	-.02904	2.489	.01039	.666	.03277	1.702	-0.34450	.657	17.13456	7, 12, 13, 15
11. Big Business:										
Good-Bad	-.00336	.275	.00224	.137	.00358	.178	1.80880	.648	16.11030	2, 6
Declining-Growing	-.01289	1.148	-.01096	.736	.00350	.189	0.03961	.55	10.75092	
Should be free-Should be controlled	.01728	1.395	-.00760	.456	.02069	1.007	4.24023	.61	13.85005	1
Pays share-Has a free ride	.00983	.605	.01107	.520	.00057	.000	4.44287	.63	14.98611	6
Socially responsible-Socially irresponsible	-.00502	.327	.01046	.521	.00254	.900	-0.74573	.665	17.37708	
Competitive-Monopolistic	.03185	1.985	-.03054	1.459	.04094	1.523	0.98870	.49	8.34440	13
12. Capitalism:										
Reality-Non-reality	-.01333	1.140	-.00383	.244	-.01752	.900	-2.55291	.68	18.66186	
Desirable-Undesirable	.00961	.622	-.01277	.617	.02059	.813	1.31247	.61	13.92109	2
Declining-Growing	-.00089	.070	.00975	.554	-.00419	.192	.45373	.71	21.83059	8

APPENDIX G
(continued)

ISSUE	AGE 1		HIGH SCHOOL 2		VSAT 3		MSAT 4		SEX 5		EXPCODE 6	
12. Capitalism (continued):												
Superior to socialism-Inferior to socialism	-.06308	.700	.03737	.388	.00040	.597	.00096	1.394	.50587	2.001	-.03133	.342
Socially irresponsible-Socially responsible	.06370	.472	-.17572	1.228	-.00096	.978	.00136	1.301	–.05518	.144	.28735	2.084
Monopolistic-Competitive	-.10932	1.199	-.02459	.252	-.00038	.563	-.00072	1.039	.31873	1.215	-.00501	.054
Politically involved-Politically uninvolved	-.11855	1.174	-.10420	.986	.00021	.286	.00052	.682	.30271	1.081	-.10859	1.065
13. Market Mechanism:												
Efficient-Inefficient	.06526	.799	-.14352	1.654	-.00017	.281	.00023	.370	.40639	1.760	-.12913	1.516
Practical-Theoretical	-.01105	.089	-.09931	.762	-.00020	.216	-.00083	.876	-.11674	.334	-.14926	1.178
Workable-Unworkable	.01312	.200	.08961	1.289	-.00063	1.331	.00084	1.699	.25899	1.408	-.03475	.518
Desirable-Undesirable	.05256	.697	.16509	2.084	-.00028	.505	.00177	3.089	.22931	1.082	.05124	.663
Abstract-Concrete	.09470	.741	-.18255	1.347	.00161	1.732	-.00117	1.204	-.08140	.221	-.11782	.894
High prices-Low prices	-.03981	.524	-.04121	.506	.00044	.798	.00007	.118	.01966	.094	-.03754	.483
Allocates-Does not allocate	-.04173	.425	-.03959	.376	.00032	.442	.00007	.089	-.04323	.137	-.17059	1.622

APPENDIX G
(continued)

Regression Results on Student Attitudes
Section 64, Economics 224

ISSUE	RELIGION 7		TUCEIMP 8		SWAT 9		ATT 10		BG1359 11		FAGE 12	
12. Capitalism (continued):												
Superior to socialism-Inferior to socialism	.18999	.955	-.00348	.282	1.51883	12.773	.71405	12.874	.03055	1.008	-.01495	1.352
Socially irresponsible-Socially responsible	.24174	.806	-.01199	.654	1.69293	8.852	.78203	10.461	-.06686	1.483	-.01716	1.024
Monopolistic-Competitive	.06238	.301	.00270	.216	1.35181	11.023	.55147	9.455	.01184	.382	-.00275	.240
Politically involved-Politically uninvolved	.26541	1.198	.01334	.975	1.54022	12.553	.85142	12.980	.03799	1.136	.00337	.270
13. Market Mechanism:												
Efficient-Inefficient	-.12683	.691	-.00759	.673	1.59537	13.685	.38918	6.103	-.02715	.993	-.00021	0
Practical-Theoretical	-.21541	.785	-.00202	.118	1.71502	13.803	.56783	8.369	.05725	1.391	.00555	.364
Workable-Unworkable	-.04714	.316	-.00688	.739	1.21200	14.390	.40265	6.898	.02091	.961	.00093	.114
Desirable-Undesirable	.01726	.104	.00512	.497	1.03534	8.337	.24696	4.068	.03466	1.394	.00420	.443
Abstract-Concrete	.21169	.736	.02831	1.620	1.58256	9.532	.63541	7.311	.02029	.477	.01955	1.234
High prices-Low prices	.08270	.483	.02201	2.129	.93176	9.156	.42597	6.881	-.03643	1.450	-.00037	.044
Allocates-Does not allocate	-.31779	1.384	.00568	.403	1.49173	8.904	.48869	6.036	.00307	.094	-.00219	.176

APPENDIX G
(continued)

ISSUE	MAGE 13		FED 14		MED 15		CONSTANT 16	R^2 17	F 18	OTHER VARIABLES 19
12. Capitalism (continued):										
Superior to socialism-Inferior to socialism	.00220	.181	-.00870	.546	-.00355	.178	.94095	.688	19.16832	5
Socially irresponsible-Socially responsible	.00552	.301	-.00347	.144	-.02758	.935	.08682	.545	10.46121	6
Monopolistic-Competitive	-.00089	.070	.01263	.778	-.01545	.766	3.21647	.60	13.19470	
Politically involved-Politically uninvolved	-.00605	.444	.03849	2.146	.02088	.959	1.24987	.665	17.35890	14
13. Market Mechanism:										
Efficient-Inefficient	-.01083	.992	.00542	.367	-.02064	1.152	.39784	.626	14.63608	2, 5
Practical-Theoretical	.00050	.031	-.02464	1.1267	.00843	.311	1.63506	.615	13.95635	
Workable-Unworkable	-.00401	.459	-.00856	.737	.01250	.868	.42683	.641	15.65633	4
Desirable-Undesirable	-.00309	.303	-.03083	2.324	.01713	1.035	- .93628	.453	7.30939	2, 4, 14
Abstract-Concrete	-.02130	1.243	.02717	1.198	.00986	.344	-2.05359	.482	8.13000	3, 8
High prices-Low prices	-.00547	.537	.01027	.767	-.00267	.161	2.19150	.46	7.57728	8
Allocates-Does not allocate	-.00224	.170	-.04083	2.334	.04887	2.201	1.69583	.516	9.16989	6, 14, 15

APPENDIX H

Attitude Questionnaire for 1974–1975 Academic Year

This questionnaire concerns the usefulness of the CAI (computer) materials that you used this semester. The information obtained will allow us to improve these materials as well as the entire education effort of this course. Please answer the questions as carefully as you can. Although we ask that you identify yourself by listing your I.D. number, the information here will in no way affect your grade in the course.

____

I.D. Number

Circle the correct or most appropriate answers in the questions below.

1. How valuable were the CAI (computer) materials in *your overall learning experience* this semester in Economics 223?

   A. Very much

   B. Considerably

   C. Some help

   D. No help

   E. Not used

2. How valuable were the CAI (computer) materials in *reviewing the Samuelson materials for a test?*

   A. Very valuable

   B. Moderately valuable

   C. Of some value

   D. Of no value

   E. Not used

3. How valuable were the discussion class teaching assistants in *reviewing the Samuelson materials for a test?*

   A. Very valuable

   B. Moderately valuable

   C. Of some value

   D. Of no value

   E. Did not attend the sessions

4. In *terms of your performance on examinations* which of the following helped the most? Rank all of the following: 1 = Highest, 4 = lowest.

   A. CAI materials______

B. Lectures______

C. Discussion Classes______

D. Text______

5. How often did you attend the lecture (note there were *25* lectures)?

   A. Missed no lectures

   B. Missed 3 or fewer

   C. Missed 4–6

   D. Missed 7–9

   E. Missed 10 or more

6. How often did you attend the discussion class (note there were 14 discussion classes)?

   A. Missed no discussion classes

   B. Missed 1 or 2

   C. Missed 3 or 4

   D. Missed 5 or more

7. On the average, how much time did the teaching assistant in the discussion class spend on discussing the Priorities book as opposed to reviewing text or lecture materials?

   A. All of the time

   B. 75 percent of the time

   C. 50 percent of the time

   D. Less than 50 percent of the time

8. On the average, how many hours per week did you spend studying for the course *excluding CAI time and excluding time in discussion classes and lecture sessions*?

   A. 1 hour per week

   B. 2 hours per week

   C. 3 hours per week

   D. 4 or more hours per week

9. Were the CAI (computer) materials the most useful in reviewing?

   A. the Institutional (descriptive) materials, or

   B. the theoretical materials, that is Income Determination and models?

10. Did you use the Review Programs, that is the multiple choice question pro-

grams (note there were 21 such programs)?

A. All of them

B. 75 percent of them

C. 50 percent of them

D. 25 percent of them or less

11. Did you use the other programs, that is the Demonstration and Simulation programs (note there were 8 such programs)?

    A. All of them

    B. 75 percent of them

    C. 50 percent of them

    D. 25 percent of them or less

APPENDIX I

Changes in Student Opinions on Economic Issues
(Standard Deviations in Parentheses)

	Economics 223				Economics 224			
	Section 61		Section 62		Section 63		Section 64	
	Controls	Experimentals	Controls	Experimentals	Controls	Experimentals	Controls	Experimentals
Decision Making for National Economic Policy								
Simple (1)–Complex (5)	0.000	-0.007	-0.150	-0.048	-0.088	-0.109	-0.177	-0.242
	(0.862)	(0.923)	(0.857)	(9.999)	(0.592)	(0.669)	(0.902)	(0.631)
Random (1)–Rational (5)	-0.043	-0.224	-0.378	-0.169	0.0	-0.172	0.131	-0.158
	(0.770)	(1.031)	(1.117)	(0.862)	(0.846)	(0.767)	(0.954)	(0.879)
Political (1)–Apolitical (5)	-0.271	0.014	-0.051	-0.145	-0.074	-0.141	0.082	0.213
	(1.062)	(1.414)	(1.271)	(1.273)	(0.951)	(1.320)	(1.126)	(1.046)
Important to me (1)–Irrelevant to me (5)	-0.956	-0.126	0.100	0.040	0.0	-0.047	-0.024	0.158
	(0.984)	(1.093)	(1.068)	(1.167)	(0.829)	(0.999)	(1.102)	(0.971)
Important to society (1)–Irrelevant to society (5)	0.043	0.126	0.250	0.320	-0.132	0.047	-0.141	0.021
	(0.908)	(1.310)	(1.038)	(1.140)	(0.929)	(0.983)	(1.114)	(0.850)
Government Spending Deficit								
Undesirable (1)–Desirable (5)	-0.648	-0.747	-0.828	-0.797	-0.029	-0.048	-0.141	-0.116
	(1.503)	(1.355)	(1.229)	(1.267)	(0.930)	(0.923)	(1.048)	(1.020)
Democratic (1)–Republican (5)	0.070	-0.007	0.051	0.0	-0.074	-0.079	0.082	-0.053
	(1.019)	(1.014)	(0.889)	(0.946)	(0.903)	(0.768)	(0.903)	(0.608)
Promotes inflation (1)–Promotes depression (5)	0.169	0.356	0.309	0.508	-0.044	-0.141	0.082	0.032
	(1.095)	(1.247)	(1.093)	(1.055)	(0.921)	(0.889)	(0.978)	(0.905)
Increases demand (1)–Decreases demand (5)	0.380	0.329	0.439	0.533	0.074	-0.016	0.129	0.011
	(1.061)	(0.910)	(0.996)	(0.981)	(0.997)	(0.968)	(0.884)	(0.881)

APPENDIX I

Changes in Student Opinions on Economic Issues
(Standard Deviations in Parentheses)

	Economics 223				Economics 224			
	Section 61		Section 62		Section 63		Section 64	
	Controls	Experimentals	Controls	Experimentals	Controls	Experimentals	Controls	Experimentals
Government Controls such as Wage-Price Freezes								
Undesirable (1)–Desirable (5)	-0.042	-0.085	0.082	-0.008	0.191	0.145	0.212	0.074
	(1.259)	(1.252)	(1.298)	(1.292)	(1.162)	(1.291)	(1.001)	(1.214)
Democratic (1)–Republican (5)	-0.141	0.064	-0.101	-0.224	0.1471	0.234	0.082	0.021
	(1.150)	(0.935)	(1.129)	(0.966)	(0.885)	(0.921)	(0.640)	(0.684)
Free enterprise (1)–Socialism (5)	-0.3571	-0.182	-0.031	0.016	0.1765	-0.143	-0.153	0.084
	(1.319)	(1.287)	(1.088)	(1.189)	(0.880)	(1.030)	(0.852)	(0.846)
Effective (1)–Ineffective (5)	0.225	0.232	0.113	0.016	-0.105	0.065	-0.226	-0.137
	(1.244)	(1.096)	(1.224)	(1.182)	(1.075)	(1.199)	(0.923)	(1.217)
Facilitates market operations (1)–Distorts market operations (5)	-9.014	0.070	-0.163	-0.236	0.0	-0.016	-0.282	-0.211
	(1.062)	(1.201)	(1.329)	(1.248)	(0.993)	(1.310)	(1.031)	(0.966)
Poverty								
Laziness (1)–Lack of opportunity (5)	-0.319	-0.359	-0.443	-0.309	-0.132	-0.078	-0.071	-0.234
	(1.157)	(0.902)	(1.030)	(0.924)	(0.862)	(0.841)	(0.828)	(0.999)
Serious (1)–Unimportant (5)	-0.183	-0.126	0.100	-0.136	0.015	0.0	0.047	0.168
	(0.661)	(0.804)	(1.059)	(0.816)	(0.635)	(0.756)	(0.596)	(0.724)
Market determined (1)–Overt discrimination (5)	0.029	-0.021	0.071	0.016	-0.424	-0.206	-0.035	0.032
	(1.076)	(1.236)	(1.256)	(1.048)	(0.824)	(1.065)	(1.219)	(0.973)
No jobs (1)–No skills (5)	0.100	0.105	0.200	0.287	-0.539	-0.318	0.071	-0.234
	(0.919)	(1.124)	(1.117)	(1.276)	(0.969)	(1.075)	(1.153)	(1.062)

Inevitable (1)–Can be eliminated (5)	-0.014	-0.252	-0.052	-0.160	-0.103	0.016	-0.024	-0.138
	(1.378)	(1.381)	(1.341)	(1.334)	(1.186)	(1.024)	(0.938)	(0.979)
Individual responsibility (1)–Social responsibility (5)	-0.191	-0.181	-0.316	-0.294	-0.141	0.049	0.047	0.0
	(1.213)	(1.204)	(1.214)	(1.160)	(1.006)	(1.146)	(0.898)	(1.022)
Inflation								
Bad (1)–Good (5)	-0.563	-0.615	-0.640	-0.464	0.239	0.500	0.141	0.337
	(1.204)	(1.156)	(1.352)	(1.202)	(0.854)	(0.943)	(0.941)	(1.088)
Recession (1)–Prosperity (5)	-0.300	-0.464	-0.440	-0.686	0.235	0.141	-0.060	0.064
	(1.408)	(1.365)	(1.566)	(1.364)	(1.447)	(1.193)	(1.253)	(1.086)
Inevitable (1)–Controllable (5)	-0.056	0.0769	0.141	0.104	0.194	0.156	0.165	-0.168
	(1.229)	(1.163)	(1.187)	(1.217)	(0.909)	(1.250)	(1.010)	(0.975)
Democratic (1)–Republican (5)	0.085	0.151	-0.110	0.072	0.059	-0.016	0.047	-0.011
	(0.751)	(0.825)	(0.863)	(0.785)	(0.596)	(0.678)	(0.596)	(0.627)
Demand pull (1)–Cost push (5)	-0.265	0.157	-0.141	-0.033	-0.061	-0.460	-0.226	-0.554
	(1.192)	(1.219)	(1.443)	(1.420)	(1.214)	(1.318)	(1.101)	(1.278)
High Unemployment								
Democratic (1)–Republican (5)	0.211	-0.036	0.0	0.065	0.0	0.016	-0.059	-0.179
	(0.860)	(0.948)	(0.926)	(0.797)	(0.457)	(0.807)	(0.643)	(0.743)
Recession (1)–Prosperity (5)	0.155	0.014	0.061	0.144	-0.044	-0.127	0.094	0.137
	(1.215)	(1.075)	(1.138)	(1.306)	(0.969)	(1.171)	(0.959)	(0.895)
Inflation (1)–Deflation (5)	-0.310	-0.147	-0.222	-0.512	0.279	0.234	-0.082	0.094
	(1.400)	(1.348)	(1.529)	(1.501)	(1.402)	(1.377)	(1.320)	(1.337)
Controllable (1)–Fact of life (5)	0.155	0.140	0.050	0.080	0.059	-0.064	-0.058	0.137
	(1.191)	(1.045)	(1.192)	(1.082)	(0.751)	(1.09)	(0.956)	(1.027)
Bad (1)–Good (5)	-0.225	-0.224	-0.060	-0.160	-0.015	-0.031	0.177	0.232
	(1.017)	(0.975)	(0.886)	(1.043)	(0.788)	(0.992)	(0.862)	(0.893)
Federal Income Tax								
Progressive (1)–Regressive (5)	0.465	0.615	0.740	0.715	-0.265	-0.250	0.047	-0.053
	(1.106)	(1.138)	(1.447)	(1.012)	(1.154)	(1.182)	(0.962)	(1.114)
Good (1)–Bad (5)	0.113	0.287	0.480	0.576	-0.294	-0.203	0.012	-0.105
	(0.838)	(1.092)	(1.267)	(0.953)	(1.023)	(0.929)	(0.838)	(1.005)

APPENDIX I

Changes in Student Opinions on Economic Issues
(Standard Deviations in Parentheses)

	Economics 223				Economics 224			
	Section 61		Section 62		Section 63		Section 64	
	Controls	Experimentals	Controls	Experimentals	Controls	Experimentals	Controls	Experimentals
Democratic (1)–Republican (5)	-0.127 (0.773)	-0.079 (0.885)	0.0 (0.841)	0.008 (0.724)	0.0 (0.546)	-0.094 (0.750)	0.129 (0.632)	0.021 (0.668)
Free enterprise (1)–Socialism (5)	0.0 (1.251)	0.119 (1.225)	0.020 (1.143)	0.080 (1.168)	-0.118 (1.113)	-0.047 (1.030)	0.024 (1.144)	-0.211 (0.999)
Too high (1)–Too low (5)	-0.414 (0.807)	-0.252 (0.960)	-0.260 (0.824)	-0.339 (0.845)	0.088 (0.707)	0.063 (0.871)	0.177 (0.743)	0.183 (0.722)
Fair (1)–Unfair (5)	0.423 (1.130)	0.322 (1.254)	0.515 (1.365)	0.608 (1.142)	-0.221 (1.183)	-0.438 (1.246)	-0.212 (1.114)	-0.147 (1.041)
Increasing the Money Supply								
Helps people (1)–Hurts people (5)	0.592 (0.950)	0.685 (1.103)	0.680 (0.984)	0.887 (1.030)	-0.294 (0.978)	-0.423 (0.832)	-0.188 (0.893)	-0.295 (0.921)
Inflation (1)–Recession (5)	-0.028 (1.108)	-0.042 (1.064)	-0.190 (1.042)	-0.144 (1.075)	0.044 (0.800)	0.031 (0.925)	0.035 (0.837)	-0.011 (0.755)
More gold (1)–More paper (5)	-0.409 (1.326)	-0.317 (1.228)	-0.343 (1.197)	-0.347 (1.197)	0.059 (1.063)	-0.127 (0.924)	-0.129 (0.923)	0.032 (0.782)
Democratic (1)–Republican (5)	0.056 (0.558)	-0.058 (0.926)	-0.010 (0.798)	-0.016 (0.665)	0.015 (0.658)	0.0 (0.777)	0.188 (0.852)	0.011 (0.664)
Free enterprise (1)–Socialism (5)	0.183 (1.046)	0.065 (1.193)	0.340 (1.224)	0.232 (1.093)	-0.147 (1.162)	-0.172 (0.935)	-0.047 (1.112)	0.190 (1.014)
Foreign Trade								
Desirable (1)–Undesirable (5)	-0.479 (0.694)	-0.168 (0.927)	-0.100 (0.835)	-0.136 (0.776)	-.338 (0.589)	0.313 (0.732)	0.224 (0.624)	0.421 (0.738)
Should be encouraged (1)–Should be discouraged (5)	-0.211 (0.877)	-0.147 (0.934)	-0.100 (0.810)	-0.177 (0.856)	0.373 (0.671)	0.423 (0.813)	0.212 (0.725)	0.358 (0.728)

Unimportant (1)–Important (5)	0.296 (0.901)	0.126 (0.933)	0.130 (0.812)	0.232 (0.881)	-0.382 (0.692)	-9.359 (0.897)	-0.188 (0.587)	-0.337 (0.752)
Should be political (1)–Should be apolitical (5)	0.225 (1.416)	0.182 (1.237)	0.010 (1.299)	0.107 (1.322)	-0.294 (1.173)	0.016 (1.109)	-0.012 (1.107)	-0.253 (1.062)
Should be free (1)–Should be controlled (5)	0.070 (1.046)	0.035 (1.451)	-0.111 (1.177)	0.104 (1.361)	0.706 (1.667)	0.406 (1.498)	0.271 (1.238)	0.0 (1.337)
Labor Unions								
Good (1)–Bad (5)	0.056 (0.924)	0.007 (1.031)	0.102 (0.958)	-0.240 (1.117)	0.059 (0.844)	0.0 (1.098)	0.082 (1.104)	0.263 (0.878)
Effective (1)–Ineffective (5)	-0.141 (1.004)	-0.049 (0.914)	-0.163 (0.796)	-0.096 (1.081)	0.015 (0.985)	-0.191 (1.120)	0.071 (0.768)	0.0 (0.816)
Important (1)–Unimportant (5)	-0.141 (0.850)	0.014 (0.856)	-0.090 (0.668)	-0.104 (0.905)	0.0 (0.773)	-0.094 (1.019)	0.129 (0.985)	0.116 (0.713)
Fair (1)–Unfair (5)	-0.028 (1.082)	-0.085 (0.871)	0.031 (0.907)	-0.064 (1.014)	0.0 (0.898)	0.031 (0.776)	0.107 (0.822)	0.147 (0.956)
Responsible (1)–Irresponsible (5)	0.028 (0.878)	-0.035 (0.922)	0.102 (0.879)	-0.088 (0.951)	-0.044 (1.165)	0.125 (0.724)	0.271 (1.005)	0.179 (0.945)
Capitalistic (1)–Socialistic (5)	-0.086 (1.271)	0.028 (1.130)	0.030 (1.147)	0.032 (1.189)	-0.058 (1.183)	0.078 (0.997)	-0.059 (1.106)	0.263 (1.178)
Greedy (1)–Selfless (5)	-0.239 (0.948)	-0.098 (0.867)	-0.170 (1.025)	0.040 (1.019)	0.044 (0.969)	0.016 (1.076)	-0.059 (0.777)	0.105 (0.928)
Necessary (1)–Unnecessary (5)	-0.268 (0.810)	-0.091 (0.863)	0.090 (0.986)	-0.048 (0.999)	-0.029 (0.880)	0.0 (1.039)	0.047 (0.925)	0.274 (0.818)
Big Business								
Good (1)–Bad (5)	-0.085 (1.038)	-0.035 (0.910)	-0.152 (0.973)	0.048 (1.054)	-0.132 (1.006)	-0.094 (0.849)	-0.318 (1.014)	0.137 (0.870)
Growing in importance (1)–Declining in importance (5)	-0.085 (0.982)	-0.084 (0.717)	-0.040 (0.942)	0.096 (1.011)	0.044 (0.818)	-0.111 (0.986)	-0.012 (0.866)	0.147 (0.757)
Should be controlled (1)–Should be free (5)	-0.229 (1.106)	0.007 (1.110)	0.263 (1.026)	-0.128 (1.047)	0.044 (0.800)	0.141 (0.833)	0.318 (1.026)	0.232 (0.905)

APPENDIX I

Changes in Student Opinions on Economic Issues
(Standard Deviations in Parentheses)

	Economics 223				Economics 224			
	Section 61		Section 62		Section 63		Section 64	
	Controls	Experimentals	Controls	Experimentals	Controls	Experimentals	Controls	Experimentals
Pays share (1)–Has a free ride (5)	0.099	0.259	0.121	0.336	0.132	-0.016	-0.329	-0.126
	(1.456)	(1.393)	(1.239)	(1.198)	(1.245)	(1.076)	(1.285)	(1.151)
Socially respoinsible (1)–Socially irrespoinsible (5)	0.257	0.231	-0.051	0.144	-0.015	-0.094	-0.388	-0.137
	(1.151)	(1.265)	(1.289)	(1.324)	(1.264)	(1.151)	(1.364)	(1.006)
Monopolistic (1)–Competitive (5)	0.324	0.280	0.450	0.296	-0.118	-0.172	-0.024	-0.277
	(1.274)	(1.340)	(1.480)	(1.218)	(0.838)	(0.901)	(1.215)	(0.955)
Politically involved (1)–Politically uninvolved (5)	--------	-1.000	-1.000	--------	0.0	0.077	0.333	0.667
	--------	(1.00)	--------	--------	(0.845)	(0.862)	(1.033)	(0.816)
Capitalism								
A reality (1)–A non-reality (5)	-0.268	0.050	-0.170	0.024	0.044	-0.016	0.0	-0.011
	(1.183)	(0.796)	(0.911)	(1.144)	(0.871)	(0.900)	(0.905)	(0.831)
Desirable (1)–Undesirable (5)	-0.014	-0.133	-0.020	0.120	0.250	0.063	0.0	0.063
	(1.007)	(0.780)	(1.050)	(0.921)	(0.817)	(0.794)	(0.831)	(0.755)
Declining (1)–Growing (5)	-0.028	-0.056	0.020	-0.072	0.059	-0.081	0.047	-0.011
	(1.230)	(1.112)	(1.073)	(1.137)	(1.006)	(1.045)	(1.112)	(0.951)
Superior to socialism (1)–Inferior to socialism (5)	0.085	-0.014	-0.060	0.024	0.206	-0.094	-0.024	0.126
	(1.204)	(0.922)	(0.993)	(0.941)	(0.856)	(0.955)	(0.740)	(0.902)
Should be controlled (1)–Should be free (5)	0.028	0.154	0.020	-0.088	0.118	0.0	-0.212	-0.126
	(1.298)	(1.128)	(1.204)	(1.115)	(1.228)	(0.976)	(1.186)	(0.878)

Efficient (1)–Inefficient (5)	-0.296	-0.007	-0.010	0.072	0.103	0.141	-0.024	0.126
	(0.868)	(0.915)	(0.979)	(0.977)	(1.081)	(0.852)	(1.000)	(0.828)
Equitable (1)–Inequitable (5)	-0.100	-0.196	-0.010	0.145	-0.044	0.016	-0.094	-0.021
	(1.009)	(1.115)	(0.879)	(1.057)	(1.028)	(0.917)	(0.921)	(1.041)
Market Mechanisms								
Efficient (1)–Inefficient (5)	0.127	0.126	0.323	0.460	0.239	-0.016	-0.012	0.263
	(1.081)	(0.956)	(1.105)	(0.940)	(0.955)	(1.031)	(0.748)	(0.913)
Theoretical (1)–Practical (5)	-0.0254	-0.140	-0.172	0.0	0.164	-0.016	0.235	0.074
	(1.204)	(1.032)	(1.429)	(1.243)	(1.463)	(1.475)	(1.120)	(1.315)
Workable (1)–Unworkable (5)	0.127	0.176	0.253	0.323	0.209	-0.016	0.024	0.032
	(0.755)	(0.861)	(0.993)	(0.907)	(0.880)	(1.000)	(0.723)	(0.831)
Desirable (1)–Undesirable (5)	0.028	0.077	0.222	0.347	0.134	-0.016	0.082	0.211
	(0.971)	(0.881)	(1.016)	(0.865)	(0.736)	(0.864)	(0.743)	(0.849)
Abstract (1)–Concrete (5)	-0.127	-0.042	0.061	-0.242	-0.164	-0.016	0.118	0.379
	(0.940)	(1.087)	(1.250)	(1.150)	(1.081)	(1.339)	(1.117)	(1.178)
High prices (1)–Low prices (5)	-0.324	-0.112	-0.051	0.008	-0.239	-0.047	-0.071	-0.095
	(0.922)	(0.848)	(0.988)	(0.844)	(0.780)	(0.881)	(0.768)	(0.864)
Allocates (1)–Does not allocate (5)	0.085	0.211	0.101	0.169	0.349	0.047	0.083	0.564
	(0.824)	(0.824)	(1.120)	(0.843)	(1.102)	(1.161)	(0.996)	(0.770)

APPENDIX J

Impact of Instructor's Position and Student's Precourse Position on Student's Postcourse Opinions Economics 223, Section 61

	R^2	R^2		Beta	
		SWAT	ATTPRE	SWAT	ATTPRE
Decision Making:					
349) Simple–Complex	.38	.04	.24	.682	.687
350) Random–Rational	.45	.04	.37	.75	.84
351) Apolitical–Political	.32	.14	.15	.73	.52
352) Important to me–Irrelevant to me	.55	.16	.33	.70	.65
353) Important to society–Irrelevant to society	.54	.42	.05	.73	.24
Government Spending Deficit:					
354) Desirable–Undesirable	.36	.20	.09	.62	.34
355) Democratic–Republican	.35	.10	.24	.67	.61
356) Inflationary–Recessionary	.38	.24	.08	.68	.35
357) Decreases demand–Increases demand	.59	.33	.21	.85	.55
Government Controls such as Wage-Price Freeze					
358) Undesirable–Desirable	.52	.05	.38	.71	.81
359) Democratic–Republican	.53	.24	.26	.78	.60
360) Socialism–Free enterprise	.41	.22	.14	.69	.45
361) Ineffective–Effective	.61	.13	.41	.81	.81
362) Distorts market operations–Facilitates market operations	.48	.15	.28	.76	.65
Poverty:					
363) Lazy–Lack of opportunity	.66	.08	.52	.67	.83
364) Unimportant–Serious	.37	.01	.30	.51	.69
365) Market determined–Overt discrimination	.48	.30	.13	.79	.42
366) No skills–No jobs	.58	.14	.38	.68	.72
367) Inevitable–Can be eliminated	.53	.12	.34	.77	.71
368) Individual responsibility–Social responsibility	.54	.07	.43	.74	.82
Inflation:					
1412) Bad–Good	.69	.22	.43	.82	.76
1413) Recession–Prosperity	.41	.13	.25	.81	.66
1414) Inevitable–Controllable	.46	.12	.29	.72	.66
1415) Democratic–Republican	.34	.08	.24	.51	.55
1416) Cost push–Demand pull	.49	.23	.18	.76	.50

APPENDIX J
(continued)

	R^2	R^2 SWAT	R^2 ATTPRE	Beta SWAT	Beta ATTPRE
High Unemployment:					
1417) Democratic-Republican	.37	.09	.23	.57	.55
1418) Recession-Prosperity	.40	.22	.16	.71	.48
1419) Inflation-Deflation	.54	.15	.33	.78	.70
1420) Not controllable-controllable	.37	.10	.25	.76	.68
1421) Bad-Good	.60	.22	.36	.78	.68
Federal Income Tax:					
1422) Progressive-Regressive	.46	.20	.21	.60	.48
1423) Bad-Good	.49	.03	.43	.82	.92
1424) Democratic-Republican	.27	.14	.12	.63	.43
1425) Socialism-Free enterprise	.51	.43	.01	.79	.17
1426) Too high-Too low	.51	.12	.32	.75	.70
1427) Unfair-Fair	.57	.11	.43	.818	.813
Increasing Money Supply:					
1428) Hurts people-Helps people	.53	.23	.29	.88	.67
1429) Inflation-Recession	.44	.24	.13	.72	.43
1430) More paper-More gold	.30	.16	.19	.55	.48
1431) Democratic-Republican	.38	.19	.13	.68	.42
1432) Free enterprise-Socialism	.45	.21	.17	.70	.48
Foreign Trade:					
1433) Desirable-Undesirable	.54	.20	.31	.71	.62
1434) Should be encouraged-Should be discouraged	.53	.16	.34	.69	.65
1435) Important-Unimportant	.49	.23	.24	.74	.55
1436) Should be apolitical-Should be political	.51	.17	.31	.75	.66
1437) Should be free-Should be controlled	.52	.04	.42	.71	.84
Labor Unions:					
1438) Bad-Good	.62	.00	.60	.96	.61
1439) Ineffective-Effective	.46	.05	.34	.63	.71
1440) Important-Unimportant	.60	.08	.47	.63	.77
1441) Unfair-Fair	.63	.07	.49	.64	.81
1442) Irresponsible-Responsible	.64	.06	.47	.59	.80
1443) Socialistic-Capitalistic	.52	.24	.44	.68	.80
1444) Greedy-Selfless	.54	.08	.38	.69	.74
1445) Unnecessary-Necessary	.58	.04	.51	.51	.79
Big Business:					
1446) Good-Bad	.51	.37	.08	.62	.71

APPENDIX J
(continued)

	R^2	R^2		Beta	
		SWAT	ATTPRE	SWAT	ATTPRE
1447) Declining–Growing	.48	.43	.02	.62	.81
1448) Should be free–Should be controlled	.42	.34	.02	.64	.76
1449) Pays share–Has a free ride	.40	.24	.13	.53	.18
1450) Responsible–Irresponsible	.56	.34	.14	.62	.65
1451) Competitive–Monopolistic	.35	.25	.04	.71	.71
Capitalism:					
1453) Reality–Non-reality	.56	.17	.35	.67	.65
1454) Desirable–Undesirable	.69	.13	.52	.67	.83
1455) Declining–Growing	.60	.17	.37	.75	.72
1456) Superior to socialism Inferior to socialism	.50	.10	.36	.62	.68
1457) Socially irresponsible– Socially responsible	.49	.05	.41	.74	.83
1458) Monopolistic–Competitive	.64	.19	.41	.72	.73
1459) Politically involved– Politically uninvolved	.54	.25	.28	.80	.61
Market Mechanism:					
1460) Efficient–Inefficient	.54	.30	.21	.77	.51
1461) Practical–Theoretical	.57	.27	.22	.69	.50
1462) Workable–Unworkable	.53	.32	.16	.72	.44
1463) Desirable–Undesirable	.49	.29	.18	.79	.50
1464) Abstract–Concrete	.57	.21	.26	.77	.61
1465) High prices–Low prices	.50	.10	.35	.79	.79
1466) Allocates–Does not allocate	.44	.15	.44	.60	.47

APPENDIX K

Impact of Instructor's Position and Student's Precourse Position on Student's Postcourse Opinions Economics 223, Section 62

	R^2	R^2		Beta	
		SWAT	ATTPRE	SWAT	ATTPRE
Decision Making:					
49) Simple–Complex	.34	.043	.209	.654	.644
50) Random–Rational	.49	.080	.341	.780	.766
51) Apolitical–Political	.27	.023	.184	.622	.629
52) Important to me–Irrelevant to me	.58	.281	.262	.730	.566
53) Important to society–Irrelevant to society	.58	.472	.093	.750	.318
Government Spending Deficit:					
54) Desirable–Undesirable	.35	.176	.132	.569	.387
55) Democratic–Republican	.45	.157	.252	.734	.600
56) Inflationary–Recessionary	.45	.158	.228	.695	.572
57) Decreases demand–Increases demand	.59	.221	.277	.827	.647
Government Controls such as Wage-Price Freeze					
58) Undesirable–Desirable	.554	.042	.476	.662	.850
59) Democratic–Republican	.590	.324	.200	.764	.501
60) Socialism–Free enterprise	.536	.189	.288	.692	.599
61) Ineffective–Effective	.619	.096	.480	.684	.786
62) Distort market operations–Facilitates market operations	.536	.227	.269	.756	.603
Poverty:					
63) Lazy–Lack of opportunity	.661	.043	.588	.816	1.010
64) Unimportant–Serious	.327	.102	.170	.622	.516
65) Market determined-Overt discrimination	.445	.241	.171	.771	.499
66) No skills–No jobs	.581	.168	.363	.830	.738
67) Inevitable–Can be eliminated	.530	.117	.375	.784	.763
68) Individual responsibility–Social responsibility	.492	.093	.376	.799	.807
Inflation:					
1412) Bad–Good	.621	.249	.335	.860	.690
1413) Recession–Prosperity	.352	.110	.187	.769	.619
1414) Inevitable–Controllable	.428	.089	.289	.675	.650
1415) Democratic–Republican	.452	.135	.249	.680	.601
1416) Cost push–Demand pull	.471	.267	.160	.809	.489

APPENDIX K
(continued)

	R^2	R^2		Beta	
		SWAT	ATTPRE	SWAT	ATTPRE
High Unemployment:					
1417) Democratic–Republican	.529	.180	.318	.702	.632
1418) Recession–Prosperity	.457	.314	.091	.715	.348
1419) Inflation–Deflation	.454	.179	.252	.806	.637
1420) Not Controllable–Controllable	.347	.131	.188	.749	.577
1421) Bad–Good	.612	.314	.249	.827	.579
Federal Income Tax:					
1422) Progressive–Regressive	.364	.194	.080	.564	.308
1423) Bad–Good	.455	.060	.327	.740	.757
1424) Democratic–Republican	.269	.103	.129	.605	.459
1425) Socialism–Free enterprise	.450	.410	.010	.728	.128
1426) Too high–Too low	.687	.096	.526	.781	.891
1427) Unfair–Fair	.614	.157	.406	.755	.738
Increasing Money Supply:					
1428) Hurts people–Helps people	.510	.079	.363	.798	.807
1429) Inflation–Recession	.485	.190	.251	.755	.605
1430) More paper–More gold	.385	.051	.286	.545	.642
1431) Democratic–Republican	.397	.074	.291	.658	.678
1432) Free enterprise–Socialism	.422	.215	.162	.706	.471
Foreign Trade:					
1433) Desirable–Undesirable	.631	.260	.353	.729	.643
1434) Should be encouraged–Should be discouraged	.637	.242	.342	.729	.642
1435) Important–Unimportant	.644	.313	.264	.738	.559
1436) Should be apolitical–Should be political	.564	.266	.226	.743	.539
1437) Should be free–Should be controlled	.520	.051	.434	.684	.810
Labor Unions:					
1438) Bad–Good	.633	.019	.550	.531	.858
1439) Ineffective–Effective	.510	.008	.471	.638	.877
1440) Important–Unimportant	.638	.092	.465	.665	.781
1441) Unfair–Fair	.657	.026	.584	.639	.923
1442) Irresponsible–Responsible	.641	.031	.543	.583	.865
1443) Socialistic–Capitalistic	.569	.124	.415	.712	.758
1444) Greedy–Selfless	.446	.098	.286	.673	.654
1445) Unnecessary–Necessary	.566	.043	.490	.682	.827
Big Business:					
1446) Good–Bad	.624	.178	.431	.696	.733
1447) Declining–Growing	.492	.082	.393	.766	.791

APPENDIX K
(continued)

	R^2	R^2 SWAT	R^2 ATTPRE	Beta SWAT	Beta ATTPRE
1448) Should be free–Should be controlled	.465	.028	.403	.697	.824
1449) Pays share–Has a free ride	.483	.079	.361	.599	.696
1450) Socially responsible–Socially irresponsible	.510	.045	.416	.665	.789
1451) Competitive–Monopolistic	.357	.044	.260	.809	.791
Capitalism:					
1453) Reality–Non-reality	.569	.204	.321	.697	.633
1454) Desirable–Undesirable	.420	.172	.206	.664	.521
1455) Declining–Growing	.617	.144	.437	.714	.759
1456) Superior to socialism–Inferior to socialism	.641	.177	.641	.659	.778
1457) Socially irresponsible–Socially responsible	.492	.047	.407	.696	.798
1458) Monopolistic–Competitive	.476	.157	.276	.712	.618
1459) Politically involved–Politically uninvolved	.609	.216	.341	.744	.689
Market Mechanism:					
1460) Efficient–Inefficient	.389	.216	.133	.655	.417
1461) Practical–Theoretical	.567	.281	.198	.718	.501
1462) Workable–Unworkable	.474	.295	.133	.701	.386
1463) Desirable–Undesirable	.422	.187	.198	.682	.513
1464) Abstract–Concrete	.518	.206	.234	.804	.588
1465) High prices–Low prices	.425	.204	.183	.788	.556
1466) Allocates–Does not allocate	.487	.229	.243	.746	.569

APPENDIX L

Impact of Instructor's Position and Student's Precourse Position on Student's Postcourse Opinions Economics 224, Section 63

	R^2	R^2 SWAT	R^2 ATTPRE	Beta SWAT	Beta ATTPRE
Decision Making:					
349) Simple–Complex	.577	.043	.414	.887	.962
350) Random–Rational	.5869	.107	.372	.818	.819
351) Apolitical–Political	.4186	.058	.1885	.520	.530
352) Important to me– Irrelevant to me	.723	.318	.378	.759	.635
353) Important to society– Irrelevant to society	.623	.407	.1395	.706	.377
Government Spending Deficit:					
354) Desirable–Undesirable	.657	.109	.391	.715	.726
355) Democratic–Republican	.418	.164	.124	.6597	.401
356) Inflation–Recessionary	.702	.172	.467	.826	.822
357) Decreases demand– Increases demand	.603	.114	.3385	.756	.772
Government Controls such as Wage-Price Freeze:					
358) Undesirable–Desirable	.5956	.156	.2915	.7505	.673
359) Democratic–Republican	.521	.1997	.184	.705	.502
360) Socialism–Free enterprise	.7135	.254	.393	.709	.705
361) Ineffective–Effective	.548	.126	.284	.653	.624
362) Distort market operations– Facilitates market operations	.588	.237	.207	.691	.493
Poverty:					
363) Lazy–Lack of opportunity	.721	.139	.523	.710	.8105
364) Unimportant–Serious	.656	.147	.440	.7295	.768
365) Market determined– Overt discrimination	.706	.256	.262	.778	.591
366) No skills–No jobs	.578	.164	.331	.620	.662
367) Inevitable–Can be eliminated	.650	.036	.464	.616	.792
368) Individual responsibility– Social responsibility	.631	.082	.401	.843	.8195
Inflation:					
1412) Bad–Good	.724	.182	.461	.489	.761
1413) Recession–Prosperity	.4235	.1575	.163	.652	.4645
1414) Inevitable–Controllable	.563	.083	.2598	.560	.543
1415) Democratic–Republican	.685	.182	.268	.6195	.544
1416) Cost push–Demand pull	.399	.165	.093	.639	.394

APPENDIX L
(continued)

	R^2	R^2 SWAT	R^2 ATTPRE	Beta SWAT	Beta ATTPRE
High Unemployment:					
1417) Democratic–Republican	.593	.216	.306	.615	.5445
1418) Recession–Prosperity	.526	.224	.206	.726	.513
1919) Inflation–Deflation	.571	.126	.3025	.694	.667
1420) Not controllable–Controllable	.4605	.118	.2015	.652	.504
1421) Bad–Good	.657	.328	.273	.797	.608
Federal Income Tax:					
1422) Progressive–Regressive	.648	.365	.189	.741	.465
1423) Bad–Good	.582	.126	.325	.602	.651
1424) Democratic–Republican	.502	.108	.219	.609	.5135
1425) Socialism–Free enterprise	.535	.107	.310	.618	.659
1426) Too high–Too low	.639	.126	.417	.708	.7815
1427) Unfair–Fair	.560	.131	.271	.694	.642
Increasing Money Supply:					
1428) Hurts people–Helps people	.416	.040	.293	.573	.637
1429) Inflation–Recession	.508	.119	.238	.683	.601
1430) More paper–More gold	.653	.256	.166	.804	.516
1431) Democratic–Republican	.406	.213	.084	.634	.342
1432) Free enterprise–Socialism	.599	.238	.176	.759	.469
Foreign Trade:					
1433) Desirable–Undesirable	.431	.064	.213	.366	.476
1434) Should be encouraged–Should be discouraged	.478	.065	.246	.4265	.534
1435) Important–Unimportant	.396	.139	.141	.529	.396
1436) Should be apolitical–Should be political	.634	.166	.325	.593	.633
1437) Should be free–Should be controlled	.439	.141	.203	.607	.544
Labor Unions:					
1438) Bad–Good	.654	.063	.415	.547	.778
1439) Ineffective–Effective	.524	.150	.254	.592	.570
1440) Important–Unimportant	.651	.3095	.239	.770	.5315
1441) Unfair–Fair	.772	.090	.508	.622	.858
1442) Irresponsible–Responsible	.727	.148	.408	.604	.741
1443) Socialistic–Capitalistic	.622	.0955	.366	.617	.6985
1444) Greedy–Selfless	.651	.206	.3245	.691	.628
1445) Unnecessary–Necessary	.609	.076	.359	.6425	.733
Big Business:					
1446) Good–Bad	.726	.225	.450	.653	.730
1447) Declining–Growing	.566	.233	.221	.665	.497

APPENDIX L
(continued)

	R^2	R^2 SWAT	R^2 ATTPRE	Beta SWAT	Beta ATTPRE
1448) Should be free–Should be controlled	.788	.130	.577	.698	.854
1449) Pays share–Has a free ride	.642	.1385	.456	.741	.768
1450) Socially responsible–Socially irresponsible	.691	.202	.431	.758	.754
1451) Competitive–Monopolistic	.666	.075	.497	.522	.706
Capitalism:					
1453) Reality–Non-reality	.741	.316	.359	.684	.6305
1454) Desirable–Undesirable	.651	.274	.310	.622	.620
1455) Declining–Growing	.673	.142	.498	.731	.829
1456) Superior to socialism–Inferior to socialism	.579	.027	.450	.588	.830
1457) Socially irresponsible–Socially responsible	.678	.050	.522	.879	1.065
1458) Monopolistic–Competitive	.598	.238	.300	.682	.595
1459) Politically involved–Politically uninvolved	.667	.192	.424	.768	.754
Market Mechanism:					
1460) Efficient–Inefficient	.054	.2795	.129	.716	.384
1461) Practical–Theoretical	.557	.372	.105	.866	.393
1462) Workable–Unworkable	.523	.319	.086	.757	.368
1463) Desirable–Undesirable	.598	.314	.179	.775	.473
1464) Abstract–Concrete	.496	.222	.169	.764	.479
1465) High prices–Low prices	.561	.169	.170	.721	.503
1466) Allocates–Does not allocate	.629	.294	.199	.787	.468

Appendix M

Impact of Instructor's Position and Student's Precourse Position on Student's Postcourse Opinions
Economics 224, Section 64

	R^2	R^2		Beta	
		SWAT	ATTPRE	SWAT	ATTPRE
Decision Making:					
49) Simple–Complex	.561	.044	.413	.730	.860
50) Random–Rational	.638	.212	.316	.702	.635
51) Apolitical–Political	.480	.131	.282	.813	.718
52) Important to me–Irrelevant to me	.685	.328	.229	.687	.501
53) Important to society–Irrelevant to society	.613	.412	.069	.739	.278
Government Spending Deficit:					
54) Desirable–Undesirable	.608	.251	.245	.688	.522
55) Democratic–Republican	.438	.088	.204	.657	.611
56) Inflationary–Recessionary	.505	.225	.230	.735	.565
57) Decreases demand–Increases demand	.632	.117	.448	.823	.844
Government Controls such as Wage-Price Freeze:					
58) Undesirable–Desirable	.635	.224	.235	.687	.528
59) Democratic–Republican	.675	.218	.431	.641	.684
60) Socialism–Free enterprise	.618	.131	.255	.562	.555
61) Ineffective–Effective	.586	.115	.341	.605	.673
62) Distort market operations–Facilitates market operations	.631	.192	.320	.618	.630
Poverty:					
63) Lazy–Lack of opportunity	.685	.187	.447	.715	.754
64) Unimportant–Serious	.667	.089	.531	.708	.848
65) Market determined–Overt discrimination	.575	.291	.213	.748	.535
66) No skills–No jobs	.603	.188	.361	.6895	.640
67) Inevitable–Can be eliminated	.724	.056	.636	.599	.882
68) Individual responsibility–Social responsibility	.661	.051	.562	.655	.876
Inflation:					
1412) Bad–Good	.656	.223	.378	.662	.650
1413) Recession–Prosperity	.498	.096	.367	.725	.717
1414) Inevitable–Controllable	.539	.025	.409	.612	.786
1415) Democratic–Republican	.539	.142	.341	.660	.677
1416) Cost push–Demand pull	.393	.210	.104	.656	.398

APPENDIX M
(continued)

	R^2	R^2 SWAT	R^2 ATTPRE	Beta SWAT	Beta ATTPRE
High Unemployment:					
1417) Democratic–Republican	.696	.267	.379	.696	.659
1418) Recession–Prosperity	.600	.447	.094	.752	.304
1419) Inflation–Deflation	.533	.139	.316	.719	.649
1420) Not controllable–Controllable	.3645	.146	.162	.741	.549
1421) Bad–Good	.478	.280	.180	.649	.449
Federal Income Tax:					
1422) Progressive–Regressive	.610	.349	.211	.765	.500
1423) Bad–Good	.466	.161	.241	.614	.532
1424) Democratic–Republican	.306	.096	.152	.4996	.432
1425) Socialism–Free enterprise	.541	.091	.349	.639	.691
1426) Too high–Too low	.565	.051	.459	.602	.799
1427) Unfair–Fair	.531	.065	.421	.644	.764
Increasing Money Supply:					
1428) Hurts people–Helps people	.375	.110	.201	.546	.491
1429) Inflation–Recession	.581	.343	.201	.770	.469
1430) More paper–More gold	.614	.278	.250	.723	.533
1431) Democratic–Republican	.286	.1148	.0345	.4245	.1585
1432) Free enterprise–Socialism	.529	.197	.213	.731	.560
Foreign Trade:					
1433) Desirable–Undesirable	.494	.073	.3747	.408	.619
1434) Should be encouraged–Should be discouraged	.468	.168	.250	.504	.511
1435) Important–Unimportant	.419	.136	.203	.482	.472
1436) Should be apolitical–Should be political	.548	.145	.378	.688	.714
1437) Should be free–Should be controlled	.4996	.089	.329	.665	.690
Labor Unions:					
1438) Bad–Good	.592	.053	.4948	.687	.855
1439) Ineffective–Effective	.391	.078	.232	.682	.604
1440) Important–Unimportant	.431	.167	.1765	.521	.451
1441) Unfair–Fair	.651	.102	.466	.709	.794
1442) Irresponsible–Responsible	.642	.112	.435	.7199	.782
1443) Socialistic–Capitalistic	.602	.145	.428	.729	.767
1444) Greedy–Selfless	.627	.155	.3846	.654	.668
1445) Unnecessary–Necessary	.657	.010	.5247	.668	.950
Big Business:					
1446) Good–Bad	.648	.308	.287	.741	.584
1447) Declining–Growing	.552	.181	.332	.6905	.664

APPENDIX M
(continued)

	R^2	R^2		Beta	
		SWAT	ATTPRE	SWAT	ATTPRE
1448) Should be free–Should be controlled	.611	.069	.4546	.739	.849
1449) Pays share–Has a free ride	.632	.174	.426	.7347	.733
1450) Socially responsible–Socially irresponsible	.6655	.159	.462	.716	.748
1451) Competitive–Monopolistic	.4905	.2065	.251	.8099	.5865
Capitalism:					
1453) Reality–Non-reality	.681	.190	.440	.7345	.762
1454) Desirable–Undesirable	.6145	.451	.078	.816	.3249
1455) Declining–Growing	.714	.195	.433	.679	.737
1456) Superior to socialism–Inferior to socialism	.689	.202	.416	.674	.701
1457) Socially irresponsible–Socially responsible	.545	.087	.409	.611	.713
1458) Monopolisitc–Competitive	.602	.2295	.286	.677	.572
1459) Politically involved–Politically uninvolved	.665	.205	.636	.749	.780
Market Mechanism:					
1460) Efficient–Inefficient	.626	.473	.114	.761	.352
1461) Practical–Theoretical	.615	.389	.605	.766	.509
1462) Workable–Unworkable	.642	.4698	.136	.805	.4046
1463) Desirable–Undesirable	.454	.256	.0796	.607	.286
1464) Abstract–Concrete	.482	.1845	.221	.711	.552
1465) High prices–Low prices	.4645	.174	.209	.702	.525
1466) Allocates–Does not allocate	.516	.228	.172	.641	.434

NOTES

Notes to Chapter 1

1. An adequate testimony to this effort and its breadth is a series of conferences on "The Use of the Computer in the Undergraduate Curricula" supported by the National Science Foundation. To date there have been six of these conferences, and the papers presented have been published.

2. For a supporting view of this assertion, see John C. Soper, "Computer Assisted Instruction in Economics: A Survey" *Journal of Economic Education* 5, 2 (Fall 1974): 5–29.

3. This criticism is also made in R. B. McKenzie and G. Tullock, *The New World of Economics* (Homewood: Richard D. Irwin, Inc., 1975), pp. 223–48.

4. There are, of course, many alternatives as well as criticisms of these standard courses. Indeed there may be as many examples of "new approaches" as there are "conventional approaches." For the curious we offer a short bibliography. R. H. Leftwich and A. M. Sharp, "Syllabus for an 'Issues Approach' to the Teaching of Economics Principles," *The Journal of Economic Education*, special issue no. 1 (Winter 1974); Rendigs Fels,"The Vanderbilt-JCEE Experimental Course in Elementary Economics," *The Journal of Economic Education,* special issue no. 2 (Winter 1974); B. Tuckman and H. Tuckman, "Toward a more Effective Economics Principles Class: The Florida State University Experience," *The Journal of Economic Education*, special issue no. 3 (Spring 1975); K. Boulding and E. Boulding, "Introducing Freshmen to the Social System," *American Economic Review Papers and Proceedings,* 64, no. 2 (May 1975): 428–30; L. Hansen, "New Approaches to Teaching the Principles Course," *American Economics Paper and Proceedings*, 65, no. 2 (May 1975): 434–37; and John G. Gurley, "Some Comments on the Principles Course," *American Economic Review Papers and Proceedings*, 65, no. 2 (May 1975): 430–33. Of special interest is "Special Issue on Teaching: Approaches to Introductory Economics Social Relations of the Classroom," *The Review of Radical Political Economics,* 6 (Winter 1975).

5. The lack of adequate range has been a criticism of CAI. See E. J. Anastasio, "The Study of the Factors Inhibiting the Use of the Computer in Instruction," *Educom* (Spring 1972): 2–10.

Notes to Chapter 2

1. The TUCE was published by the Psychological Corporation and is available from the Joint Council on Economic Education, 1212 Avenue of the Americas, New York, N.Y. 10036.

2. As a matter of fact little use was made of the demonstration and game-simulation routines by the experimental students in both semesters. This is established in Chapter 6.

3. For a description of the TUCE, see *Manual Test of Understanding in College Economics* published by the Psychological Corporation and available from the Joint Council on Economic Education.

4. There is some question concerning what these categories actually represent. See Darrel Lewis and Tor Dahl, "The Test of Understanding College Economics and Its Construct Validity," *Journal of Economic Education* (Spring 1971): 77–85.

5. The national norming data are also contained in the *Manual Test of Understanding in College Economics.*

6. For an earlier version of this view of the learning process, see F. J. Bonello, W. I. Davisson, and K. Jameson, "Alternative Approaches to Introductory Economics." This paper was presented at the Joint Council for Economic Education session at the American Economic Association meeting for 1974.

7. The diminishing-returns concept is usually explained as the impact of a continued decrease in the ratio of fixed to variable inputs. Whether or not this condition holds in education depends on the definition of the production period. Thus we are less likely to obtain diminishing returns if we deal with an entire semester as opposed to a single day of the semester, that is, human capital is more likely to be fixed for the case of a day but less likely to be fixed over the course of a semester.

8. In fact, examinations may, in part, be justified in terms of influencing a student to increase his utilization rate.

9. For a discussion of these possibilities, see R. B. McKenzie and G. Tullock, *The New World of Economics*, pp. 235–41.

10. Contract grading may also be viewed as a solution to this dilemma.

11. This might be an interpretation of the TIPS. See Allan Kelley, "Individualizing Instruction through the Use of Technology in Higher Education," *The Journal of Economic Education* (Spring 1973): 77–89.

12. A complete empirical restatement is reserved for the regression section of Chapter 3.

13. This is revealed by an examination of the various empirical articles in the *Journal of Economic Education.*

14. For a description of the Scholastic Aptitude Test, see *The SAT.* Copies are available from the College Board, Box 592, Princeton, New Jersey 08540.

15. *The SAT,* p. 10.

16. *The SAT,* p. 4.

17. The remarks that follow might be interpreted as criticisms of the

Scholastic Aptitude Test. This would be unfortunate because our remarks are not directed to the test itself but to the manner it is used in evaluating education innovation.

18. For an example, see D. Paden and M. Mayer, "The Relative Effectiveness of Three Methods of Teaching Principles of Economics," *Journal of Economic Education* (Fall 1969): 33–45.

Notes to Chapter 3

1. See R. Crowley and D. Witlan, "A Preliminary Report on the Efficiency of Introductory Economics Courses," *Journal of Economic Education* (Spring 1974): 103–8; and J. Soper, "Programmed Instruction in Large Lecture Courses," *Journal of Economic Education* (Spring 1973): 125–29.

2. Note that this is an option inherent in our implementation of CAI.

Notes to Chapter 4

1. At the end of the 223 course, it was determined that more specific information regarding both the discussion classes and the CAI system would be useful, and this instrument was subsequently developed.

2. B. S. Bloom, ed., *Taxonomy of Educational Objectives,* 2 (Ann Arbor: Edwards Bros., 1964).

3. The fall 1974 issue of the *Journal of Economic Education* contains a number of articles dealing with teacher-course evaluations.

4. Note that we did not distinguish between patterns of responses like conservative or liberal, but we did distinguish between types of semantic differentials. In the latter context we will refer to kinds of semantic differentials as: political such as "Democratic–Republican," content or analytic such as "cost push–demand pull," and value-laden such as "good–bad" or "fair–unfair."

5. One aftermath of Watergate is that some educators have taken the position that normative issues, particularly in the social sciences, should be raised explicitly. Such a position was taken by Alan J. Pifer of the Carnegie Foundation in his spring 1975 commencement address at the University of Notre Dame.

6. There has been some research in this area. Fred A. Thompson, "The Interaction of Cognition and Affect: The Issue of Free Trade," *Journal of Economic Education,* 4, no. 2 (Spring 1973): 11–15; William R. Mann and Daniel R. Fusfeld, "Evaluation of Teaching Effectiveness: Attitude Sophistication and Effective Teaching in Economics," *Journal of Economic Education,* 1, no. 2 (Spring 1970): 111–29; Lewis Karstensson and Richard K. Vedder, "A Note on Attitude as a Factor in Learning Economics," *Journal of Economic Education,* 5, no. 2 (Spring 1974): 109–11; Mitchell P. Rothman and James H. Scott, Jr., *Journal of Economic Education,* 4, no. 2 (Spring 1973): 116–24; Marilyn Kourilsky, "Learning through Advocacy: An Experimental Evalu-

ation of an Adversary Instructional Model," *Journal of Economic Education* 3, no. 2 (Spring 1972): 86–93; Robert V. Horton, "Values and the Economics Principles Course," *Journal of Economic Education* 3, no. 2 (Spring 1972): 118–23; and Jerome Rothenberg, "Relating the Study of Economics to the Problems of Modern Society," *Journal of Economic Education* 2, no. 2 (Spring 1971): 119–26.

7. This is not to say that all students would respond in the same way. If the student views the tax simply from the rate structure, he may indeed respond *progressive*. If, on the other hand, he is also noting loopholes and the like, he may respond *regressive*.

Notes to Chapter 5

1. As before, statistical significance is determined by a t test at the 5-percent leve.

2. This procedure may seem ambiguous–that using information on the dependent variable as part of the construction of an independent variable. However, the correlation coefficient between these variables were quite low.

3. The minimum F-Ration required for an equation of 10 and 192 degrees of freedom to be significantly different from zero is 2.32.

4. As a matter of general interest, in all instances for Economics 223 and Economics 224, the adjusted R^2 was approximately .02 less than the R^2.

5. This is a curious effect, and a final conclusion must be reserved for the analysis of Economics 224. Except for the market mechanism, the professors did not lecture on the microeconomic issues during Economics 223, and thus, less revision in the student's opinion might be expected. See Appendix D.

6. Aside from the coefficients of determination, there is the question of the relative importance of the explanatory variables. This is resolved by using the beta-weight concept. The beta-weight in regression is known as the *standard* partial regression coefficient as contrasted with the b-weight, which is the partial regression coefficient. The b-weight indicates the change in the dependent variable as a result of a given change in the appropriate independent variable. The problem is that the b-weight for the various independent variables reflects the nature of the measure or scale of the independent variables. For instance, some of the independent variables in the given regression are binary variables, some are measured on a five-point scale, and some are measured on a much larger scale such as VSAT and MSAT. Therefore it is difficult to measure the actual weight of the independent variable in the equation by looking at the b-weight when the independent variables are measured on different scales.

The beta weight simply is a measure of the partial regression coefficient after all the independent variables are converted to standard scores. Thus the question of scale measurements does not enter, and the beta-weights measure more accurately the actual weight or strength of the variable in the regression equation. For instance, from Appendix D, row 1, the DECISION-MAKING FOR NATIONAL ECONOMIC POLICY, for the first semantic differential:

Simple–Complex. In columns 9 and 10 the b-weight for the instructors' position is 1.076 and the b-weight for the students' precourse attitudes is .584. This would make sense, in that the instructors' attitudes are measured on a binary scale and the students' precourse scores are measured on a five-point scale. It would take a greater relative change in the binary variable to obtain the same change in the dependent variable than could be obtained in the dependent variable for a smaller change in the five-point-scale variable. We hypothesize that if both of these independent variables were measured on the same scale they would be much closer together. This is shown in column 4 of Appendix J where the beta-weight for the instructor's position is .682, and the beta-weight for the students' precourse position is .687 (column 5). Suffice to say that the differences in the b-weights from the original regression equations become much more comparable when viewed as beta-weights based on standard scores for the variables.

7. The minimum F-Ratio required for an equation with 10 and 185 degrees of freedom is 2.32. The adjusted R^2 is approximately .025 less than the R^2. For instance, the coefficient of determination for the first regression of Economics 223, Section 62 (Appendix E), is in Row 1, Column 11, and is .340. The adjusted R^2, not indicated in the table, is .309.

8. For a regression with 14 degrees of freedom in the numerator and 78 degrees of freedom in the denominator, the minimum required F-Ratio is 1.89.

9. For a regression with 14 degrees of freedom in the numerator and 134 degrees of freedom in the denominator, the minimum required F-Ratio is 1.85 for the equation to be statistically significant.

Notes to Chapter 6

1. This is an activity whose time has come. For example, see: D. R. Lewis and C. Orvis, "A Training System for Graduate Student Instructors of Introductory Economics," *Economic Education Experiences of Enterprising Teachers* 11, pp. 102–11. In addition, the Alfred P. Sloan Foundation has given a substantial grant to the Joint Council for Economic Education to prepare materials and strategies that might be employed in such activities.

2. Chapter 7 presents a cost comparison but does not include these additional costs.

3. The interviews were taped (with the knowledge of the students) and transcribed. We would also like to acknowledge the assistance of Ms. Jean Byrne, Ph.D., who arranged and conducted the interviews.

4. The variation in the quality of the graduate teaching assistants previously documented was also obvious from the interviews. Indeed the rankings that could be derived from the interviews would correspond to those previously presented.

5. This is another indication of another type of breakdown which occurred in the experimental design. If a student is to use two terminals at the same

time he must have two different user numbers, and consequently the time data recorded for his assigned number in the course is incorrect. This would suggest that the evaluation of cognitive achievement presented in Chapter 3 may have understated the impact of CAI on the performance of experimentals on examinations. Indeed access to these materials by the controls may have contributed to their performance.

Notes to Chapter 7

1. At present, the cost algorithm for time sharing appears as follows:

Job Cost = (Rate (1) X CPU Time) + (Rate (2) X Disk Controller and Channel Time) + (Rate (5) X Core Allocation Time) + (Rate (11) X TPUTS) + (Rate X (12) X TGETS) + (Rate (13) X Connect Time) + (Rate (10).

RATES

Rate (1)	=	$142.00 per hour
Rate (2)	=	$100.28 per hour
Rate (3)	=	$ 51.00 per hour
Rate (4)	=	$ 16.57 per hour
Rate (5)	=	$ .10 per K. hour
Rate (6)	=	$ .021 per 50 lines printed
Rate (7)	=	$ .0012 per card read
Rate (8)	=	$ .0047 per card punched
Rate (9)	=	$ 5.00 per wall clock hour (2400 Baud Rate)[a]
Rate (10)	=	$ .21 per Job or Logon
Rate (11)	=	$ .0016 per TPUT
Rate (12)	=	$ .0016 per TGET
Rate (13)	=	$ 1.02 per wall clock hour (110–300 Baud Rate)[b]

[a]This connect time charge applies only to high speed remote entry jobs submitted via HASP.
[b]This connect time charge applies only to TSO.

Source: The Patch (University of Notre Dame Computing Center Newsletter) 3, no. 16 (June 30, 1975): 4.

2. This is a true marginal cost because a graduate student may be assigned to these or other activities. We reject the notion that only the cash stipend represents the marginal cost of assigning a graduate student to the discussion class. This latter view might arise from the fact that a graduate student may obtain a tuition scholarship without doing any teaching but obtain both the tuition scholarship and the cash stipend if he does teach.

3. The basis for this suspicion is the following explanation of cost determination.

> In spite of inflationary rises in the total cost of computing, increased productivity has allowed the computing center to announce a substantial computer-rate reduction. The following rates will be in effect for the fiscal year 1974–75. This change will take place Tuesday, July 1, 1975. All rates are determined by dividing the budgeted costs for computer resources by the anticipated usage of those resources.
>
> Several users usually share the various computer resources in a multiprogramming operating system. While it is difficult to develop a charging algorithm that exactly identifies that portion of the resources that each user has used, the center has developed a cost-allocation algorithm that has the following objectives:
>
> To distribute all operating costs of the center to the budget areas of the University using its services.
>
> To distribute costs to individual users for the cost of those resources that he alone required.
>
> To try and have the cost allocation repeat each time a program is run without any changes.
>
> Our algorithm is based on those resources for which we are able to obtain a reliable measure of use. (*The Patch*, University of Notre Dame Newsletter, 3, no. 16 (July 30, 1975): 3.)

4. This refers to budgeted costs. Increasing either the number of discussion classes taught or their size may lead to a reduction in their "quality."

5. D. Lewis and C. Orvis, "A Training System for Graduate Instructors of Introductory Economics," *Economic Education Experiences of Enterprising Teachers* 11 (1974): 102ff.

Notes to Chapter 9

1. This chapter was written with the assistance of Kenneth Jameson. A revision of this chapter was presented at the Joint Council for Economic Education session at the American Economics Association meeting in San Francisco, December 1974.

2. See John C. Soper, "Computer Assisted Instruction in Economics: A Survey."

3. The objective functions may differ in terms of what is maximized (or minimized). For example a department may choose from among the following alternatives: maximize the number of students who take introductory courses, maximize the economic knowledge of the students who take the introductory courses, maximize interest in economics as a major, maximize the usefulness of introductory economics with respect to either the general educational background or vocational orientation of the student, and so on. Each one of these seems to imply a different pattern of offerings or at least a variation in the content of a given pattern.

4. Frank J. Bonello, William I. Davisson, Kenneth P. Jameson, "Teaching Introductory Economics with the Computer as Laboratory." *Proceedings*, Conference on Computers in the Undergraduate Curricula, 5th Annual Conference, Pullman, Washington, 1974, pp. 147–51.

5. One of the student papers that started as an independent research paper for the second semester has been published by the *American Economist.*

6. Once the educational side has been determined, questions regarding institutional requirements and resource constraints would then be addressed. For instance, the educational tradeoffs may be acceptable to us as a department but not to the College of Business. On the other hand, the hardware facilities necessary to process 600 students through a 101–102 type sequence may preclude its adoption as the norm for the traditional introductory sequence.

7. Differences in the characteristics of students—for example, their human capital measured by VSAT and MSAT and related variables—will be taken into consideration in the regression section by including these as independent variables. However, no such adjustment or consideration will be made in the following discussion.

8. The success of Economics 101 in these areas is measured by the students' abilities to attain behavioral objectives set prior to the course. In general the students do succeed in attaining these goals.

9. It should be pointed out that in Economics 102 and 224 the TUCE results roughly patterned the results which we found for the Economics 101 and 223 courses. In addition we found that the gap between the courses (the tradeoff) is less—for example, the Economics 102 TUCE postcourse test was 23.19 compared with the Economics 224 score of 23.58, with t = .8. This result was to be expected, since there is much more direct concentration on economic content in both the lecture and the laboratory of Economics 102. In Economics 102, philosophy of science and computer statistical programming are not taught.

10. Note that the ordering of effects here is similar to the ordering on the cognitive results. This suggests that indeed this measure is part and parcel of cognitive achievement.

11. It is necessary to admit that no impact for a continuing "3" may be a misnomer. What may have in fact occurred is that the student established a solid foundation for a middle-of-the-road position, changing in effect from no opinion to a middle-of-the-road position.

12. Note that CE9 suffers from the same problem as UR; the question used to obtain the teacher evaluation is phrased in a relative sense. CE15 and CE16 seem to avoid this problem.

13. OPI for the student is defined as $(\sum_{j=1}^{5} |0_A - 0_B| j)$ where 0_A is the postcourse (after) opinion and 0_B is the pre (before) opinion and j represents a seecific semantic differential listed under the DECISION MAKING FOR NATIONAL ECONOMIC POLICY issue.

14. See Frank Gery, "Is There a Ceiling Effect to the Test of Understanding College Economics?" *Research Papers in Economic Education* (New York: Joint Council on Economic Education, 1972), pp. 34–49. The gap closing is

defined as TUCEPOST-TUCEPRE/33-TUCEPRE or the ratio of actual improvement to potential improvement.